westermann

Exploring History

1

Moderated by
Dr. Christa Lohmann

Written by
Rolf J. Kröger
Dr. Deanna Nebert
Dr. Barbara Nerlich
Thomas Söhrnsen

Druck A[6] / Jahr 2023
Alle Drucke der Serie A sind im Unterricht parallel verwendbar.

Redaktion: Christoph Meyer
Druck und Bindung: Westermann Druck GmbH, Georg-Westermann-Allee 66, 38104 Braunschweig

ISBN 978-3-14-**111810**-0

04 INDUSTRIALIZATION 82

05 EUROPE IN REVOLT – THE STRUGGLE FOR UNITY AND LIBERTY (1815 – 1849) 112

06 IMPERIAL GERMANY 138

07 THE NEW IMPERIALISM AND THE SCRAMBLE FOR AFRICA 164

08 THE FIRST WORLD WAR 186

M 1 **Louis XIV**

Painting by Hyacinthe Rigaud, about 1700

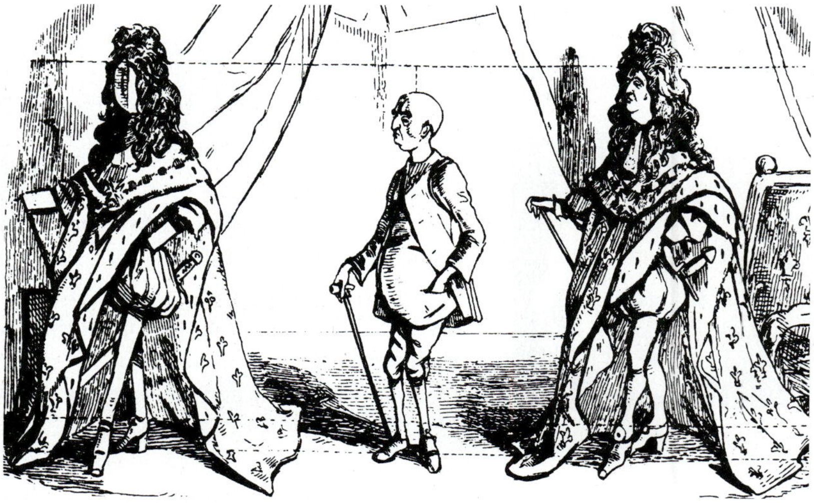

M 2 **The Demasking**

Caricature by W. Thackeray, about 1840

M 3 **Hall of Mirrors at the Palace of Versailles today**

01 THE AGE OF ABSOLUTISM AND ENLIGHTENMENT

New Ways of Government

Since the 16th century France had been involved in a lot of inner conflicts, which came up after the Reformation changed the landscape of religion forever. France took part in the Thirty-Years'-War until 1648. Moreover, long periods of bloody civil wars over religion, which led to economic crises and misery, made people think their world was upside down. They wished for order and security in their lives, which corresponded with the ideas of philosophers and rulers alike. What God was for the universe, they wanted the king to be for the state.

Louis XIV of France became the symbol of the era and a role model for many other princes in Europe. But wasn't it too much to ask of one person to be the strong leader who would change everything to the better? Was it possible at all to organize things in a structured way so that people got what they were looking for?

At the same time things in England developed differently even though there had also been a lot of problems after Henry VIII's death. But his daughter Elizabeth I had somehow stabilized the country before she died in 1603.

When philosophers came up with the ideas of the **Enlightenment** many people saw that there was a better way towards peace in society. Their ideas led to new ways of governing in countries like Austria and Prussia.

Historical Terms

Enlightenment: Aufklärung

absolutism: Absolutismus

This chapter deals with many questions such as:

- What did **absolutism** mean and what did it look like?
- What role did Louis XIV play?
- How did he want to be seen?
- How was French society organized?
- How did the new system of the economy work?
- What did Louis's fight for hegemony mean for Europe and for France herself?
- What form of government did the English have?
- What did the Enlightenment mean for politics and people?
- What influence did the Enlightenment have on Prussia?

Vocabulary

to crush: to defeat sb. completely

benediction of God: blessing, approval of God

interest: money you have to pay when you have borrowed money

warrant: certificate, license

Louis XIV – The Sun King

More Power to the King

At the end of the 16th century Henry IV ended the wars of religion in France. In 1598 he published the Edict of Nantes, granting relative religious freedom to the Protestants (the "Huguenots"), who had been persecuted for a long time. After the horror of the wars people hoped that a more powerful king would bring lasting peace to France. But Louis XIII was weak because of financial problems. Cardinal Richelieu, his new and powerful Prime Minister, whose motto was "the end justifies the means" proved to be more successful. He and his successor Cardinal Mazarin, Prime Minister from 1642 on, educated the son of the king to be more powerful. They also *crushed* dangerous rebellions by different groups, including the "Fronde", an aristocratic uprising against a more powerful government.

Louis XIV – a new type of king

After Mazarin's death in 1661 Louis XIV took over himself. His idea of government did not allow for people to speak out against him, so he crushed all kinds of opposition. Even the aristocratic centres of law ("parliaments") had to follow the king's will.

A new system of administration was introduced, in which "intendants" executed the King's orders directly, so that the noble governors of the provinces lost nearly all of their power. In this way laws, the police and the civil service were standardized. The "intendants" belonged to the **Third Estate** and entirely depended on the king as he gave them their positions for a certain time only. So they supported him without reservations – just like the rich landowners and merchants, who bought aristocratic titles from him.

Louis wanted to be in control of French society, so he invited the high nobility to live at his court and gave them high-sounding titles and profitable jobs in order to keep them away from politics and power.

Above all he was certain that he had the *benediction of God* and that he symbolized the nation.

Historical Terms

Third Estate: Dritter Stand

M 1 **Louis XIV welcomes Frederick August I, the Elector of Saxony and King of Poland, in 1714**

Painting by Louis Sylvestre

Financial Difficulties

All these measures did not solve the financial problems Louis had inherited from his father. He had to borrow money from the rich, who received privileges and monopolies in return apart from high *interest* rates. He offered people the chance to buy a certain position in his administration, including the collection of taxes and customs. Even the state's income from agricultural activities, markets, and mining were leased out. Rich people could buy "lettres de cachet", blank arrest *warrants* which the owner could fill in himself. It still wasn't enough, as the state spendings were enormous. So one of his ministers set up a new economic system to raise more money for the state.

Info

Absolutism

The word comes from the Latin "Rex legibus absolutus est" – the king does not have to obey the laws ("lex"). He gets all his power from God and is only responsible to God's rules ("ius"). In this political system the monarch is supposed to hold total power and have complete authority over the lives of the people. He makes the laws and nobody is allowed to resist or check him. But in real life his power was limited by influential advisors, by the fact that he could not be everywhere and by his constant lack of money.

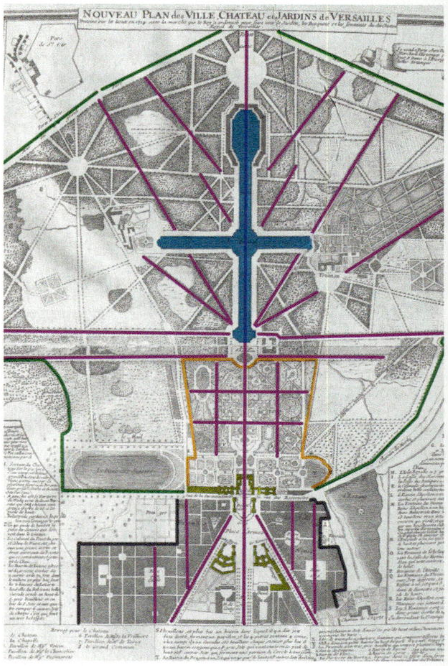

M 2 **Versailles**
Plan of the grounds

M 3 **Versailles**
Painting by Pierre Patel, 1668

Louis XIV – the Sun King

M 4 The Sun

Costume of the 13-year-old king for a performance of the "Ballet de la Nuit", 1653

M 6 Le "Roi Soleil"

Medal from 1674 with Louis's motto: "Nec Pluribus Impar" ("Not unequal to many" which means: there is nobody like him)

M 5 Louis's Memoirs

In his memoirs Louis XIV revealed his motives:

"As my emblem I have chosen the sun, which according to the rules of *heraldry* is the noblest sign. It is without any doubt the liveliest and the most beautiful emblem of a great prince, because it is *entirely* unique, because of the light it gives to the other stars, which almost form its court, because of the fair distribution of its light to all the different parts of the sky, because of the many favours it does everywhere, because of the life, the joy and the activity it arouses, because of its *perpetual* motion and its radiation of a sense of calm at the same time, because of its constant and unchangeable way.
God, who has set the kings over their subjects, wanted them to be acknowledged as his representatives. He has reserved the right to himself to judge on them. It is his will that those who have been born as subjects, have to totally submit."

Ludwig XIV., Memoiren, Kompass: Basel/Leipzig 1931, p. 187, 271. (transl. by Rolf J. Kröger).

Vocabulary

heraldry: the study of the coats of arms and of old families
entirely: totally, completely
unique: there is only one of it
perpetual: never-ending

M 7 Louis's Lever (Getting up)

Louis XIV's bedroom was the central room in the palace of Versailles. Saint-Simon, a nobleman who lived at the court, wrote a report about his getting up at eight o'clock sharp, which was enacted like a ceremonial:

"He was woken up by his valet de chambre, who had slept in the bedchamber. The chief physician, the chief surgeon and Louis's childhood nurse all entered the room at the same time. The nurse kissed him and the night chamberpot was removed. At a quarter past eight the grande entrée began. The privilege to be a part of it was restricted to nobles and could be bought. The king stayed in bed in his nightshirt. The Grand Chamberlain of France presented holy water to the king and his morning clothes were laid out. Then the Master of the Bedchamber and the First Servant, both high nobles, pulled the king's nightshirt over his head. The Grand Chamberlain presented the day shirt, which was changed only sometimes. At this stage the nobles could try to have a brief private word with the king, which they would have rehearsed beforehand. Then they withdrew and the king held a short private prayer. Then the première entrée began, which included persons of lesser privilege. They watched the king getting dressed and getting shaved. He was given a dressing gown and a mirror was held for him while he dressed underneath the gown. Other privileged courtiers entered while the king was putting on his stockings and his shoes. During this entrée de la chambre the king's readers and his director of festivities also entered. The fourth group to arrive in the king's bedroom were his ministers and secretaries, who were allowed in at the entrée du chambre.
A fifth entrée admitted ladies for the first time, and a sixth entrée admitted the king's children, legitimate and illegitimate, who entered through a special backdoor."

Adapted by Rolf J. Kröger from http://en.chateauversailles.fr/ and https://en.wikipedia.org/wiki/Louis_XIV_of_France [Oct. 2017].

The Garden at Versailles – a baroque garden

M 8 The Garden at the Palace of Versailles

Current photos

Baroque gardens were also called "French Formal Gardens". They were designed on a big scale in order to impress people by their sheer size and show that "man" dominates nature which he can even manipulate as he likes. Their design followed geometric patterns like straight lines, circles and triangles and other features like symmetry and a central axis. Even trees and bushes were trimmed into ornamental shapes, planting beds designed in square or rectangular patterns and surrounded by coloured gravel.

The place of the palace in a formal garden was chosen in a way that made the house seem bigger than it was. The use of water in a large number of basins, canals and fountains with statues and tricks gave people the impression of control of nature. Grottos and hidden gardens were included to surprise the visitor.

Tasks

1. Louis XIV – the Sun King

a) Describe the problems France had before Louis XIV took over the government (text).

b) Explain how Louis defined his role in society and what he thought a good king should do (M5).

c) Analyse what the sources say about Louis and his view of himself (M4, M6, M7)

2. Versailles

a) Describe the layout of the palace and the gardens of Versailles (M2, M3).

b) Work out the features of a typical baroque garden as seen in the photos (text, M8).

c) Show what the palace and the gardens of Versailles say about Louis XIV.

M 9 Louis XIV

Painting by Hyacinthe Rigaud, about 1700. Rigaud received orders to paint a life-size picture of the king. The painting was meant to be sent to Spain, where Louis XIV's grandson was about to become king. However, the king liked the painting so much that he only sent a copy to the Spanish court.

Vocabulary

Useful words and phrases

sword of Charlemagne (Karl der Große)

column with relief

dancemaster – step appears artificial

left hand is put on the king's hip

necklace with the Order of the Golden Fleece (Goldenes Flies = ein Orden)

red shoes were only worn by the nobility

Vocabulary

earnest and reserved official expression of the face

robe falls in folds (Umhang)

lion-like wig (Perücke) makes person appear taller

canopy of red velvet (Samt) frames the painting like a vault (Gewölbe, Himmel)

sceptre in right hand is placed on table with crown and "main de justice" (Hand der Gerechtigkeit)

table covered with blue velvet which shows the golden lily of the Bourbons (Lilie der Bourbonen = Kennzeichen des Adelsgeschlechts der Bourbonen)

Analysing Paintings

Historical paintings provide information about the past. As with all other sources some critical questions must be asked when you want to use a painting as a source of information. In addition you must know that paintings do not show reality but a painter's view of it. There have been times when painters were simply not interested in what reality looked like, so they painted what they liked to see or what their customer told them he wanted to see. Another obstacle is that the fashion of painting changed.

What is the advantage of paintings as historical sources then? In former times fewer people could read. But they were very well-trained in understanding signs, codes and symbols. The language of images was widespread. That is why the elements in most paintings show a message. So the ruler of a state had himself painted in order to show people what he wanted them to see and to believe. And that is why paintings can be so valuable as historical sources, if only you have the means to find out.

Portraits of Louis XIV

From early childhood Louis XIV stood in the limelight. So he saw the opportunity to create his own image. Not only did he use the ceremonies at court, but he also had all sorts of paintings, tapestries, statues, poems and other works of art done for him that presented him as an antique god, as Apollo or even as the sun. His aim was to inform people about his political activities, but also about his personality. His subjects were to see that he was an outstanding person who was at the same time dangerous and powerful, always close but nevertheless unreachable.

When Louis XIV invited a group of painters (among them Rigaud) to his court in 1655, he practically founded his own public relations agency. These painters developed a new style of representational portrait and created a new fashion, which quickly spread to other parts of Europe.

Historical Workshop

Analysing Paintings

1. Description

a. Give your first impression on what the picture shows.
b. Name the painter.
c. Write down when it was painted.
d. Find out about its original size (Internet).
e. Find out according to whose orders it was painted and who paid for it.

2. Finding Information

a. Analyse the way the main person looks and how he is positioned.
b. Explain all the elements of his dress (with the help of an encyclopaedia or the Internet).
c. Look for the symbols of the king's power and explain their significance.
d. Examine from what position the observer of this painting looks at the king.
e. Investigate why the painting was made.

3. Interpreting the Painting

a. Taking into account all the information you have collected, assess the painting as a work of art but also as a historical source.
b. Give reasons why you think this painting is worth investigating or not.
c. Show what message Louis XIV wanted to convey with this painting.

The Three Estates

Historical Terms

estates: Stände
clergy: Personen der Kirche
nobility: Adel
taxes: Steuern

Since the Middle Ages the French population had fallen into three groups, called **estates**.

The First Estate – the clergy

Being a true Catholic and the protector of his Church, Louis set up the principle of "one king, one law, one belief" ("un roi, une loi, une foi") and in 1685 cancelled the Edict of Nantes, which protected the Protestants. So the Catholic confession was the state religion again.

The **clergy** consisted of the high clergy appointed by the king. They were mostly rich and had some influence on him. The bigger part in numbers belonged to the low clergy, whose members were mostly poor and badly-trained for the job. They were often not even paid by the church, but had to live on what their community gave them. Together less than one percent of the population belonged to the clergy. They took over parts of the state administration with their church registers and had to pay almost no taxes.

The Second Estate – the nobility

M 1 The Three Estates
Doves and rabbits the farmer wasn't allowed to hunt eat the harvest. On the sabre it says "red from blood", on the stick "drained in tears". Caricature, 1789

Less than two percent of the people belonged to the **nobility**. They either inherited their titles, were appointed by the king or received their titles because of a certain job they had done. Like the clergy they had to pay hardly any taxes. Their income came from the land they owned and from contributions of the peasants. Taking part in business or trade did not fit in with the view of their role. The aim of the high nobility was to be as close to the king as possible, so many of them lived at the royal court at Versailles.

The low nobility depended on the development of the economy and on the harvests, which led to the fact that some noblemen's financial situation was difficult at times. However, they did not lose their privileges.

The Third Estate – the people

Nearly 98 percent of the population belonged to the Third Estate, which meant everybody from a rich banker, who would look very similar to a nobleman, to a starving farmhand. Most of this estate lived in the country and worked on the land. But only the big landowners and the rich farmers earned a good living. Another well-off group were the civil servants whose positions were entirely dependent on the king.

By centralizing and standardizing his administration Louis took away power from the nobles and gave it to well-trained and loyal civil servants from the Third Estate, who were not from the areas where they were sent to work and who owed their careers only to him. To get even more control he transferred them to other districts from time to time.

For most of the ordinary farmers life was extremely hard as they had to pay half of their income in **taxes** and they had other duties to fulfil, e.g. working for the landowners. Going hunting or fishing was forbidden and they often had to become soldiers in the wars. Some of them were only able to survive.

M 2 **Traditional Costumes of the Three Estates**
Illustration from 1788

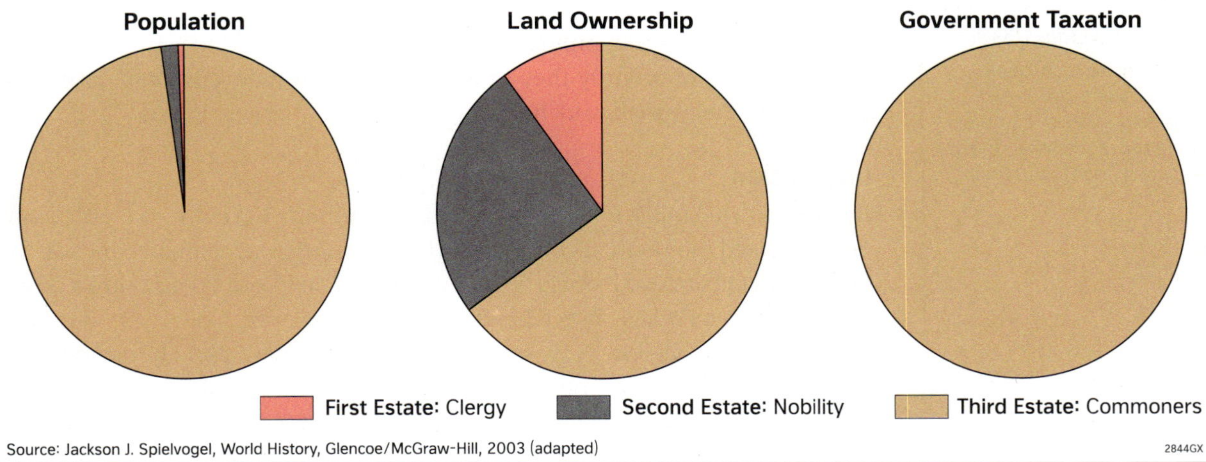

Source: Jackson J. Spielvogel, World History, Glencoe/McGraw-Hill, 2003 (adapted)

M 3 **The Three Estates in Pre-Revolutionary France**

Tasks

1. French Society
a) Explain the structure of French society.
b) Work out the changes in society during Louis XIV's reign.

2. The Three Estates
a) Say what the meaning of the caricature is (M1).
b) Describe the clothes the members of the three estates are wearing (M2).
c) Compare the two illustrations and find out what they tell you about the situation in France (M1, M2).

Vocabulary

to convert: to change religion
to revoke: to cancel
intimidation: frightening, threatening

The Huguenots – Accepted or Persecuted

Henry, the Protestant Duke of Navarre, had *converted* to Catholicism in order to marry a Catholic princess and become King of France. He wanted to make peace at last. In 1598 he published the Edict of Nantes which gave the Protestants in France ("the Huguenots") a kind of religious freedom and some safe places, where they could live in peace. Many of these hard-working people stayed in France and became successful in business.

But when Louis XIV took over the government in 1661 the tide turned. His idea of absolute monarchy did not accept any other belief than Roman Catholicism. After 1680 the persecution of the Huguenots began again. Things became worse when Louis *revoked* the Edict of Nantes by publishing the Edict of Fontainebleau in 1685.

This resulted in the destruction of Huguenot churches, the closing of Protestant schools and increased pressure and *intimidation* to convert to Catholicism. Those who refused were often driven out of their houses or even killed. Many Huguenots tried to flee.

M 1 "Chignon" Bible of the French Huguenots 1753/4

Women carried their small Huguenot Bible, which was forbidden in France, with them in their topknot on their heads. Compare its size to the coin.

Refugees in Europe

More than 250,000 Huguenots tried to get to the parts of Europe which were dominated by the Protestant belief. They were very welcome in England, in Switzerland, in the Netherlands and in religiously tolerant Prussia, where Elector Frederic William was happy to personally greet the first who came. He even attracted them by giving them numerous privileges. In return they brought much capital into Prussia as well as new crafts, among them the silk and textile production. They also introduced unknown vegetables like beans, sweet peas, asparagus and Brussels sprouts.

But most importantly they brought with them their enormous economic activity and their will to work hard.

Integration

By 1686 in the small town of Erlangen in southern Germany the Huguenots outnumbered the Germans by 1000 to 317. In Berlin it was estimated in 1700 that every third person was French. A great number of people in Prussia spoke French and there was a French church in nearly every town.

When Louis died in 1715, the Huguenots could have gone home to France again. But they changed from refugees into immigrants instead. French influence in their lives slowly became less important. By 1750, they had adapted to the German language and culture and at the end of the 18th century they were completely German. The last French-speaking church service was held in 1822.

Historical Terms

Great Elector: Großer Kurfürst

Info

In his **Edict of Potsdam** in 1685 the **Great Elector** granted privileges to the Huguenots, among others:

free and safe refuge, permission to bring anything with them for free, unoccupied land in towns for free, citizenship at once, farmland in the country for free, jobs for nobles in the army and in the administration, French preachers paid by the state

M 2 Persecution of the Huguenots in France 1621

Contemporary etching by Jan Luyken, coloured later

M 3 "Refugees welcomed by the Great Elector (1640–1688)"

Segment of the relief at the French Cathedral in Berlin 1935

M 4 French Cathedral, Berlin

Built for the Huguenots by Louis Cayart from 1701–1705. Photo 2016

Tasks

1. **The Huguenots in France**
   a) Describe their role in France before Louis XIV (text).
   b) Say in your own words what changed under Louis XIV (text).
2. **The Huguenots in Europe**
   a) Write a short newspaper article about the meeting of the Huguenots and the Prussian monarch (M3).
   b) Explain why they were welcome in many parts of Europe (text, info, M3, M4).
   c) Find out whether there are any families in your area with a Huguenot background.
   d) Compare and contrast the situation of the Huguenots to refugees today.

Vocabulary

intervention: getting involved in order to help

blueprint: draft, model

Mercantilism

In the mid 17th century about twenty million people lived in France, 90 per cent of whom led a miserable life full of hard work. On the other hand there was the court of Versailles, which was a symbol of luxury and thoughtless spending of money.

When Louis XIV took over the government in 1661, the state income of the following three years had already been spent. So something had to be done. Louis's minister of finance, Jean Colbert, developed an economic system for France which was not really new. The Dutch and the English had been using it for quite some time.

State *Intervention*

The king needed more money for his army, his luxurious lifestyle, his palaces, his civil servants and his wars. Taxes could not be raised as most of the people already had major problems paying them. Colbert supported the new factories financially and freed them from taxes, so that they produced goods more cheaply. Besides, work was completely reorganized – split up, so that workers became specialists. The goods were sold abroad in order to get more money into France. Colbert's aim was a positive balance of trade, which he achieved by the following measures:

- most raw material for the production of goods came from the French colonies where it was cheap
- export of raw material was forbidden or made extremely expensive
- high customs duties were put on imported goods
- transport in France was improved and became cheaper
- units of measure and weight were standardized
- rich Frenchmen were "persuaded" to invest in the new factories.

Winners and Losers

Colbert's system worked quite well and production increased. Trading boomed and merchants earned a lot. A part of the profit, especially the money the state had invested and some consumption taxes, had to be returned. But the owners of small workshops did not benefit from the system. They suffered from the competition of the factories and went bankrupt. Also, many farmers became poorer, because they had to sell their produce at fixed low prices. As Louis XIV did not care about the state of his finances the country lost out as well. When he died in 1715 he left behind a country that was regarded as the *blueprint* of a successful state by many other leaders in Europe. But behind the façade it stood on the brink of financial collapse.

M 1 The Production of Playing Cards in a Factory
Painting, 17th century

M 2 Memorandum

In 1664 Jean Baptiste Colbert wrote the following memorandum:

"If we had factories in France then we would not have to buy goods from Holland for our own use – but we would produce enough goods ourselves to have some left over for our own export, which would in turn give us more money. This alone is the only goal of trade.

An annual sum should be spent each year for the founding of factories and improvement of trade. In addition *subsidies* should be paid to everyone who buys or builds ships. The country roads should be improved, new bridges should be built, the customs barriers on the rivers removed, [...] the rivers should be made navigable and the idea of a canal should be considered carefully."

J. B. Colbert, Lettres II, Paris 1863, p. 226f. (adapted and transl. by Rolf J. Kröger).

Vocabulary

subsidies: money the state gives people for investment

M 3 Jean Baptiste Colbert (1619 – 1683)

He served his king faithfully for 22 years. Everybody at the court treated him with respect although he wasn't a nobleman. Their "sweet life" depended on the success of his system of mercantilism.

M 4

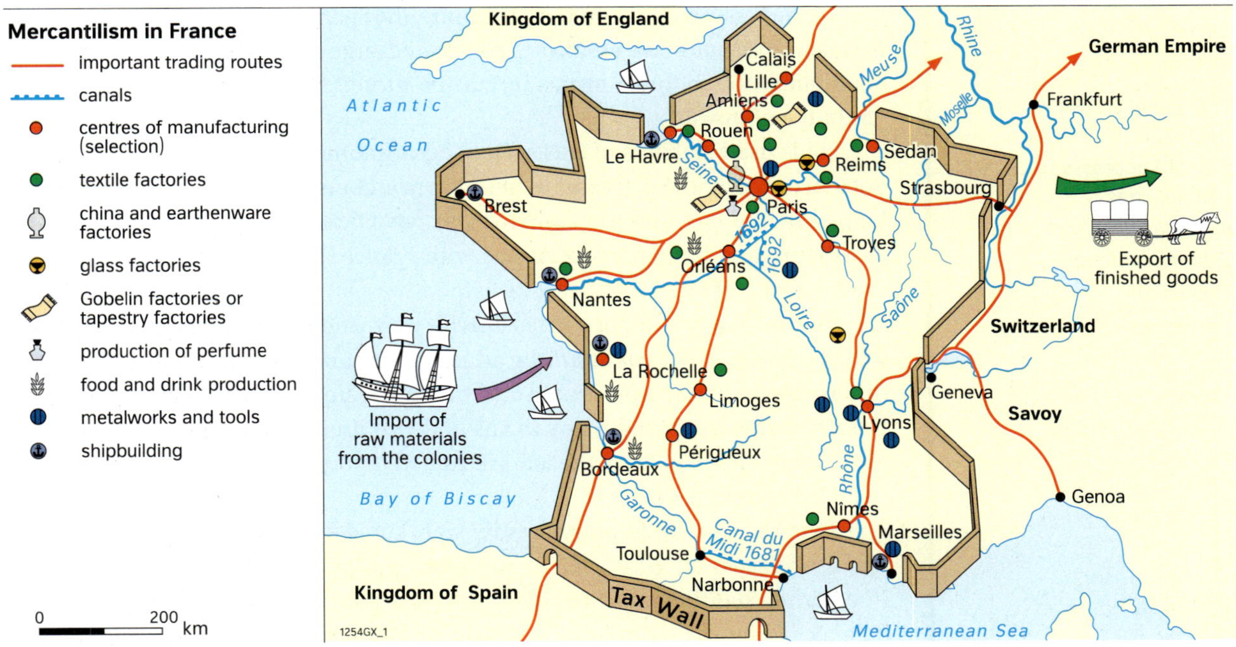

Tasks

1. Mercantilism

a) Cottage industry – manufacturing – industrial mass production are three steps of the development of man's production of goods. Explain which of them was taken in the time of absolutism (text, M1).

b) Explain how manufacturing was an improvement.

c) Describe the map (M4).

d) Compare Colbert's ideas with what was actually done in France (M2, M4).

e) Assess Colbert's system.

Louis's Wars

Vocabulary

to encircle: to surround, form a circle

mercenary: a soldier who will fight for anybody for money (Söldner)

shelling: shooting with big guns

Palatinate: Pfalz

arsonist (in M1): sb. who sets things on fire (Brandstifter)

Preparing War

Louis XIV wanted to make France the dominant power in Europe, which led to a long series of wars. He also thought that war was the best way to demonstrate the power of a sovereign. Moreover, he believed that the House of Habsburg tried to *encircle* France. However, the other European states were not willing to give in to his aggression.

The formation of a standing army with a strict hierarchy was his first step. As commander-in-chief he gained control over the nobility, who traditionally served as officers. All soldiers had the same uniforms and exercised together in manoeuvres, so that they were much better trained than the *mercenaries* before. As most people were poor, it was no problem to recruit soldiers – they joined the army simply to earn money.

At the same time Louis made the northern and western borders of France safer with a line of 300 fortresses and fortifications of a new type. His engineer Vauban designed them in a way that they even resisted *shelling*.

Inside France Louis had the last old city walls and fortifications destroyed so that resistance in his country became impossible.

France – the number one in Europe?

Louis wanted to integrate the land on the left bank of the Rhine into France. So his main enemies were the Holy Roman Empire, the Spanish Netherlands and Holland. At first he was quite successful and conquered large areas of land. But the more he conquered, the more countries in Europe turned against him and united for a "**balance of power**".

Historical Terms

balance of power: Mächtegleichgewicht

War of Succession: Erbfolgekrieg

hegemony: Vorherrschaft oder Hegemonie

Louis used all kinds of tricks. He made diplomats and jurists find out about ancient claims and documents in "reunion chambers". Based on their findings and helped by the fact that the emperor was busy fighting the Turks, he "reunited" Strasbourg and large parts of Alsace with France. This area remained disputed until the 20th century.

He also invented all sorts of reasons for wars when he wanted them. In the **War of Succession** in the *Palatinate* he attacked the country in the name of his sister-in-law Liselotte of the Palatinate and tried to occupy the southeast of Germany. French troops destroyed many towns and vast areas of land because Louis had given them orders to leave the land so ruined that it could never become a threat to France again.

Trying to gain **hegemony** over Europe, Louis went too far in the "War of the Spanish Succession" (1701–1713). Nearly all European powers united against him in a grand coalition and beat him. But as Britain still wanted to keep the old balance of power, France remained a major power in Europe. When Louis died in 1715 he had made France bigger but he had also ruined the finances of his country.

M 1 French Military Growth

Date	1661	1664	1672	1672	1703
Soldiers	12500	45000	120000	290000	400000
Warships	–	30	200		

M 2

M 3 War in the Palatinate

The war in the Palatinate left its scars. On 19 October 1688 a part of Louis XIV's army occupied the town of Oberwesel and stayed until March 1689. The official town chronicles contain the following account by a man called Schwarz:

"The commander-in-chief General Marquis de Bretèche took quarters at the Schönburg. The abbeys and the monasteries had to hand over nearly all of their treasures for his court.

In the town were 1400 foot soldiers, 200 knights, most of higher rank, and 416 horses. The people had to give them their pay and food. Three thousand tons of grain and 1575 tons of oats, the last bale of hay and straw, the last cow and the last pig, everything was requisitioned.

When the troops left they destroyed gates, towers and Schönburg castle. Then they set the town on fire, thus destroying both town halls, two nobles' mansions and 115 town houses as well as most of the hospital church."

www.regionalgeschichte.net/mittelrhein/region/orte/orte-o/oberwesel.html (adapted and transl. by Rolf J. Kröger) [Oct. 2017].

M 4 The French General Melac

A leaflet showing the French General Melac in front of the burning palace at Heidelberg. The text introduces him as a murderer and an *arsonist*. Some people in the Palatinate still call dangerous dogs "Melac". Engraving, 1689.

Tasks

1. The Wars and France

a) Analyse the role of the military in Louis's France (text, M1).

b) Find the towns of Oberwesel and Heidelberg on the map and explain why and how Louis's wars were fought there (M2, M3).

c) Assess the final outcome of the wars for France (text, M1).

2. The Wars and Europe

a) Talk about what the people of the area east of the French border have gone through (M3, M4).

b) Compare the European borders of 1715 to those of today (M2, Atlas).

M 1 **The State Opening of Parliament by Queen Elizabeth II on May 8th, 2013**

England – An Absolute Monarchy as Well?

M 2 **Magna Charta Libertatum 1215**

Even today the State Opening of Parliament marks the beginning of the parliamentary year. Although the Queen doesn't have any real power anymore, she still belongs to the institutions which rule the country.

Since the Magna Carta in 1215, when King John had to hand over special rights to the high nobility, the barons, England had been ruled by a monarch, who received advice from but also faced opposition by the meeting of the barons called Parliament. The right to decide on finances and in legislation had to be shared by the two parties. During the reign of Elizabeth I (1558–1603) a third group had come to influence – the gentry, a mixture of low nobility and merchants, who were the backbone of Elizabeth's economy and of her foreign policy. They had prepared England for the fight against Spain, the dominant sea power until England took over this role after the victory over the Spanish Armada in 1588. King Charles I, however, wanted to govern the country in the same style as his French colleagues, but the political situation stood against it. The conflict began in two fields: religion and finances.

Info

The English Parliament

The English Parliament consisted of two parts, called chambers. The House of Lords with all the great noblemen of the country had a lot of influence on the king's decisions. The House of Commons, where the gentry and the merchant classes met, also had to agree to the raising of taxes. From here protest came against unpopular measures of the king. Its members often ran the risk of court action, fines and even the loss of their property. But many of them were Puritans, so principles were more important than material aspects.

The Problem of Religion

England had been a Protestant country since 1534, when Henry VIII had founded his own state church, the Anglican Church, turning his back on the pope in Rome and Catholicism. His daughter Mary forced England to return to Catholicism, her successor Elizabeth changed things again, but when the English throne passed to the Stuart dynasty from Scotland in 1603, the new king wanted to return to Catholicism. Most people did not want to follow him, but wanted to remain Protestant. Some fled to North America in order to exercise their religion freely, but others opposed James I's wish.

The most powerful group were the Puritans, who stood for simplicity of the church and a modest style of life. Many Puritans belonged to the gentry and had been very successful in business. They had also begun to play an important role in Parliament, where they started to oppose the king now. It became a more powerful body. In particular they wanted to stop the king appointing only Catholics as members of the government.

The Problem of Finances

When the king wanted to raise taxes he had to ask Parliament for consent. In 1628 Parliament only gave the king what he wanted after he had signed a *Petition* of Right, which included fundamental civil rights and granted the political rights of Parliament. But the king was tired of having to ask for money, so he raised taxes without calling Parliament into session between 1629 and 1640, just like his absolute colleague in France. He became very unpopular because of the new taxes, but also because he created special courts without *juries*, so that his judges could decide alone.

Civil War

In 1640 Charles I had to call Parliament again because an open war had broken out with the Scots. Instead of giving him the money he needed for the war, Parliament accused him of tyranny. Soon after a brutal civil war broke out which ended with the victory of Parliament under Oliver Cromwell, a Puritan, and the execution of Charles I. From 1649 to 1660 England was a republic, but Parliament did not rule for a long time as Oliver Cromwell dissolved it in 1653 and made himself "Lord Protector", which in effect meant military dictator. He turned down the offer of becoming king. After his death England returned to the old system of government again and made the son of the old king the new monarch as Charles II. But the old conflicts returned as well soon.

The "Glorious Revolution"

Only parts of Parliament supported the king, but when Catholic James II came to the throne in 1685 and joined forces with France and Louis XIV they feared that absolutism would come to England. Even though James granted religious freedom to everybody, Parliament allied with William of Orange from Holland, who was the husband of James's daughter Mary. Parliament invited him to invade England, offering him the crown. After William had driven James II out of the country, Parliament made him and Mary sign a declaration of the rights of the people of England before handing over the crown to them . This "Bill of Rights" from 1689 made England a parliamentary monarchy and a model for other states.

Info

Petition of Right 1628

1. No taxes could be *levied* without Parliament's consent
2. No English subject could be imprisoned without *cause* – thus reinforcing the right of *habeas corpus*
3. No *quartering* of soldiers in citizens' homes
4. No *martial law* may be used in peacetime

M 3 **Meeting of Parliament** without a king whose place has been taken by the speaker. Seal from 1651.

Vocabulary

petition: an official document asking for sth. to be done

jury: a group of people, usually 12, who judge a court case

to levy: (here) to ask for

cause: reason

habeas corpus: legal principle that a court must decide whether sb. can be imprisoned

to quarter: to give soldiers a temporary home

martial law: law of war

The English Way of Solving Problems

M 4 **The Execution of King Charles I in 1649**

Copper etching from 1649

M 5 Extract from the "Bill of Rights"

The Bill of Rights forms one part of the unwritten English constitution (1689):

"4. That *levying* money for or to the use of the crown [...], without grant of parliament, for longer time or in other manner than the same is or shall be granted, is illegal.

5. That it is the right of the subjects to petition the king, and all commitments and prosecutions for such petitioning are illegal.

6. That the raising or keeping a standing army within the kingdom in time of peace, unless it be with consent of parliament, is against the law.

7. That the subjects which are Protestants may have arms for their defense suitable to their conditions, and as allowed by law.

8. That election of members of parliament ought to be free.

9. That the freedom of speech, and debates or proceedings in parliament, ought not to be [...] questioned in any court or place out of parliament. [...]

13. And that for *redress* of all grievances, and for the amending, strengthening and preserving of the laws, parliament ought to be held frequently."

Quoted from: David C. Douglas (ed.), English Historical Documents Vol. 8, Eyre & Spottiswode: London 1955, p. 122f.

Vocabulary

to levy: (here) to use official authority to collect payments

redress: payment for sth. wrong that has happened to people

M 6 **William of Orange (1650 – 1702) and Mary**
accept the crown from Parliament in 1689. Contemporary painting.

Info

Constitution

Most states have a written document, which contains all the general rules of government and of organisation of the state (e.g. our basic law = Grundgesetz). The constitution of Great Britain is an unwritten one, which means that it consists of four different sources:

1. Statute laws (laws passed by the two houses of Parliament and the king/queen)
2. Common laws (laws made by court decisions)
3. Parliamentary conventions (some of which are very old like the Bill of Rights from 1689)
4. Works of authority (interpretations of the constitution by experts)

Parliamentary **Supremacy** and the rule of law are the most important principles.

Historical Terms

Constitution: Verfassung

Supremacy: Vorrangstellung, Vorherrschaft

Tasks

1. Monarchy in England

a) Collect reasons why England became more and more powerful in the 16th century (text).

b) Make a timeline from the second half of the 16th to the end of the 17th century, write the names of the rulers above the line and the actions of parliament below (text, M3, M4, M5, M6).

c) Describe the photo of the State Opening of Parliament (M1) and the painting of William and Mary (M6).

2. The English Way of Solving Problems

a) Describe the scene of the execution of the king (M4).

b) 1215 – 1628 – 1640/49 – 1689. Say how the problems of government were solved (M1, M3, M4, M5, M6).

c) Say why England did not become an absolute monarchy like France. Assess the role of Parliament in this context, especially in the 17th century.

M 1 Immanuel Kant (1724–1804)

Drawing, about 1790. Immanuel Kant became famous for the following definition:

"Enlightenment is man's emergence from his self-imposed *immaturity* ... Have courage to use your own understanding! – that is the motto of enlightenment."

The Age of Enlightenment

A New Way of Thinking

At about the time of the discovery of America, groundbreaking ideas had been made especially in the natural sciences. Some absolute monarchs founded academies and universities whose aim it was to develop the knowledge of mankind. Diderot and d'Alembert, two French philosophers, wrote the first "Encyclopedia", which included everything people knew at that time in 34 volumes. A new way of thinking spread in the homes of educated people in Europe. One of the most important issues people thought and talked about especially in Germany was religion, because people understood there was no general truth in a single religion and so they came up with the idea of religious tolerance.

The Theory

In the 17th and the 18th centuries some philosophers began to investigate the nature of the state and the nature of power. Their ideas were based on the *conviction* that people were born free. They all had one principle in common to direct people's way of life and the actions of the state alike – reason. They did not accept the old style of ruling based on the "grace of God". Whereas Montesquieu was convinced that a new kind of monarchy was best, one that was limited by laws and by a constitution, Rousseau went further and claimed that the people should be the origin of all power. This form of government is called a "republic".

Vocabulary

conviction: a strong opinion or belief

superstition: the belief that particular events bring good or bad luck

to modify: to change sth. slightly

immaturity (in M1): the state of not being fully developed

The Consequences

As a result of the new way of thinking knowledge grew, also because large numbers of people learned to read and write. Owning books became fashionable.

At the universities sciences gained importance whereas astrology and alchemy disappeared. There was no longer room for *superstition*.

Of course, some monarchs were not amused at first, when they heard about the development that was going on. However, some were interested and wanted to learn more themselves. So they invited philosophers to live at their courts and teach them. They understood that the new ideas could help them modernize their states. Some of them, like Catherine II of Russia and Emperor Joseph II of Austria, were even willing and able to *modify* their own role in their states carefully.

M 2 A Reading in Paris, 1755

Parisian high society meets in Madame Geoffrins's salon, Montesquieu and Rousseau among the guests. Contemporary painting.

M 3 The Enlightenment

a) John Locke (1690):

"The state is a union of people created for the sole purpose of representing, *asserting* and developing their civil interest."

John Locke, Two Treatises on Government, University Press: Cambridge 1960, p. 286ff.

b) Charles de Montesquieu (1748):

"Every state holds three powers: the power to legislate, the power to carry out what has been legislated, and the power to enforce the law. The second power is called the executive function and the third power, which enables the ruler to punish [...] citizens, is called the judicial function. All would be lost if a single man or authority [...] should succeed in combining the three powers. In a free state, every rational individual would ideally rule himself, but [...] this is impracticable in large states."

Charles de Montesquieu, On the Spirit of the Laws (1748), p. 162ff. (adapted by Rolf J. Kröger).

c) Jean-Jacques Rousseau (1762):

"Man is born free; and everywhere he is in chains [...] Since no man has a natural authority over his fellow, and force creates no right, we must conclude that conventions form the basis of all legitimate authority among men [...] To *renounce* liberty is to renounce being a man, to *surrender* the rights of humanity and even his duties. This is incompatible with man's nature."

Jean-Jacques Rousseau, Le Contrat Social, adapted by Rolf J. Kröger from: www.fordham.edu/halsall/mod/rousseau-contract2.html [Oct. 2017].

Vocabulary

to assert: to state firmly

renounce: to state formally that you no longer have a particular belief or position

to surrender: to give up sth. when forced to

M 4 "Tolerance"

"Tolerance, a female with a helmet and an aura of light protects the people of all religions."

Copper etching by Chodowiecki, 1791

Tasks

1. The Enlightenment – the big change?

a) Explain the new ideas of the three philosophers (M3).

b) Say what would happen if Montesquieu's three powers were in the hands of one person (M3b).

c) Compare Kant's statement to the other three (M1, M3).

2. The Enlightenment and Religion

a) Explain the influence of the Enlightenment on the church (text).

b) Describe the copper etching in detail and discuss its meaning (M4).

c) Show why the idea expressed in "Tolerance" is still valid and important today (M4).

Enlightened Absolutism and Prussia

M 1 Frederick as Military Commander
Equestrian statue in Berlin, Unter den Linden, by Christian Rauch, 1851

After the Thirty Years' War (1618–1648) Brandenburg-Prussia became more and more important in central Europe. Her rulers modernized the administration and created a big, well-trained army. They ruled the country as absolute princes. But in comparison to the "Big Four" in Europe (England, France, Russia, and Austria) their country was regarded as second class.

Frederick II – two personalities?

When he was young Frederick had a big problem with his father, who regarded him to be too weak for his future position. Frederick was interested in music and philosophy, but not so much in the military. He thought of reforms for his country. But his father brutally broke his will and forced him to pursue a military education. So during Frederick's entire life these two aspects remained important: reforms and the good sides of life on the one hand and wars and aggression on the other.

Reforms in Prussia

Although Frederick ruled the country like an absolute monarch, he thought himself to be the "first servant of his country". His reforms were deeply rooted in the ideas of the Enlightenment. He invited immigrants into the country in order to settle in formerly unsettled parts like the Oder area which he had turned into farm land by draining the swamps. He introduced the potato as a basic food and reformed the judicial system by simplifying it and having the laws written down. He also tried to improve the school system. With all these measures he wanted everybody to live in their own way, something that he personally did. He invited the French philosopher Voltaire to live at his court, he composed and played music and spent much time with his dogs. But he did not even think of handing over power to the people. However, by changing things to the better for many of them, he won the support of his people.

Biography

Prussian Rulers

1640–1688 Frederick William, the Great Elector

1688–1713 Frederick I, King in Prussia

1713–1740 Frederick William I, the Soldier King

1740–1786 Frederick II, the Great

Frederick II – the Great or not?

Contrary to what he had said before he became king, he attacked Silesia, which belonged to Austria. In a long series of wars he conquered land, but also risked the existence of his state. He was a very able military commander, but sometimes pure luck saved him from losing everything. At the end of his reign he had made Prussia the fifth great power in Europe. For a long time he was seen as Frederick the Great. But he used his troops in a reckless way for his aims and that has caused many people to come to a different opinion of his "greatness".

M 2 Frederick II, the Fluteplayer
Painting by Adolph von Menzel, 1852

M 3 **Frederick II, the Soldier, Battle of Zorndorf, 1758**

Painting by Carl Röchling, 1904

M 4 **Frederick II and Voltaire**

Frederick II and the French philosopher Voltaire having a discussion at Sanssouci.

Copper etching by Pierre Charles Baquoy, 1800

M 5 **Frederick II and Farming**

The painting "King Everywhere" shows Frederick II checking on his orders about planting potatoes.

Painting by Robert Warthmüller, 1886

Tasks

1. **Enlightened Absolutism and Prussia**
   a) Describe the pictures and find out about their main messages (M1 – M5).
   b) Find out about Frederick II's contribution to the growth of Prussian territory (text).
   c) Explain why people's opinions of Frederick II are mixed.
   d) Discuss whether Frederick II can or cannot be a role model for politicians today.

1640 1655 1670 1685 1700

1648: Peace of Westphalia

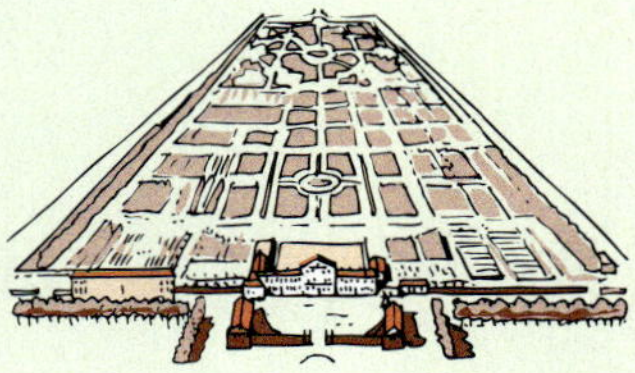

1661–1715: Louis XIV rules

Glorious Revolution

Edict of Fontainebleau

The Age of Absolutismus and Enlightenment – the historical map

1730 | 1745 | 1760 | 1775 | 1790

The Enlightenment

Frederick the Great

1756 – 1763:
Seven Years' War

French Revolution

Summary

From the second part of the 17th century onwards the French King Louis XIV became the absolute ruler of his country. He limited the influence of the old elite, founded his power on a standing army, on dependant civil servants, a new system of government, and on a newly organized economy. He saw himself as God's hand on earth and only responsible to God. In daily life, however, his power was not quite as "absolute" as in theory.

Nevertheless, he and his way of governing quickly became the role model for many princes in Europe. But when The Enlightenment, a new way of thinking, appeared, some of the princes integrated it into their style of ruling.

King Frederick II of Prussia was an especially successful monarch in the 18th century, when more and more people became enlightened, understood that their roles were changing and that they had basic civil rights.

In England some of these basic human rights became laws as a consequence of the struggle between the monarchs and important groups in society like the nobility and the members of parliament. So England did not become an absolute monarchy and slowly developed into a parliamentary monarchy instead.

DATES

1648: Peace of Westphalia

1661 – 1715: Louis XIV rules

1756 – 1763: Seven Years' War

HISTORICAL TERMS

Enlightenment
absolutism
Third Estate
estates
clergy
nobility
taxes
Great Elector
War of Succession
hegemony
balance of power
The English Parliament
Petition of Right
constitution
supremacy

PERSONS

Louis XIV

Frederick the Great

HISTORY WORKSHOP

Analysing Paintings

M 1 **Jefferson Hands over the Declaration of Independence. Painting by John Trumbull, 1787–1818**

M 2 **At a Slave Auction about 1850**

M 3 **"Agony" by Charles Deas, 1845**

M 4 **Stamps Showing US Flags**

02 THE AMERICAN REVOLUTION

The Rise of a New Nation

In the 18th century a new country, the United States of America, was founded. She began as a group of British colonies in North America, which later fought a War of Independence against Britain (1776 – 1783). By the end of the 20th century she was a world power. The rise of the new nation came about through some unusual factors, which this unit examines.

Founding a new country was difficult. At first, settling the new territory was the most important task. Homes, farms, churches, schools, roads, and businesses all had to be built. Even governments had to be founded. After the early settlements succeeded, the country grew dramatically. When the population was counted for the first time in 1790, there were nearly 4 million people living in the country. In 2017 there are about 325 million. The territory of the USA also expanded westward. Today the land claimed by the country extends from the Atlantic to the Pacific Ocean and includes Alaska, Hawaii, and other US territories. This dynamic growth meant that many people had to be taken in and find their places in a new society. Some newcomers found it hard to adapt to the conditions of life in a new country, some were not welcomed by those who had come earlier. At the same time, natives who already lived on the territory of the new nation were removed or even killed. This chapter looks especially at how Native Americans, blacks, and women were integrated into US society.

After the US Constitution was written in 1787, national unity seemed secure. But the Civil War from 1861 to1865 called this unity into question. Although the North defeated the South, the conflict still had an effect on American political life for many years. The goal from the Declaration of Independence that "all men are created equal" has been difficult to achieve.

This chapter deals with many questions such as:

- What European settlements were there in North and South America?
- Why did settlers move to the colonies?
- How did European settlers and natives interact?
- What problems came up on the Mayflower passage in 1620?
- What in the situation of the British colonists led them to declare their independence?
- What are the main features of the US Constitution?
- What conflicts came about because of slavery?
- What were the goals of the women's movement?

Historical Terms

Pilgrim: Pilger
constitution: Verfassung

A New Beginning in a Foreign Land

European Settlements in the Americas

When Christopher Columbus landed in the Caribbean in1492, he claimed the new lands he found for Spain. Then other Spanish explorers set out for the new territory to search for riches and to convert natives there to Christianity. Soon Portuguese explorers followed. By the 16th century, Spain claimed land in most of South America and in North America from the West Coast to Florida. Portugal claimed mostly Brazil. In the 17th century, the French, Dutch and British moved along the east coast of North America to Hudson Bay. Denmark claimed Greenland. Russia moved into Alaska and along the northwestern coast of North America in the 18th century.

The European powers competed with native peoples and with each other for the new lands. At the same time, the Europeans also allied with natives in fighting their enemies in the colonies. Britain, the Netherlands, Spain, and France fought wars in the Americas. The French and Indian War (1754–1763) in North America was called the Seven Years' War in Europe (1756–1763). It ended when Britain and Spain defeated France and divided the French colonies in the New World between them.

First British Colonies

It was not until 1584 that Sir Walter Raleigh founded the first English settlement, which he named Virginia after his "Virgin Queen" Elizabeth I. After her death, political and religious *persecution* led to more and more Protestants leaving England for America. Among them were a group of about forty religious "Separatists" and sixty non-religious settlers, who reached the coast of what was

M 1 **Mayflower II**

A copy of the Mayflower in Plymouth, Mass., USA

to be Massachusetts on board the "Mayflower" on 21 November 1620. Today we call them the **Pilgrims**.

The New Settlers in North America

As a result of the political and economic turbulence which shook Europe in the course of the Thirty Years' War and the Civil War in England, more and more emigrants left their mother countries hoping for a better future or at least the end of their hardship. Many people had lost their land because it had been destroyed by official troops or *mercenaries*. Others had been forced to join an army and wanted to get away. A large number of those who left Europe belonged to a religious minority and had been *persecuted* in their home countries. But there were also shipowners who saw their chance of becoming rich by persuading people to go to America. They used all sorts of tricks and promises to get passengers. Some emigrants went because of a spirit of adventure. Beggars and criminals were *deported*. Those who could not pay for the voyage were allowed to go as *indentured servants*, which meant that they had to work for the person who had paid for their voyage for three to seven years after their arrival.

Natives Weakened by Disease

The natives who had lived where the Pilgrims landed had died from a terrible disease they may have got from other Europeans on an earlier visit. Historians do not know what the disease was. In the three years before the Pilgrims landed it had killed between 90 and 96% of the natives living on the New England coast. In the fifteen years afterwards, outbreaks of disease, which were probably smallpox, killed more of the natives. The natives had lived isolated from Europeans, so they were not immune to the diseases brought by the settlers. The Pilgrims believed that the natives' deaths were a sign of God's grace and proof that they should have the land they now claimed.

Getting Organized

Many immigrants worked very hard, not only because they wanted to survive and have a better future but also because they thought God's blessing showed in the success of their work. This religious belief became a strong driving force in the economy. The first years were extremely hard as the newcomers had to adjust to differences in the living conditions, especially the climate.

By 1700 colonial government had been established by the British in thirteen colonies on the East Coast. All followed the example set by Connecticut in 1639 and gave themselves **constitutions**. *Free colonists* had the same rights as British citizens, but women, slaves, natives, and all those who were not members of the church had no rights.

The "First" Thanksgiving, 1621

In the autumn of 1621, the fifty-three Pilgrims who were still alive celebrated at a harvest festival with about ninety Wampanoag natives. The natives hunted five deer to help feed everyone at the festival. This "first" Thanksgiving in the British colonies has become a legend in US history. But the Pilgrims did not introduce Thanksgiving to America. Native tribes had celebrated harvests for many hundreds of years before the settlers arrived. Thanksgiving became a US national holiday in 1863, during the Civil War. The Pilgrims did not become part of the "tradition" until the 1890s.

Vocabulary

mercenary: a soldier fighting for sb. who pays him

to persecute: to treat sb. in a cruel or unfair way

to deport: to send away to a foreign country by force

indentured servant: person who agrees to work for sb. for a number of years to pay back money borrowed (here the money was usually borrowed to pay for passage to America)

free colonist: a colonist who was not an indentured servant and therefore had the right to vote

A New Beginning in a Foreign Land

Info

Problems Among the Mayflower Passengers

Passengers on the Mayflower had to deal with serious problems. First of all, the trip did not start until September 1620. Weather conditions in the autumn made the journey difficult. The ship did not land in Virginia as planned, but historians today do not agree on the reasons for this. When the Mayflower finally reached Massachusetts after sixty-six days at sea, snow had already fallen. The cold winter was much harsher than the settlers expected, so they waited out the winter on board the ship. By spring only fifty-three of the passengers and one-half of the crew were still alive, thanks to natives who helped them survive. Many of the non-religious passengers complained about reaching the wrong destination. The settlers had to ask the English king to give them a patent for a colony in the area where they landed. While they waited for this patent, forty-one men on board the ship signed the Mayflower Compact, an agreement to act together for the safety of the colony.

M 2 Mayflower Compact

Forty-one men on the Mayflower signed the following compact (1620):

"In the name of God, Amen. We [...] having undertaken for the glory of God, and advancement of the Christian faith, and honor of our King and country, a voyage to plant the first colony in the northern parts of Virginia, do by these presents solemnly and mutually, in the presence of God and one another, *covenant* and combine ourselves together into a civil body politic, for our better ordering and preservation, and furtherance of the ends aforesaid; and by virtue hereof do enact, constitute and frame such just and equal laws, ordinances, acts, constitutions and offices, [...] AD 1620."

Quoted from: Thomas V. DiBacco, Lorna C. Mason, Christian G. Appy, History of the United States, Houghton Mifflin Company: Boston 1991, p. 16. (adapted by Rolf J. Kröger).

M 3 God's Will?

John Winthrop, governor of Massachusetts Bay Colony, in a letter to a friend, 1634:

"But for the natives in these parts, God hath so *pursued* them, as for 300 miles space the greatest part of them are swept away by the smallpox which still continues among them. So as God hath thereby cleared our title to this place, those who remain in these parts, being in all not 50, have put themselves under our protection [...]."

Quoted from: James W. Loewen, Lies My Teacher Told Me, Touchstone: New York 1995, p. 81.

M 4 An Account of Pennsylvania

A politician from Pennsylvania described four reasons why people settled in the new territory:

"The true reason why the people of this country buy more and more land is their success in trade. And there is a lot more cheap land to buy. Most of the new Christian land owners are farmers and have large cattle herds. Many of them must now go further up into the country because they can find cheaper and better land there for their cattle.
It is also the part of the land where skins, furs, and other animal products are traded in from the Indians. The third advantage of that land is the existence of copper and iron mines. When it was first examined only heathens and very few Christians lived there and hardly anybody wanted to go there because it was wild and dangerous."

Gabriel Thomas, An account of Pennsylvania, adapted by Rolf J. Kröger from: Daniel J. Boorstin (ed.), An American Primer, Meridian: Chicago 1966, p. 56f.

Vocabulary

to covenant: to legally agree to do sth.
to pursue: to follow and persecute sb.

Tasks

1. **The Mayflower**
   a) List the problems the ship had crossing the Atlantic (text, infobox).
   b) Explain why the forty-one men signed the Mayflower Compact (text, M2).
2. **Disease Among the Natives**
   a) Describe the effects of disease on the native peoples near Plymouth, Massachusetts, from 1617 to 1620.
   b) Tell in your own words what William Bradford reports about the natives in 1634 (M3).
   c) Explain why the English settlers believed that God had given them the land they claimed in Plymouth.
3. **An Account of Pennsylvania**
   a) List the four reasons why people settled in the new territory (M4).
   b) Explain what made the territory "wild and dangerous" (l. 12).

The First Thanksgiving – finding mistakes in a historical painting

M 5 **"The First Thanksgiving"**
Oil painting by Jean Leon Gerome Ferris, about 1912

Vocabulary

useful words and phrases to discuss the painting:

some people are "guests" and others are "hosts" in the painting

food: a pot of soup or porridge

bowls of meal

a plate of baked goods

a pitcher of water (beer was rare)

Vocabulary

the painting is historically inaccurate, because

- the Wampanoag did not wear feather headdresses
- the Wampanoag would not sit on the ground as shown
- Wampanoag and Pilgrim clothes looked different
- Pilgrims did not build log cabins

Tasks

1. "The First Thanksgiving"
  a) Describe the painting (M5).
  b) Point out how the "guests" and the "hosts" are shown in the painting.
  c) Make a list of what the artist shows that is not historically accurate.
  d) Explain why the artist made these mistakes.

M 1 **Thomas Jefferson (1743–1826)**

The author of the Declaration of Independence. He later became the third president of the USA.

The Road to Independence

Money Problems

From 1755 to 1763 war *raged* in both America and Europe. The "Seven Years' War" in Europe was called the "French and Indian War" in America. Britain won after the surrender of the French in Canada. In the Treaty of Paris, France had to hand over most of Canada and the territory east of the Mississippi River to Britain. But the war had been very expensive for the British so they raised taxes or simply invented new ones. These taxes also applied to the colonists, who found many of them unfair, especially because they had no representatives in the British Parliament to oppose them. They claimed "no taxation without representation" and protested strongly. As a reaction the British cancelled most of the taxes except for the tax on tea, but the protests went on. They culminated in the Boston Massacre in 1770, in which five Americans were killed by British soldiers.

Fighting for Independence

In 1773 Bostonians disguised as Indians threw the cargo of three tea clippers into the harbour, which was closed afterwards by the British. Behind the scenes representatives of the thirteen colonies discussed their *options*. They met at the First Continental Congress in Philadelphia in 1774 and decided not to trade with Britain any longer.

At the same time the colonists founded their own militia, the "Minutemen". The first armed clash in 1775 developed into the War of Independence. Thomas Paine wrote and issued a *pamphlet* with all the arguments the colonists needed for the separation. But it was not before 4 July of the following year that some of the colonists formally declared their independence. One third remained neutral, others stayed loyal to the British king and supported the British troops, as did most of the Indians and about 13,000 mercenaries from Hesse and Brunswick who had been hired out to England by their princes.

The army of only 13,000 colonists was trained by the Prussian General Steuben and commanded by George Washington. Their allies were Holland, Spain and France, whose absolute monarch Louis XVI wanted to take revenge on the British for the defeat of France twenty years earlier. George Washington proved to be a very *skilful* commander, but the colonists also had other advantages. All the farmers knew and used their own guns. They were strong believers in the cause and nearly all of them were well educated for the time, so communication worked well. They were also encouraged by a free press in the colonies. After several defeats the British surrendered and recognized American independence in the 1783 Treaty of Paris.

It took the Americans another four years until they were able to agree on a federal constitution for the United States of America. The differences among the thirteen former colonies were a main *obstacle* in this process.

Vocabulary

to rage: to continue in a violent way

option: sth. you can choose to have or do

pamphlet: (here) a leaflet containing a political message

skilful: good at doing sth.

obstacle: sth. that hinders you

M 2 **Yorktown 1781**

George Washington discusses the situation with the Duke of Rochambeau and the Marquis de Lafayette.

M 3 **"Join or Die"**

Caricature by Benjamin Franklin, 1754

M 4 "Time to Part"

Thomas Paine, who emigrated to America in 1774, wrote a pamphlet in which he laid out the only solution to the problems between England and the colonies:

"But Britain is the parent country, say some. Then the more shame upon her conduct [...]
This new World *hath* been the asylum for the persecuted lovers of civil and religious liberty from EVERY PART of Europe. Hither have they fled, not from the tender embraces of the mother, but from the cruelty of the monster [...] I challenge the warmest advocate for *reconciliation* to show a single advantage that this continent can reap by being connected with Great Britain. I repeat the challenge; not a single advantage is derived. Our corn will fetch its price in any market in Europe, and our imported goods must be paid for – buy them where we will [...] Because, any [...] dependence on Great Britain, tends directly to involve this Continent in European wars and quarrels, and sets us at variance with nations who would otherwise seek our friendship, and against whom we have neither anger nor complaint. As Europe is our market for trade, we ought to form no partial connection with any part of it.
Every thing that is right or reasonable *pleads* for separation. The blood of the *slain*, the weeping voice of nature cries, 'TIS TIME TO PART'. Even the distance at which the Almighty hath placed England and America is a strong and natural proof that the authority of the one over the other, was never the design of Heaven."

www.ushistory.org/PAINE/commonsense/sense4.htm [Oct. 2017].

M 5 The Declaration of Independence

Thomas Jefferson wrote in the Declaration of Independence:

"We hold these truths to be self-evident. That all men are created equal. That they are endowed by their creator with certain *unalienable* rights. That among these are life, liberty and the pursuit of happiness. That to secure these rights governments are instituted among men deriving their just powers from the consent of the governed. That whenever any form of government becomes destructive of these ends it is the right of the people to alter or to abolish it and to institute new government [...]."

www.ushistory.org/declaration/document/index.html [Oct. 2017].

Vocabulary

hath: has
reconciliation: end to a quarrel and start of a good relationship again
to plead: to ask urgently
the slain: the people who were killed
unalienable: sth. that cannot be taken away from you

Tasks

1. **Money Problems**
   a) Show reasons why the British raised taxes on the colonists (text).
   b) Explain the colonists' reactions to the taxes (text).
   c) Point out Benjamin Franklin's message to the colonists in the caricature (M3).
2. **Fighting for Independence**
   a) Make a timeline of the events of the American Revolution (text).
   b) Find countries which helped the colonists fight the British (text, M2).
   c) Comment on these foreign interests in helping the colonists (text).
3. **The Colonists' Arguments for Independence**
   a) List Thomas Paine's arguments for fighting against Britain (M4).
   b) Underline the rights of everyone, according to Thomas Jefferson (M5).
   c) Show how the Declaration of Independence gives the colonists the right to rebel against the British government (M5).
   d) Decide whether the War of Independence was a revolution or only a rebellion. Point out facts to support your argument (text).

The USA – A New State

M 1 **The Presidential Seal of the USA**

A New Type of State

After the war had been won, the thirteen former colonies were only linked by a confederation that had coordinated activities against the British. The confederation had no president, no court system, no government agencies, and no way of raising taxes efficiently. The army and navy could not be paid for, veterans of the Revolutionary War could not get the pensions they had been promised. Even though the political representatives of the individual states saw the *necessity* of some sort of central government there were different opinions on how to organize it so that every single state would be satisfied:

- What rights should the individual states have?
- How should elections be organized and how many representatives should be elected to represent each state?
- How should federalism be set up?
- How could abuse of power be prevented?

Apart from these questions there were practical obstacles like huge distances, the differences in climate and lack of roads, which the British were certain would hinder the states from uniting.

Common Ground

But representatives of the states also held some principles in common. So they met at a federal convention in 1787 to work out a constitution for the United States. The discussions were influenced by the French philosopher Montesquieu, among others. His writings had been sent to America by its *ambassador* to France, Thomas Jefferson, who tried to influence the results of the convention, as he wanted his ideas in the Declaration of Independence *to prevail*. As in the constitution of the Roman Republic, power was to be shared so that no one could have complete power. Human rights were to guide all laws. One group of representatives at the convention thought one house in the new Congress, elected by the people, was sufficient; another group did not want to hand over too much influence to the mass of the people. However, no one wanted to copy the British Parliament.

Problems and Results

But all feared that the other states might gain more power and influence than their own, so they chose a system with two chambers. Each state had two senators. The number of representatives in the second chamber was decided according to the population of the state. A *census* took place every ten years. Only men who were citizens could vote, but women, children, slaves (a slave counted as only 3/5 of a person) and non-citizens were counted in the census. The Electoral College elected the president and vice-president indirectly by electors, not by popular vote.

It took the convention more than a year to agree on a solution. Some delegates even left early in disgust. As it was not certain whether the states would ratify the new constitution, a Bill of Rights was added and a campaign was organized to gather support. By June 1788 nine states had ratified. The last two of the original thirteen colonies – North Carolina and Rhode Island, which had not even taken part in the convention – ratified only after the swearing-in-ceremony of the first president, George Washington.

Vocabulary

necessity: the fact that sth. must happen

ambassador: an official who represents his country in a foreign one

to prevail: to dominate

census: an official count of the people with details such as age, sex, occupation, etc.

life tenure: holding a job for as long as sb. lives

impeachment: the act of formally accusing a public official of a serious crime

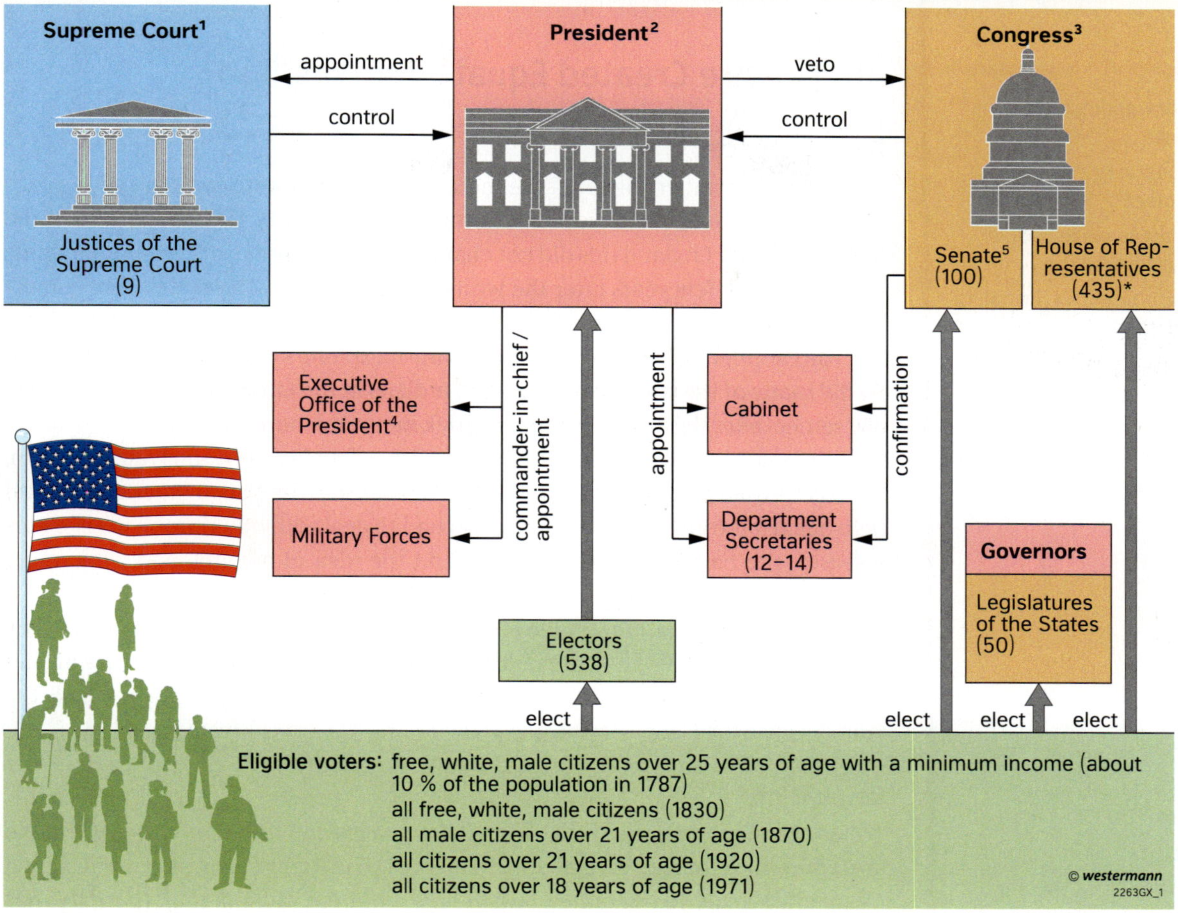

M 2 The Constitution of the United States, 17 September 1787 to today

1. The justices of the Supreme Court are appointed by the president and confirmed by the Senate for *life tenure*. *Impeachment* is possible, although this has never happened to date. The Supreme Court decides disputes among the individual states and is also the final court of appeal in the judicial system.

Since the beginning of the 19th century, the Supreme Court has established its right to interpret federal law, including the Constitution.

2. A president can prevent a law from going into effect by vetoing it. This veto can be overridden by a two-thirds majority in both houses of Congress.

3. The main duty of the Congress is to pass laws. These must be signed by the president to go into effect. The Congress decides about taxation and can declare war. (* There are five other delegates from US territories, but they have no voting rights in the chamber.)

4. The president depends upon competent advice in many areas. The Executive Office of the President was created in 1939 to allow advisors from outside the departmental bureaucracy of the Cabinet to assist in such areas.

5. Each state elects two senators. The seats in the House of Representatives are set by the census, which is taken every ten years. The House of Representatives has the right to impeach a president by voting to send the case to trial in the Senate. Then the Senate decides either to convict the president or not.

Tasks

1. The USA – A New State

a) Discuss the necessity for the states to unite. Find at least three arguments for and against unity (text).

b) Explain why it took the states so long to form the United States (text).

2. The US Constitution (M2)

a) Explain how the three branches of government work together and also control each other.

b) Show how the number of eligible voters grew from 1787 to 1971.

c) Assess the difference between the Senate and the House of Representatives.

d) Comment on the method of electing the president in 1787 and today.

Vocabulary

curious: wanting to know about sth.

ferocious: very aggressive and violent

to stir up: to make people feel strong emotions

savage: a primitive, brutal, or cruel person

relocation: moving to a new place

All Men Are Created Equal – Indians, Too?

Big Differences

When the new settlers first met the Indians, the natives were *curious* and friendly. The Pilgrims could not have lived through the first winter without help from the Indians. In New England this did not change until 1638. But in other colonies fights began within a few years after the white settlers arrived. The fights were usually over land.

Christopher Columbus and other Spanish explorers treated the Indians badly. So did many of the later settlers. In 1622 Indians in the Jamestown area massacred 350 settlers after the Virginia Company took more and more land for tobacco farms. Such massacres helped create the myth of the *ferocious* and uncivilized Indian, which was used *to stir up* hate against these "*savages*". The Native Americans had to fight against the armed whites. They also had to deal with other problems like new diseases, the bad influence of alcohol and the idea of owning land, which was unknown to them.

The natives could not understand the settlers' greed for land or the way they took it. Natives believed no one could possess any of the four elements water, air, fire and earth. The whites, on the other hand, thought that they had the right to take the land because the Native Americans of the prairie did not cultivate it.

Relocation

Tribes of Indian "nations" with different languages and different customs tried to keep the white settlers from taking their lands. The American government signed treaty after treaty to guarantee Indian lands, but few settlers took these treaties seriously. In the 18th and the 19th centuries many tribes from the East, the South and the Southwest were relocated to the West by the government. One of the worst relocations was the Cherokee "Trail of Tears" in 1838.

Often the Indians agreed to move when the US government offered them money or new land. Some of the agreements were dishonest and gave the Indians only poor-quality land. When Congress passed the Indian Removal Act in 1830, the government had the right to force all Indians to move to reservations whether they agreed or not. After the whites wiped out the buffalo in most parts of the prairie, some tribes, which had lost their whole way of life, went peacefully. But a number of tribes banded together and fought to stay on their ancestors' land. Then the US Army showed it was stronger than the Indians, who were all resettled by 1900. Although the Fourteenth Amendment to the US Constitution (passed in 1868) said that "all persons born or naturalized in the United States" were citizens, Native Americans did not receive US citizenship until Congress passed the Indian Citizenship Act in 1924.

M 1

Indian Territory in the USA

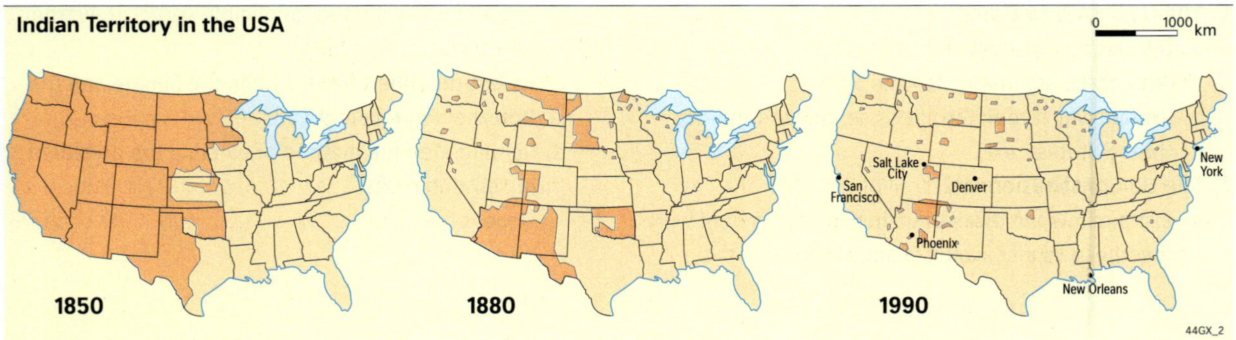

M 2 "Trail of Tears"
The removal of the Cherokee Indians to the West in 1838, oil on canvas by Robert Lindneux. Painting, 1942

M 3 Four Indian Chiefs Try to be Heard

a) Wahunsonacock (King Powhatan) in 1609:

"Why should you take by force what you can have by love? Why should you destroy us who have provided you with food? What can you get by war? We can hide our provisions and fly into the woods; and then you must consequently *famish* by wronging your friends. What is the cause of your *jealousy*? You see us unarmed, and willing to supply your wants, if you come in a friendly manner, and not with swords and guns as to invade an enemy."

Quoted from: A. LaVonne Brown Ruoff, American Indian Literatures, The Modern Language Association of America: New York 1990, p. 51.

b) Shawnee Chief Tecumseh in 1811:

"Where today are the Pequot? Where are the Narrangansett, the Mohican, the Pocanet, and other powerful tribes of our people? They have *vanished* before the *avarice* and oppression of the white man, as snow before the summer sun [...] Will we let ourselves be destroyed in our turn, without making an effort worthy of our race? Shall we, without a struggle, give up our homes, our lands, *bequeathed* to us by the Great Spirit? The graves of our dead and everything that is dear and sacred to us? [...] I know you will say with me, Never! Never!"

Ibid, p. 51.

c) Chief Joseph of the Nez Perez in 1877:

"Our chiefs are killed. The little children are freezing to death. My people have no blankets, no food. Hear me, my chiefs; I am tired; my heart is sick and sad. From where the sun now stands, I will fight no more."

Ibid, p. 57.

d) Young Sioux Black Elk in 1890 after surviving Wounded Knee:

"Something else died there [...] A people's dream died there. It was a beautiful dream."

Quoted from: Anne Zeman and Kate Kelly, Everything you need to know about American Homework, Scholastic: New York 1997, p. 52.

Vocabulary

to famish: to die of hunger, to starve
jealousy: wanting sth. belonging to another person
to vanish: to disappear
avarice: greed, extreme desire for wealth
to bequeath (formal): to give sb. property

Tasks

1. **Differences Between Settlers and Native Americans**
   Show how the relationship between the white settlers and the Native Americans changed (text).
2. **Relocation**
   a) Describe the loss of Indian territory from 1850 to 1990 (M1).
   b) Look up the Cherokee "Trail of Tears" on the Internet. Report back to your class.
   c) Write two reports about the painting from the points of view of
   – a Cherokee woman, and
   – a US Cavalry soldier.
4. **Four Indian Chiefs (M3)**
   a) List the arguments that the Native Americans make in their statements.
   b) Discuss the differences among the statements.
   c) Assess the changes in Native American life shown in the texts.

M 1 **Abraham Lincoln**
President from 1861–1865.
Photograph, about 1863

All Men Are Created Equal – Blacks, Too?

Slavery

By the end of the 18th century half a million slaves had been taken to the USA from Africa by means of the "Atlantic Triangle", a system of trade organized by the British and other Europeans. Many slaves, who were handcuffed and chained to each other during the voyage, died before they reached America. The survivors were bought by planters and farmers mainly in the southern states.

Slavery and Territorial Expansion

Slavery together with the movement to the West created political problems for the United States. In the northern states more and more people rejected the idea of slavery, so it was gradually prohibited. But in the South slaves were needed to work on the cotton plantations and tobacco farms. Without the work of the slaves these crops were not profitable. As more settlers went to the new lands in the western territories, the question of whether slavery would move with them came up repeatedly.

Even though the slave trade was forbidden in 1808, the number of slaves grew steadily, keeping pace with the production of cotton. As new states joined the union, Congress had to decide whether they would join as "slave" or "free" states. Because each state selected two Senators, it was important to keep a balance between the two groups. Otherwise, both sides feared they would be constantly outvoted. In 1820 the Missouri Compromise decided that states north of the Missouri Territory's northern border could join the Union as free states, while those south of it could join as slave states. But in the Kansas-Nebraska Act of 1854, Congress decided to let the voters decide about slavery in the future states of Kansas and Nebraska directly. This *repealed* the Missouri Compromise. The result was "Bleeding Kansas", as slaveowners from Missouri tried to drive out free-soil farmers, or at least keep them from voting. Kansas became a (free) state in 1861, just before the Civil War began. Nebraska joined the Union in 1867, after the Civil War had ended. The Kansas-Nebraska Act also meant that the Midwestern native tribes who had been driven from their lands under the Indian Removal Act of 1830 were now forced to move on to other areas farther west, such as in Oklahoma.

Fugitive Slaves and the Underground Railroad

Slaves tried to become free by crossing into non-slave states. When Frederick Douglass escaped in 1837 and became the first "fugitive slave" lecturer in America and abroad, the abolitionist movement grew, even organizing civil rights demonstrations. The Underground Railroad organized people to help fugitive

M 2 **Slaves Picking Cotton on a Southern Plantation**
Engraving, about 1861

slaves on escape routes to free areas. Harriet Tubman, an escaped slave woman, made thirteen trips to southern states to lead slaves into free states and Canada. The 1850 Fugitive Slave Act passed by Congress made it legal for slave owners to look for their fugitive slaves in the free states and have "their property" returned.

Dred Scott Casts a Shadow on the Future

An important development in the slavery debate was the Supreme Court decision in the Dred Scott case in 1857. Declaring "a Negro had no rights a white man was bound to respect," the court made what historians call its worst decision ever. Dred Scott, a slave, had *sued* his owner for his freedom when he was taken to a free state. But the court said a Negro, whether slave or free man, could not be an American citizen and had no right to sue his owner. In addition, the court stated that owners could take their slaves to free states (which Congress had tried to forbid by law), because slaves were property and Congress could not restrict an owner's right to this property. The decision seemed to mean that slavery could spread legally throughout the entire United States in the future. It led to strong opposition among those who opposed slavery and pushed the country closer to civil war.

M 3 Public Punishment
Photograph, about 1860

The Civil War and its Legacy

Abraham Lincoln was elected president in 1860. He wanted to keep the Union together and stop the spread of slavery to new states. Slavery was not the only issue which divided the North and the South. Although most people still lived and worked on small farms, circumstances had changed completely. In the North many people worked in factories in the cities, whereas the South remained rural. The economy of the North was based on free labourers who received wages and worked where they wanted to. The South was based on slave labour. Moreover, the southern states argued that it was possible to leave the Union if a state voted to do so. The North denied that states had such a right. Seven southern states (four more joined them later) declared their secession from the Union. In April 1861, these Confederate States attacked the Union army at Fort Sumter, South Carolina, in the first battle of the Civil War. The war lasted until 1865 and cost 600,000 American lives.

In 1863 Lincoln freed the slaves with the Emancipation Proclamation. The Union victory at Gettysburg was the turning point in the war. A week after the main Confederate army surrendered, Lincoln was assassinated. The 14th Amendment to the Constitution made all former slaves US citizens in 1868. The southern states opposed the amendment bitterly, but were forced to agree in order to get seats in Congress once again. In the South, slavery was replaced by racial segregation. Voters in various places had to pay a "poll tax" to vote, or prove their grandfathers had voted earlier. The Supreme Court ruled that public facilities could be segregated if they were "separate, but equal" in 1896. "*Jim Crow*" laws enforced segregation for schools, toilets, drinking fountains, railroad cars, and buses. These laws from the end of the 19th century stayed in effect until the Civil Rights Act of 1964. Only then were African-Americans granted full equality. Although the Supreme Court declared the segregation of public schools unconstitutional in 1954, change came only slowly. It took pressure from a strong civil rights movement led by the *NAACP* and its leader Dr. Martin Luther King, Jr. to improve the situation of blacks in the USA.

Vocabulary

to repeal: to state officially that a law has ended

to sue: to make a legal claim

Jim Crow: an unpleasant name for Negro

NAACP: National Association for the Advancement of Colored People

All Men Are Created Equal – Blacks, Too?

M 4 Extract from "Uncle Tom's Cabin"

In her famous book "Uncle Tom's Cabin" Harriett Beecher-Stowe included a conversation between Mr Shelby and his wife:

"Mr Shelby, you cannot be serious."

"I'm sorry to say that I am," said Mr Shelby. "I've agreed to sell Tom."

"What? Our Tom? – that good faithful creature! – been your faithful servant from a boy! O, Mr Shelby! – and you have promised him his freedom, too, – you and I have spoken to him a hundred times of it. Well, I can believe anything now, – I can believe now that you could sell little Harry, poor Eliza's only child!" said Mrs Shelby, in a tone of grief and indignation.

"Well, since you must know all, it is so..."

"Why sell them, ... if you must sell at all?"

"Because they will bring the highest sum of money – that's why..."

Harriett Beecher Stowe, Uncle Tom's Cabin, John P. Jewett and Company: Cleveland/Ohio 1852, chapter V.

M 5 "Cornerstone Speech"

Alexander Stephens, Vice President of the Confederacy, from the "Cornerstone Speech", at Savannah, Georgia, on 21 March 1861:

[The Confederacy's] corner-stone rests upon the great truth, that the negro is not equal to the white man; that slavery – subordination to the superior race – is his natural and normal condition. This, our new government, is the first, in the history of the world, based upon this great physical, philosophical, and moral truth.

https://en.wikisource.org/wiki/Cornerstone_Speech [Oct. 2017].

M 6 "The Gettysburg Address"

Abraham Lincoln, "The Gettysburg Address", 19 November 1863. Lincoln spoke where the armies of the North and the South fought from 1 to 3 July 1863 at the Battle of Gettysburg, which is considered the turning point of the Civil War. Nearly 51,000 soldiers died there. It was the most costly battle in U.S. history:

Fourscore and seven years ago our fathers brought forth on this continent a new nation, conceived in liberty and dedicated to the proposition that all men are created equal. Now we are engaged in a great civil war, testing whether that nation or any nation so conceived and so dedicated can long endure. We are met on a great battlefield of that war. We have come to dedicate a portion of that field as a final resting-place for those who here gave their lives that that nation might live. It is altogether fitting and proper that we should do this. But in a larger sense, we cannot dedicate, we cannot consecrate, we cannot hallow this ground. The brave men, living and dead who struggled here have consecrated it far above our poor power to add or detract. The world will little note nor long remember what we say here, but it can never forget what they did here. It is for us the living rather to be dedicated here to the unfinished work which they who fought here have thus far so nobly advanced. It is rather for us to be here dedicated to the great task remaining before us – that from these honored dead we take increased devotion to that cause for which they gave the last full measure of devotion – that we here highly resolve that these dead shall not have died in vain, that this nation under God shall have a new birth of freedom, and that government of the people, by the people, for the people shall not perish from the earth.

https://www.loc.gov/exhibits/gettysburg-address/ext/trans-nicolay-inscribed.html [Oct. 2017].

Tasks

1. **Slavery**
   a) Explain why slavery continued in the South, although northern states prohibited it (text).
   b) Discuss why slavery was inhumane (M2, M3).
   c) Assess why "Uncle Tom's Cabin" became so popular when it was written (M4).
2. **Slavery and Territorial Expansion**
   a) Show why slavery was a problem as the USA moved to the West (text).
   b) Work in small groups. Comment on how Congress tried to solve the problem through laws (text).
   c) Assess how the slavery problem affected Native Americans (text).
3. **The Civil War**
   a) Give reasons for the outbreak of the Civil War (text).
   b) Point out what Confederate Vice President Stephens states is the "cornerstone" of the Confederacy (M6).
   c) Explain why Abraham Lincoln is considered one of the greatest US presidents today (text).
   d) Read Lincoln's Gettysburg Address (M7). State the goals he sets for the USA in the speech.

M 7 "Truth: Remarks on the Removal of Confederate Monuments in New Orleans"

In June 2015, nine people were shot in a black church in South Carolina. The killings started a discussion of Confederate symbols in the South. In New Orleans, four Confederate monuments have been removed, among them statues of the Confederate President Jefferson Davis and of the Confederate Generals Robert E. Lee and P. G. T. Beauregard. The mayor of New Orleans, Mitchell J. Landrieu, explains why the removals were necessary in his speech, 19 May 2017:

The soul of our beloved City is deeply rooted in a history that has evolved over thousands of years; rooted in a diverse people who have been here together every step of the way – for both good and for ill. [...] New Orleans is truly a city of many nations / a melting pot / a bubbling cauldron of many cultures. There is no other place quite like it in the world that so eloquently exemplifies the uniquely American motto: e pluribus unum – out of many we are one.

But there are also other truths about our city that we must confront.

New Orleans was America's largest slave market: a port where hundreds of thousands of souls were brought, sold and shipped up the Mississippi River to lives of forced labor, of misery, of rape, of torture.

America was the place where nearly 4000 of our fellow citizens were lynched, 540 alone in Louisiana; where the courts *enshrined* 'separate but equal' [...].

So when people say to me that the monuments in question are history, well what I just described is real history as well, and it is the *searing* truth. [...]

The historic record is clear, the Robert E. Lee, Jefferson Davis, and P. G. T. Beauregard statues were not erected just to honor these men, but as part of the movement which became known as The Cult of the Lost Cause. This 'cult' had one goal – through monuments and through other means – to rewrite history to hide the truth, which is that the Confederacy was on the wrong side of humanity.

M 8 Robert E. Lee Monument in New Orleans
City workers remove the statue from its pedestal, photograph, 2017

[...T]hese men did not fight for the United States of America, they fought against it. They may have been warriors, but in this cause they were not patriots. [...]

These monuments purposefully celebrate a fictional, *sanitized* Confederacy; ignoring the death, ignoring the enslavement, and the terror that it actually stood for.

After the Civil War, these statues were a part of that terrorism as much as a burning cross on someone's lawn; they were erected purposefully to send a strong message to all who walked in their shadows about who was still in charge in this city. [...]

Surely we are far enough removed from this dark time to acknowledge that the cause of the Confederacy was wrong. [...] So [...] let us again state the truth clearly.

The Confederacy was on the wrong side of history and humanity. It sought to tear apart our nation and subjugate our fellow Americans to slavery. This is the history we should never forget and one that we should never again put on a pedestal to be revered. [...]

http://www.nola.com/politics/index.ssf/2017/05/mayor_landrieu_speech_confeder.html [Oct. 2017].

Vocabulary

to enshrine: to make sth. seem important
searing: powerful (so strong it feels like burning)
to sanitize: to make sth. clean

Tasks

1. **The Legacy of the Civil War**
   a) List the changes in the USA which came about because of the Civil War (text).
   b) Show the long-term reaction to many of these changes in the South (text).
   c) Explain why racial equality in the USA has been so difficult to achieve (text).
   d) Underline the reasons Landrieu gives for removing Confederate monuments in New Orleans in 2017 (M7).
   e) Agree or disagree with Landrieu, giving your reasons for your opinion.
   f) Suggest a monument for New Orleans as an alternative to those which have been removed.

Vocabulary

temperance: drinking alcohol in moderation

prohibition: forbidding sth. by law (here: alcoholic drinks)

Info

Prohibition

The 18th Amendment to the US Constitution prohibits the making, sale, import, and transport of alcohol in the USA (passed January 1919).

But the sale and use of alcohol did not stop. Instead, the business itself became illegal and criminal activity increased.

By 1933 it was clear that Prohibition had failed. The 21st Amendment then replaced the 18th, making alcohol legal in the USA again.

All Men Are Created Equal – Women, Too?

Women played important roles in three movements for political reform in the USA in the nineteenth century. Women worked to make slavery illegal in the abolition movement. They tried to prevent alcoholism in the *temperance* movement, which later led to *Prohibition*. They also worked for women's rights. Some women were active in at least one of these movements, while many were active in all of them.

The Women's Rights Movement

In 1848 a group met in Seneca Falls, New York, to discuss the social, civil, and religious situation of women in the USA. It was the first public meeting to deal with women's rights in the western world. For the meeting, Elizabeth Cady Stanton wrote a "Declaration of Sentiments" based on the text of the US Declaration of Independence. Three hundred women and some men attended the convention. They agreed to support nearly all of the changes mentioned in the declaration, but the right to vote seemed too controversial. Some found it unnecessary, others thought it was ridiculous. It only passed by a close vote when Frederick Douglass, the abolitionist and former slave, reminded the convention that the right to vote was fundamental to all other rights.

Similar meetings discussed women's rights after 1848, but groups within the movement did not agree on basic strategy. Some thought activists should pass laws for women's rights in the separate states. Others thought a national right to vote was more important. Suffragists disagreed on questions of equal pay, access to education, workers' rights, racial equality, and marriage equality. Strict social customs at the time also held women back: It was impolite for women to speak in public. Women's clothing made it hard to move freely. Wearing trousers and riding bicycles were thought indecent.

M 1 Session of the National Woman's Suffrage Association During Its Political Convention in Chicago, 1880

Elizabeth Cady Stanton and Susan B. Anthony formed this group after breaking with the earlier American Equal Rights Association.

Info

Suffragists Lose Their Patience

Alice Paul (1885–1977) lived in Britain for ten years. She turned the militant tactics she learned there to the women's rights struggle in the USA. Paul organized a suffrage parade on the day before Woodrow Wilson was sworn in as President in 1913. When the march nearly became a riot, the public showed more interest in the women's movement. Paul organized the first demonstrations ever held in front of the White House. "Silent *Sentinels*" stood with signs demanding women's right to vote, even after the USA entered World War I. American suffragists suffered just as the British suffragettes had: They were arrested, sent to prison, and force-fed when they went on hunger strikes. Public opinion began to support the suffragists.

At the end of the war, it was clear that the USA could not insist on civil rights all over the world if American women did not have them. The 19th Amendment to the Constitution gave women the right to vote in 1920.

M 2 **Alice Paul (1885–1977)**
Photograph, 1915

Black Men Gain Rights, but not women

After the Civil War, amendments to the Constitution guaranteed black men equality and the right to vote. Some suffragists agreed that former slaves needed these rights and should be given priority. But Stanton and her fellow suffragist, Susan B. Anthony, disagreed because women were left out. The disagreement divided the women's movement. However, even though black men got the right to vote, later "Jim Crow" laws passed in southern states kept them from being able to do so. Also, southern states opposed women's suffrage – if women could vote, there would be no reason to keep blacks (men and women) from doing so.

Women's rights in the USA came about by changing laws in the separate states, one by one. The first reforms dealt with married women's rights to own property and administer it themselves. Women got access to education when colleges for only women were founded and public universities gradually accepted them for studies. Women were allowed to enter some professions and to get trade certificates. But the right to vote stayed out of reach for most women. Some western states allowed women's suffrage in the 19th century, while eastern and southern states did not. Before World War I, women in Montana could vote but women in New York could not. However, the 19th Amendment to the Constitution gave women the right to vote in 1920.

Vocabulary

sentinel: (here) guard

Equal Rights – some successes, some failures

In 1923 Alice Paul wrote an Equal Rights Amendment to the Constitution to guarantee women the same rights as men in the USA. Although a revised amendment was passed by Congress in 1972, not enough states approved to add it to the Constitution. Opposition to the amendment first came from the labour movement, which feared that women could lose their protections in the workplace. Later others worried that women might not be supported by their husbands, privacy rights might be overturned, women might serve in the military, abortion and same-sex marriage might become legal. (These issues may not seem as pressing in American society today, but they influenced public opinion at the time.)

In 1964 the Civil Rights Act made it illegal to discriminate because of race, colour, religion, sex, or national origin. It was the first national law stating equal rights for women. However, there is still no constitutional guarantee of equal rights for women.

Historical Terms

suffrage: Wahlrecht

suffragist (US), suffragette (GB): Kämpferin für das Frauenwahlrecht

All Men are Created Equal – Women, Too?

M 3 "Declaration of Sentiments"

From the Seneca Falls "Declaration of Sentiments", 1848:

"We hold these truths to be self-evident; that all men and women are created equal; that they are endowed by the Creator with certain inalienable rights; that among these are life, liberty, and the pursuit of happiness."

Stanton continued with a list of complaints about how men treated women (just as the original Declaration of Independence listed complaints against the government of George III in 1776), which included the following:

- married women were considered legally dead
- women did not have the right to vote
- women had to obey laws but they had no voice in passing them
- married women could not own property
- husbands were legally responsible for their wives; they could beat them or imprison them if they wished to do so
- men decided questions of divorce and child custody, women had no rights in such matters
- most occupations were closed to women; those who worked were paid far less than men
- women could not enter professions such as medicine or law
- women were not accepted to study at colleges or universities
- with a few exceptions, women could not play a public role in church affairs
- men robbed women of self-confidence and self-respect, making them completely dependent beings.

Report of the Woman's Rights Convention, held at Seneca Falls, N.Y., July 19th & 20th, 1848. Printed by John Dick at the North Star Office: Rochester 1848. (adapted)

M 4 Suffragist *Picketing* in Front of the White House
Photograph, about 1917

M 5 Susan B. Anthony on Bicycling

Susan B. Anthony (1896):

"Let me tell you what I think about bicycling. I think it has done more to emancipate women than anything else in the world. It gives women a feeling of freedom and self-reliance. I stand and rejoice every time I see a woman ride by on a wheel [...] the picture of free, *untrammelled* womanhood."

https://www.goodreads.com/quotes/10789-let-me-tell-you-what-i-think-of-bicycling-i [Oct. 2017].

M 6 Equal Rights Amendment, 1972

This amendment has never become part of the U.S. Constitution.

Section 1. Equality of rights under the law shall not be denied or abridged by the United States or by any State on account of sex.
Section 2. The Congress shall have the power to enforce, by appropriate legislation, the provisions of this article.
Section 3. This amendment shall take effect two years after the date of ratification.

http://equalrightsamendment.org/history.htm [Oct. 2017].

M 7 German Basic Law

From the German Basic Law (as in the 1949 version):

Article 3 [Equality before the law]
(1) All persons shall be equal before the law.
(2) Men and women shall have equal rights.
(3) No person shall be favoured or disfavoured because of sex, parentage, race, language, homeland and origin, faith, or religious or political opinions.

https://www.gesetze-im-internet.de/englisch_gg/englisch_gg.html#p0028 [Oct. 2017].

M 8 Alice Paul's warning about political reforms

Paul spoke with Robert S. Gallagher about her life in an interview for American Heritage in February 1974. Paul did not live to see that the Equal Rights Amendment passed by Congress in 1972 did not become part of the US Constitution when it was not approved by enough of the separate states:

I feel very strongly that if you are going to do anything, you have to take one thing and do it. You can't try lots and lots of reforms and get them all mixed up together. [...] I have never doubted that equal rights was the right direction. Most reforms, most problems are complicated. But to me there is nothing complicated about ordinary equality. Which is a nice thing about our campaign [for the Equal Rights Amendment of 1972]. It really is true, at least to my mind, that only good will come to everybody with equality. If we get to the point where everyone has equality of opportunity – and I don't expect to see it, we have such a long, long way ahead of us – then it seems to me it is not our problem how women use their equality or how men use their equality.

Robert S. Gallagher: An interview with the famed suffragette Alice Paul, American Heritage, Volume 25, Issue 2, February 1974; http://www.americanheritage.com/content/"i-was-arrested-course..." [Oct. 2017].

Vocabulary

to picket: to take part in a protest
untrammelled: not limited or controlled

Tasks

1. **Women's Rights**
   a) Read the "Declaration of Sentiments" from the Seneca Falls meeting in 1848 (M3).
   b) Decide which three of the complaints in the declaration you think are the most important for the women's movement to work on.
   c) Formulate a strategy to solve the three problems you have chosen (text, own opinion).
   d) Explain why women having the right to vote was controversial (text).
   e) Assess Frederick Douglass's opinion on the right to vote (text).
   f) Point out the social limits all women had to overcome to be active in public (text).
   g) Agree or disagree with Susan Anthony's opinion on bicycling (M5).
2. **Black Men Gain Rights, but not Women**
   a) Show how black men gained the right to vote, but then lost it (text).
   b) Explain why black men getting the right to vote divided the women's movement (text).
3. **Suffragists Lose Patience**
   a) Point out the strategy American women used to get their rights at first (text).
   b) Compare and contrast with the strategies women used later (M1, M4, text).
   c) Assess how effective the suffragist's demonstration is in winning public approval for her cause (M4).
4. **Equal Rights Amendments**
   a) Compare the Equal Rights Amendments of 1972 (M6) and Article 3 from the German Basic Law of 1949 (M7). Contrast the situation of women in Germany with women in the USA.
   b) Explain why the amendment did not become part of the US Constitution (text).
   c) Comment on the progress of women's rights in the USA since 1848 (text).

Analysing Texts

Working with Written Documents

Written documents may be either primary or secondary sources. Primary sources were made at the same time as the events happened. There are many kinds of primary sources, such as notes, diaries, memoirs, literary works, speeches, and even political programmes.

Secondary sources, like histories or textbooks, were written after the events happened. They may use both primary and secondary sources to prove their arguments. Older secondary sources can even become primary sources when they show how people or events were interpreted in earlier times.

Historians use different methods for different types of written sources. However, there are some basic rules which historians use for all of them. The following tasks show how to work with such written documents.

Historical Workshop

Analysing Texts

1. Describing the Text

a. Name the author and the role he or she played when the text was written.

b. Define the text type (e.g. letter, note, speech, pamphlet, law, etc.).

c. Describe the situation in which the text was written.

d. Find out who the audience is for the text.

e. Sum up the main points of the text in your own words.

2. Analysing the Text

a. Analyse the text in detail and state the author's intentions.

b. Examine the facts the author mentions and those he or she does not mention.

c. Point out misconceptions in the text, if there are any.

d. Look at the content and the language of the text. Show what both say about the author.

e. In this text, rhetorical questions are used. Explain their effect on the audience.

3. Evaluating the Text

a. Assess how much influence the text had on its audience.

b. Find arguments you approve or disapprove of.

c. Discuss the validity of the arguments.

d. Comment on how much you learn from the text.

e. Explain why Americans today think this text is important.

M 1 "Ain't I a Woman?" (1851)

Isabell Baumfree was born a slave to a Dutch American landowner in New York state. When New York outlawed slavery in 1827 and her master refused to free her, she walked away from the farm. She became an abolitionist, a travelling preacher, a women's rights activist and called herself Sojourner Truth (1797–1883). Her speech at the Woman's Rights Convention in Akron, Ohio, on 29 May 1851, is one of the most famous in American history. No audio or written record was made during the speech, so there are different written versions of it. The following version is from a monument to Truth run by the US National Park Service.

"Well, children, where there is so much *racket* there must be something *out of kilter*. I think that twixt the negroes of the South and the women at the North, all talking about rights, the white men will be in a fix pretty soon. But what's all this here talking about?

That man over there says that women need to be helped into carriages, and lifted over ditches, and to have the best place everywhere. Nobody ever helps me into carriages, or over mud-puddles, or gives me any best place! And ain't I a woman? Look at me! Look at my arm! I have ploughed and planted, and gathered into barns, and no man could *head* me! And ain't I a woman? I could work as much and eat as much as a man – when I could get it – and bear the lash as well! And ain't I a woman? I have borne thirteen children, and seen most all sold off to slavery, and when I cried out with my mother's grief, none but Jesus heard me! And ain't I a woman?

Then they talk about this thing in the head; what's this they call it? [member of audience whispers, "intellect"] That's it, honey. What's that got to do with women's rights or negroes' rights? If my cup won't hold but a pint, and yours holds a quart, wouldn't you be mean not to let me have my little half measure full?

Then that little man in black there, he says women can't have as much rights as men, 'cause Christ wasn't a woman! Where did your Christ come from? Where did your Christ come from? From God and a woman! Man had nothing to do with Him.
If the first woman God ever made was strong enough to turn the world upside down all alone, these women together ought to be able to turn it back, and get it right side up again! And now they is asking to do it, the men better let them.
Obliged to you for hearing me, and now old Sojourner ain't got nothing more to say."

https://www.nps.gov/wori/learn/historyculture/sojourner-truth.htm [Oct. 2017].

Vocabulary

ain't: verb form of isn't or aren't (considered grammatically incorrect today, but acceptable in Truth's day)
to outlaw: to make sth. illegal
sojourner: (literary) traveller
racket: noise, illegal doing
out of kilter: not right in some way
to head: to get ahead of sb.
lash: whip or a hit with a whip

M 2 Sojourner Truth Statue at Battle Creek Michigan Monument Park

Contemporary photograph

1580 | 1610 | 1640 | 1670 | 1700

First English settlement founded called Virginia

Pilgrims arrive

settling the continent

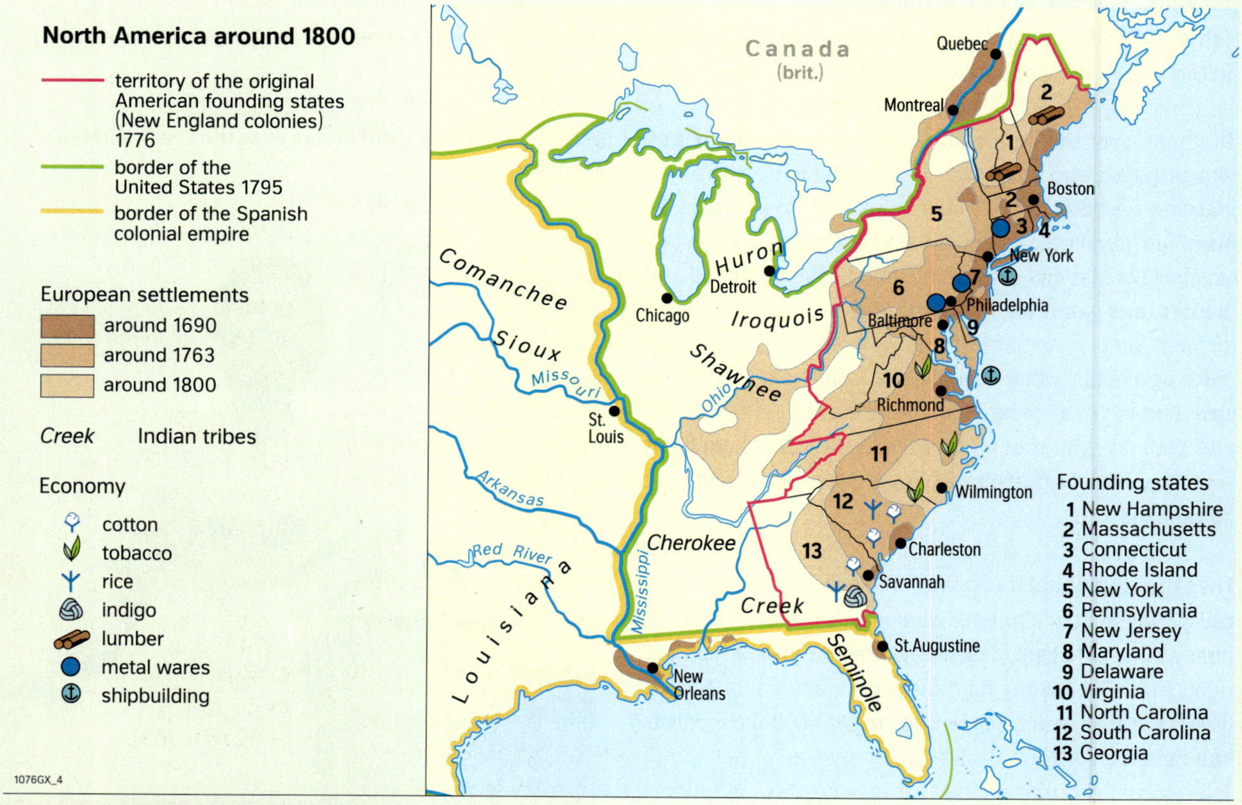

The American Revolution – the historical map

1760 | 1790 | 1820 | 1850 | 1880

1755–1763: French and Indian War

1776: Declaration of Independence

1838: Cherokee "Trail of Tears"

1861–1865: Civil War / War of Secession

1860 Abraham Lincoln elected President of the USA

Summary

From the early colonial times, the USA has grown rapidly. At first the colonists had to overcome existential difficulties while making a new life in a new country. The thirteen British colonies had to found their own government after the War of Independence ended in 1783. As the country grew in size and population, various immigrant groups had to be integrated into American society. At first the idea from the Declaration of Independence that "all men are created equal" did not apply to some groups. Native Americans, blacks, and women struggled for equal rights for many years, because they were not citizens in a country made for white, Anglo-Saxon, Protestant men.

Political leaders of the new nation wrote the US Constitution in 1787. The document has given stability to the country. However, problems came up when the Constitution no longer fit a country which changed in ways not seen in 1787. For example, the problems with slavery were not resolved. After years of compromise the issue of slavery finally led to the Civil War from 1861 to 1865. The war nearly tore the country apart. When the northern states defeated the South, national unity was saved. Still, the USA continues to be affected by the Civil War and the social and political resentments it left behind. Discussions about flags, statues, or heroes today reveal these historical resentments.

Nevertheless, the Civil War began a long process leading to civil rights. Slavery was abolished and former slaves were set free. Black men got the right to vote in 1868. But political equality for blacks took much longer to achieve, because racial discrimination went on for many years. Women began their struggle for equality as early as 1848, but a mixture of social movements such as abolition, temperance, family, and workers' rights kept women from concentrating on a single goal of voting rights. American women finally got the right to vote nation-wide in 1920. With even fewer supporters than blacks or women, Native Americans did not become citizens until 1924. In spite of the progress these groups have made since 1787, there is still room for improvement of the idea that "all men are created equal" in the USA.

DATES

1620: Mayflower colonists land in Massachusetts

1776: Declaration of Independence

1787: U.S. Constitution written

1830: Indian Removal Act passed by Congress

1868: black men have the right to vote in the USA

1920: women in the USA have the right to vote

1924: Indian Citizenship Act states that all Native Americans are U.S. citizens

HISTORICAL TERMS

Pilgrim
constitution
suffrage
suffragist (US)
suffragette (GB)

PERSONS

George Washington

Abraham Lincoln

Sojourner Truth

Frederick Douglass

HISTORY WORKSHOP

Analysing Texts

M 1 **The Declaration of the Rights of Man and the Citizen. Painting by J. J. LeBarbier, 1790**

M 2 **The Execution of Louis XVI, Paris, 1793**

03 THE FRENCH REVOLUTION

Radical Change?

The political system of France changed dramatically within a few years. In 1789 France was an **absolute monarchy**. Then the government became a **constitutional monarchy**, a **republic**, and a **dictatorship** which tried to rule through terror. After the terror, a directory ruled the country for a short time before France became a monarchy again. This time an emperor ruled, but finally the old royal dynasty returned to power. These political ups and downs made it hard for all kinds of people to survive even though one of the major achievements of the revolution was the introduction of the rights of man and the citizen.

This unit explains why the revolution came about, what it was like, and what consequences it had for France and Europe. Also, the unit looks at why the French Revolution is still regarded as a very important historical event.

This chapter deals with many questions such as:

- How and why did the revolution come about?
- What were the three different starting points?
- What were the rights of men (and women?)
- Why did the political system change?
- What happened to the royal family?
- What were the consequences of terror as a means of government?
- How did Napoleon come to power?
- How did Napoleon change France and the map of Europe?
- How can maps be sources of historical information?
- Why did Prussia benefit from the French occupation?

Historical Terms

Forms of Government

monarchy: Monarchie

absolute monarchy: absolutistische Monarchie

Historical Terms

constitutional monarchy: konstitutionelle Monarchie

republic: Republik

dictatorship: Diktatur

M 1 **A Farmer Pays his Dues**
Etching, about 1650

From the Old Regime to a New Age

Louis XVI under Pressure

Louis XVI became King of France when he was 19. At the age of 15 he had married 14-year-old Austrian Princess Marie Antoinette for political reasons. She later on became very unpopular with the people of France and was often called "the German". Louis invested a lot of money in the navy because he wanted to compete with Britain on the seas. He took part in the War of Independence on the side of the Americans, which meant he won the war against Britain. The peace treaty was signed in Paris. But there were problems: the victory cost too much money and the French soldiers who came home brought the ideas of the American rebellion with them. Some of the nobles and the parliaments whose members had read the ideas of the philosophers from the Age of Enlightenment opposed the king. Louis lost his popularity with most of his people in France.

A Political and Economic Crisis

After Louis found out that he didn't have enough money to rule in the way he wanted to because France was practically bankrupt, he planned to raise taxes. But he needed the three estates to agree to that, so he invited the Estates-General to a meeting – for the first time since 1614.

In many parts of the country the poor people *suffered hardship* because there were bad harvests and harsh winters. The price of bread went up. Many people wrote lists of complaints, which they gave their deputies in the Estates-General to discuss with the king. The rich citizens from the Third Estate were also angry because they had to pay high taxes but had no influence on politics.

However, the First Estate, the clergy, hardly paid taxes at all, a privilege that they shared with most of the noblemen, who formed the Second Estate. Within the three estates there were huge social differences.

M 2 **Opening the Estates-General**
Versailles, 5 May 1789

M 3 **The Three Estates in Their Festive Clothes**
Painting, 1780

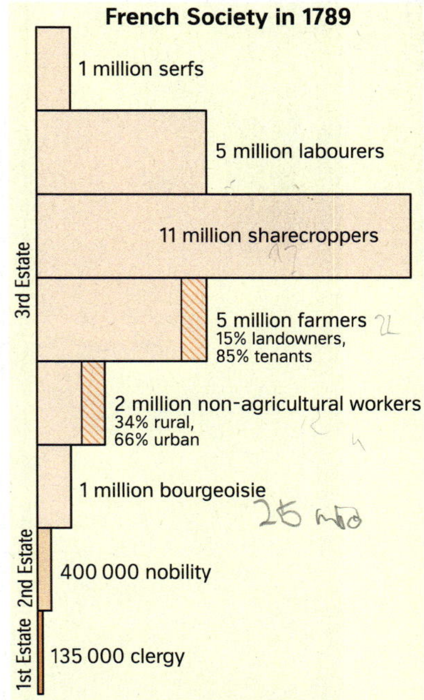

Derek Heater, Presenting the Past, Book 3; Oxford 142GX

M 4

The Summer of 1789 – three revolutions

- The Tennis Court Oath: At the opening of the Estates-General Louis welcomed 291 deputies of the clergy, 270 of the nobles and 578 of the Third Estate. The Third Estate had forced him to invite twice as many of their deputies as he originally wanted. Then he tried to play a trick on them. He changed the voting *procedures* from one vote per head to one vote for each estate. The Third Estate became angry and moved out of the assembly. On 20 June they met in a nearby indoor tennis court and swore to stay there until a constitution was written. Quite a few members of the other estates joined them as time went on. On 27 June the king gave in and accepted this group (now called the National Assembly) as the legal French parliament.
- The Storming of the Bastille: But the problems of the poor were not solved. They were still hungry and felt disadvantaged. Riots broke out and some tried to get hold of weapons as they feared the king's reaction. On July 14 an angry crowd stormed the Bastille, Louis's prison and armoury in Paris.
  To re-establish order the king gave the rioters permission to set up their own militia, the National Guard, and to form their own government, the Paris Commune. Towns all over France followed this example.
- The Great Fear: Violence also spread to the country. Landlords began to live in fear of their own *peasants*, who took revenge for what their masters had done to them and destroyed the *records* of their *dues*. A "Great Fear" lay its grip on the country.

Louis – king and prisoner

On 4 August the nobles gave up their privileges. The National Assembly took measures against the violence in the country and suggested radical changes to society. But the king didn't like the ideas and resisted. When rumours spread that the king was gathering more soldiers in Versailles, crowds of market women armed themselves and marched on the palace of Versailles. They took the royal family by force to the capital on a cattle cart in order to show them how bad the situation was there. The king and his family had to live in the Palace of the Tuileries from then on.

Vocabulary

serf (in M4): a person who is tied to the land he works on

sharecropper (in M4): a worker who works on sb. else's land and has to give them a big part of the harvest

tenant (in M4): a farmer who rents land and has to pay for it

Vocabulary

to suffer hardship: to have really bad times

procedure: the way sth. is done

peasant: a farm worker of low status

record: written document

dues: charges, money that you owe sb.

Three Revolutions as Shown in Pictures

M 5 **Tennis Court Oath, 1789**
Painting by Jacques-Louis David, 1791

M 6 **Storming of the Bastille, 14 July**
Drawing, 1789

M 7 **The Great Fear**
Drawing, 1789

What is the Third Estate?

Biography

Abbé Emmanuel Joseph Sieyès (1748 – 1836)

Abbé Sieyès became a priest in 1774, but turned to politics soon after. He was interested in the writings of the Age of Enlightenment and started writing political pamphlets of importance himself. In 1789 he was elected to the Estates-General for the Third Estate and had a lot of influence on the first constitution. As a member of the National Assembly he could not become a member of the constitutional assembly afterwards. So he worked in the political background for some time. As a member of the National Convention he voted for the execution of the king in 1793. After surviving the Reign of Terror he took over various government positions after 1795, e.g. working together with Napoleon in the directory. When the old royal family returned to power after 1816 he had to live in exile because of his vote in 1793.

M 8 **Emmanuel Joseph Sieyès**
Painting by Jacques-Louis David, 1817

M 9 What is the Third Estate?

The text is a political** pamphlet **written in January 1789, before the outbreak of the revolution. Abbé Sieyès wrote it to plan how the Estates-General should be organized:

"The plan of this work is quite simple. We have three questions to ask ourselves.
1. What is the Third Estate? – Everything.
2. What has it been so far in the political order? – Nothing.
3. What does it ask to be? – Something.

We shall see if these are the right answers. Meanwhile, it would be wrong to say that these truths have been *exaggerated* when you have not yet seen the supporting evidence. Next we shall examine the measures that have been tried, and those that must [still] be taken, for the Third Estate to actually become something.

Thus we shall state:
4. What ministers have tried to do in the interests of the Third Estate, and what the privileged themselves propose to do for it;
5. What should have been done;
6. And finally, what remains to be done for the Third Estate so that it can take up the place that is its due [...]."

www.age-of-the-sage.org/historical/biography/abbe_sieyes.html [Oct. 2017].

Vocabulary

pamphlet: a leaflet, flyer to influence people
to exaggerate: to overdo, overdraw

Tasks

1. **Louis's Situation**
   a) Explain how the situation of the king changed in 1789 (text).
   b) State how Louis XVI could have stayed in control of the situation (text).
2. **The Outbreak of the Revolution**
   a) Describe the pictures (M5–M7) and match them with the three phases (text).
   b) Show which social groups support the different phases (text, M3, M4).
   c) Find more reasons for the outbreak of the revolution.
3. **The Third Estate**
   a) Say what Abbé Sieyès wants to express about the French society (M9).
   b) List the main ideas of the text (M9).
   c) Discuss what people might learn from the life of Abbé Sieyès (M8 and biography).

The Rights of Men – And Women?

M 1 **Olympe de Gouges (1748–93)**

Biography

Olympe de Gouges
- born in 1748
- had to marry at 17
- became a writer
- fought for the right of women to lead independent lives
- was against the death penalty
- executed in 1793

After the privileges of the nobles and the clergy were abolished the National Assembly had a debate on civil rights. It had started long before the revolution. During the revolution "liberté, égalité, fraternité" (liberty, equality, fraternity) became the *slogan* of the people. The National Assembly changed its name to "Constituante" in order to show that its task was to write a constitution.

Liberty

In the second half of the eighteenth century a number of writers set out their ideas to improve society. The philosopher Voltaire wrote that France was not free as long as the king of France was an absolute monarch. He was impressed by the English example and wrote in 1750 that the English people had a king and a parliament, which guaranteed people the freedom to go where they wanted, to read what they liked, to follow the religion they chose and to be tried properly by law. This was what he wanted to achieve for France as well.

Equality

Some writers thought that equality was even more important than freedom. Jean Jacques Rousseau claimed in his book "The Social Contract" ("Du contrat social") that all men were born free, but they were in chains everywhere. In 1760 he wrote in "Kings and Republics" that a republic is always better than a monarchy. He said that even the best kings do what they like, but people in a republic choose only men of talent and experience for the highest posts. He also said that all men were born equal and should remain equal. He put women on a different level. They disturbed political life and distracted the citizens (= the men) from politics.

Fraternity

The ideas and results of the American revolution influenced the development in France. Organizing a state in a peaceful and cooperative way was what the revolutionaries wanted. Everybody was to be everybody else's brother. A wave of patriotism swept over France extending the ideas of the revolution to the rest of Europe.

The Rights of Man and the Citizen – but not for women!

The French saw the American Declaration of Independence as the death certificate of absolutism. It became the foundation of the constitution the Assembly created afterwards. The deputies in the National Assembly wanted the document to be valid throughout the entire world. It went even further than the English Bill of Rights of 1689 and marked a new beginning in the relationship between the individual and the state. In effect it turned out to be the very document which recognized rights as high values. Even nowadays people refer to this document in their fight for human rights all over the world.

But it needed a very courageous woman to point out that these rights had to apply to women as well. Olympe de Gouges, a butcher's daughter and a writer, published her "Declaration of the Rights of Woman and the Citizeness" in September 1791 – but the male dominated constitution was already in place, so that she had no chance to influence it. Later on she was charged with treason and executed, also because the male leaders of the state saw her ideas as a *disturbance*.

Vocabulary

slogan: a short phrase easy to remember and often used by a political party

disturbance: trouble, disorder

preservation: keeping sth. the way it is

sovereignty: independent power

M 2 **The Declaration of the Rights of Man and the Citizen**

Painting by J. J. LeBarbier, 1790

M 3 Extracts from the "Declaration of the Rights of Man and the Citizen"

The National Assembly began its work to write a constitution by making a "Declaration of the Rights of Man and the Citizen" (August 1789):

"1. Men are born and remain free and equal in rights.
2. The aim of all political association is the *preservation* of [...] liberty, property, security, and resistance to oppression.
3. The power to rule comes from the whole nation...
4. Liberty consists in the freedom to do everything which injures no one else...
5. Law can only prohibit such actions as are hurtful to society. Nothing may be prevented which is not forbidden by law.
6. Law is the expression of the general will. It must be the same for all.
9. Every man is innocent until he has been declared guilty."

http://avalon.law.yale.edu/18th_century/rightsof.asp [Oct. 2017].

M 4 Extracts from "The Declaration of the Rights of Woman and the Citizeness"

Olympe de Gouges wrote the "Declaration of the Rights of Woman and the Citizeness" in 1791. Later on she turned against the leading revolutionaries and was executed:

"1. Woman is born free and remains equal to man in rights. [...]
2. The purpose of all political association is the preservation of the natural [...] rights of woman and man. These rights are liberty, property, security, and especially resistance to oppression.
3. The principle of all *sovereignty* rests essentially in the nation, which is but the reuniting of woman and man. [...]
4. Liberty and justice consist in restoring all that belongs to another; hence the exercise of the natural rights of woman has no other limits than those that the perpetual tyranny of man opposes to them; these limits must be reformed according to the laws of nature and reason.
6. The law should be the expression of the general will. All citizenesses and citizens should take part, in person or by their representatives, in its formation. It must be the same for everyone. All citizenesses and citizens, being equal in its eyes, should be equally admissible to all public dignities, offices and employments, according to their ability, and with no other distinction than that of their virtues and talents.
11. The free communication of thoughts and opinions is one of the most precious of the rights of woman [...]"

http://chnm.gmu.edu/revolution/d/293/ [Oct. 2017].

Tasks

1. The Declaration of the Rights of Man

a) Explain what the painter may have thought of the Rights of Man (M2).
b) Check in which way the Rights of Man oppose absolutism (M3).
c) Compare this declaration to the American Declaration of Independence (Chapter 2).
d) Find out about any connections between this declaration and the ideas of the Enlightenment.

2. The Declaration of the Rights of Woman

a) Make a list of equal and different Rights of Man and Rights of Woman (M3, M4).
b) Find out more about the role Olympe de Gouges played in the revolution (M1, Internet).
c) Decide which of the Rights of Man/Woman you find important and give reasons why (M3, M4).

M 1 **Sansculotte**

Sansculottes – radical Paris citizens from the lower classes, whose clothes were not the fashionable clothes of the time. It is a French expression meaning without (sans) short trousers (culottes). Painting by Louis-Léopold Boilly, 1792

France Becomes a Republic

The New Constitution – too new for some

In order to pay back the state debts the National Assembly *confiscated* all church land and made the priests swear an oath to the state. This led to *resistance*, also from the king. Finally the new constitution was put into place on 3 Sept. 1791. It divided the citizens into "active citizens", four million men over 25, who paid high taxes and were allowed to vote, and "passive citizens", two-thirds of the people. These did not pay enough taxes to vote, were under 25 or women. They could not take part in politics.

The basis of the constitution was Montesquieu's principle of the separation of power into three branches. The king was part of the constitution and still had a lot of influence. But he was against the limitations that were now placed on him.

The King's Flight

By 1791 about 40,000 nobles fled the country, most of them to border towns in Germany. They hoped to find support from the nobles there and wanted to organize resistance against the new order in France. On 21 June 1791 Louis and his family tried to flee to Germany in order to join forces with the emigrants. But they were stopped in Varennes and *escorted* back to Paris. By the time the royal family arrived, the sansculottes, a very radical group of citizens, had put up a poster at the city palace: "Flat for rent". The deputies first wanted to deny the king a position in the new constitution, but as it was nearly finished they changed their minds and only made him swear an oath to the constitution. Because of his attempt to flee the king lost a lot of public support even from those who had stayed loyal to him.

War Breaks Out and More Radical Changes

Louis's position became weaker when the monarchs of Austria and Prussia declared in 1792 that they would save the French monarchy with military action if necessary. This declaration caused the French to unite against them and the king. A large majority in the National Assembly declared war on Austria and Prussia. But the war did not go well at first and France was invaded. The Prussian High Command threatened to completely destroy Paris if the king was harmed. Louis was then suspected of working together with the enemy, like a traitor.

The sansculottes stormed the Tuileries and killed the royal guard. Throughout the month of September they massacred thousands of opponents of the revolution. A new stage began – much more violent this time. The National Assembly dismissed the king and put him and his family in prison. Then it gave a new National Convention the task of writing a republican constitution and dissolved itself. The new parliament was elected by all French men over 21, who could live on what they earned. As a result, it became much more radical. One of the first discussions in this new parliament was about the king. He was tried for **treason** and finally executed in public on 21 January 1793. Queen Marie Antoinette was also executed later in the same year.

Vocabulary

to confiscate: to officially take away sb.'s possessions

resistance: opposition

to escort: to go with sb. to keep him from escaping

Historical Terms

treason: Verrat

Tasks

1. **France Becomes a Republic**
   a) Describe the role that the king played during the revolution (text).
   b) Assess whether Louis XVI worked together with the enemies of France (text).
   c) List the different political assemblies of people between 1789 and 1792 (text).
   d) State the aims of each of these assemblies (text).

The Case of the King in Pictures

Biography

Louis's Last Months

10 Aug 1792 Louis imprisoned

10 Dec 1792 trial begins with charges

11 Dec 1792 more charges and cross-examination of the king

12 Dec 1792 defence council chosen

26 Dec 1792 response by the defence

15 Jan 1793 unanimous verdict: guilty

16 Jan 1793 380 to 310 for execution

21 Jan 1793 public execution (guillotine)

M 2 **The King in the Cage of the Constitution**
Cartoon, 1791

M 3 **King Louis XVI,** painting, about 1777

Tasks

1. Louis's Image

a) Describe how Louis is portrayed in each picture (M2 – M3).

b) Explain the elements the artists have used (symbols, clothing, background).

c) Analyse how the king looks and how he is positioned.

2. The Artists' Intentions

a) Look for symbols of the king's power and explain how the artists have used them (M2 – M3).

b) Analyse why the artists made the pictures and say what they wanted to point out.

c) Interpret the pictures as historical sources.

France Becomes a Republic – two constitutions

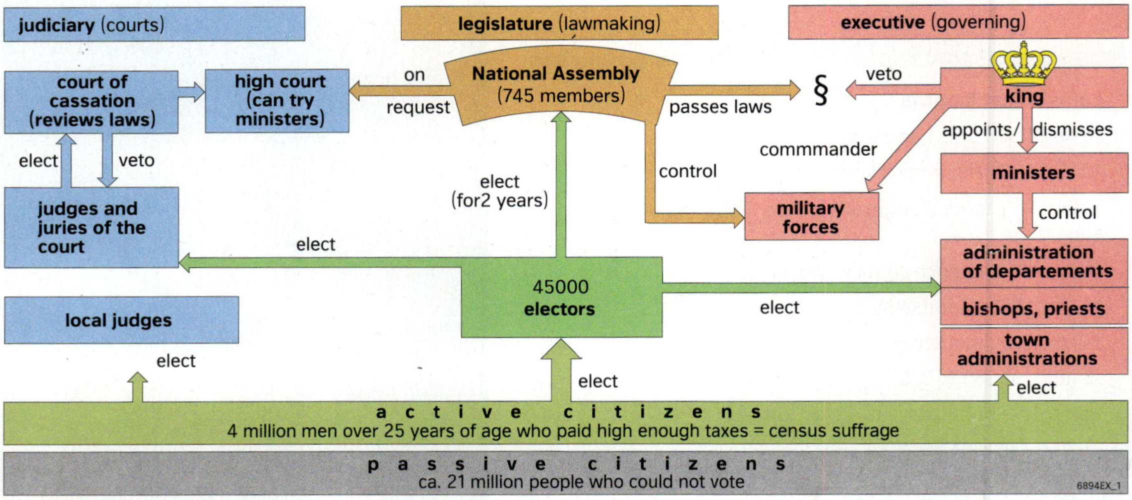

M 4 **The Constitution of 1791**

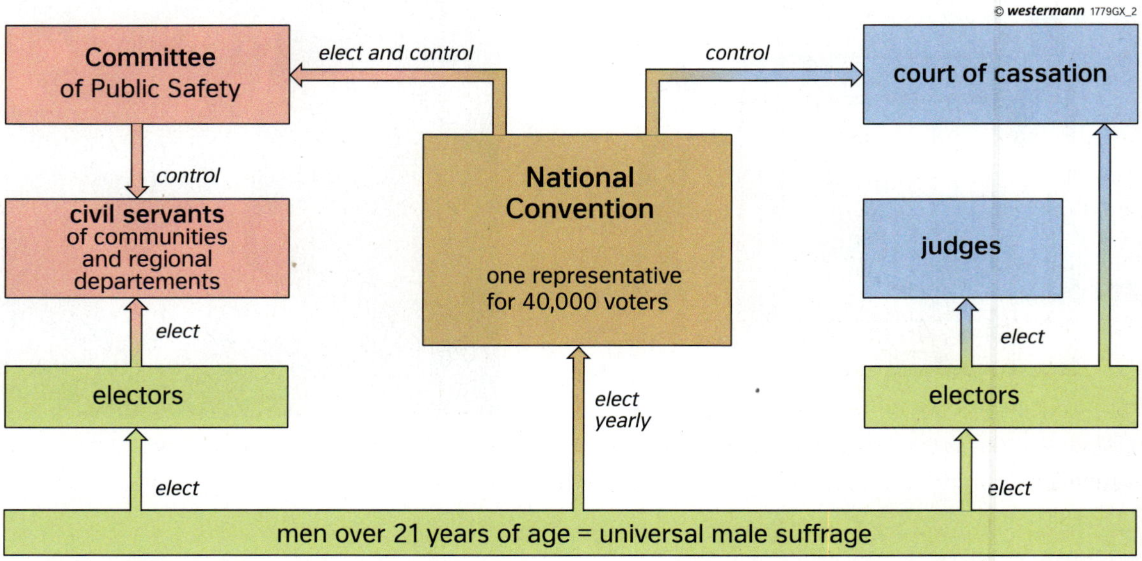

M 5 **The Constitution of 1793**

Tasks

1. France Becomes a Republic – two constitutions

a) Look at the title and name the topic of the diagrams and their content.

b) Describe the elements of the diagrams. Pay attention to colours, symbols and printing.

c) Explain the relations between the different elements with the help of lines, arrows and other features.

d) Talk about the information the diagrams contain as to the system of government and compare them. Also look at the opening page of this chapter (p. 57).

The Execution of Louis XVI

M 6 The Debate in the Convention

a) In the first of two speeches Saint Just wanted to prove to the members of the Convention that they had the political authority to try the king:

"I shall undertake, citizens, to prove that the King can be judged. One day men will be astonished by the fact that humanity in the eighteenth century was less advanced than in the time of Caesar. Then a tyrant was slain in the midst of the Senate [...].
And today we respectfully conduct a trial for a man who assassinated a people, caught *in flagrante delicto*, his murderous hands soaked with blood!"

b) After the king himself had spoken, Saint Just spoke again, this time urging the deputies to condemn Louis XVI:

"Today will decide the fate of the Republic. It is doomed if the tyrant goes unpunished. The enemies of the common good will reappear, meet, and hope. The forces of tyranny will pick up their pieces like a reptile renewing its lost tail. [...]."

a) and b) https://chnm.gmu.edu/revolution/d/320/ [Oct. 2017].

c) As a member of the Convention British-born Thomas Paine, who had become a French citizen, answered Saint Just in the debate over the king's fate:

"[...] He [Louis Capet] cannot be made responsible for the situation if the national assembly that restored him to the throne without the consent of the people is not made responsible as well. The people have beat down royalty, never, never to rise again; they have brought Louis Capet to the bar. There remains only one question to be considered: what is to be done with this man? For myself, I freely confess that apart from all the corruption of his reign there is one circumstance in his life which ought to cover for some of his wrongdoings. Without his support the United States of America would never have been able to shake off the unjust and terrible yoke. Let then these United States be the safeguard and asylum to Louis Capet."

Thomas Paine, Reasons for Preserving the Life of Louis Capet, adapted by Rolf J. Kröger from: http://thomaspaine.org/essays/french-revolution/reasons-for-preserving-the-life-of-louis-capet.html [Oct. 2017].

M 7 The King's Execution

An eyewitness report by Henry Edgeworth, Louis XVI's priest:

"Whatever can be said of Louis XVI's performance during his reign and the early parts of the French Revolution, there can be no doubt he died bravely and like a king.
It had taken two hours for a large escort of cavalrymen to bring him to the Place de la Revolution through a massive crowd that had gathered to witness the historical moment. Three soldiers moved to take off his brown coat to prepare him for the blade. But he *repulsed* them with *haughtiness* - he undressed himself, untied his neckcloth, opened his shirt, and arranged it himself. The path leading to the scaffold was extremely rough and difficult to pass; the King was obliged to lean on my arm, and from the slowness with which he *proceeded*, I feared for a moment that his courage might fail; but what was my astonishment, when arrived at the last step, I felt that he suddenly let go my arm, and I saw him cross with a firm foot the breadth of the whole scaffold. By his look alone the crowd was silenced and then the king spoke in a loud voice: 'I die innocent of all the crimes laid to my charge; I pardon those who have occasioned my death; and I pray to God that the blood you are going to shed may never be visited on France'. [...]"

www.napoleonguide.com/guillotine_louis.htm [Oct. 2017].

Vocabulary

in flagrante delicto: in the very act of doing wrong
to repulse: to push back
haughtiness: pride
to proceed: to carry on

Tasks

1. **The Execution of Louis XVI**
   a) Collect the reasons given for and against the execution of the king (M6).
   b) Comment on the arguments for and against his execution (M7).
   c) Say in your own words what the eyewitness wants to express (M7).
   d) Define the relationship between the eyewitness and the king (M7).

Vocabulary

welfare: well-being

suspect: a person who is thought to have committed a crime

virtue: high moral standards

incorruptible: honest, fair; cannot be made dishonest

character trait: good/bad character traits make a person what they are like

prairial: 9th month in the calendar of the French Revolution

Reign of Terror – Violence as a Means of Government

Politics in Paris Become More Radical – Jacobins and Girondins

After the execution of the king the situation in Paris became more violent. It began, when "patriotic federations" like the "Club of the Friends of Human Rights", started to look closely at the way the authorities dealt with human rights. The leaders of this club were Georges Danton and Jean Paul Marat, two followers of Rousseau's philosophy. Both of them were **demagogues**.

Together with other groups like the Jacobins, the Cordeliers and some men from the Gironde, who called themselves Girondins, they formed the Democrats in the first National Assembly. The leader and most influential member of the Jacobins was Robespierre.

War or Peace?

The Jacobins and the Girondins disagreed over the question of war against the European monarchies. In this situation Robespierre's suggestion was accepted that no member of the Constituante could be elected to the Legislative Assembly in 1791. As a result more radical revolutionaries were elected to the new parliament, so that a majority then voted for war. They were also in favour of electing a new parliament in 1792 after the war began and the king was suspected of working together with the enemy. So an even more radical republican parliament ("the Convention") was elected this time. Robespierre, who had not been in the Legislative Assembly, was back on the political stage. As a member of the Convention he voted for the execution of the king.

Historical Terms

demagogue: Demagoge

emergency decree: Notstandsgesetz

Crisis of the State

In September 1792 Robespierre increased his attacks on the Girondins and supported an uprising in Paris. After Danton was murdered, his rival Robespierre became the leader of the Convention's Committee of Public Safety, also called "the *Welfare* Committee". This group of twelve revolutionaries ruled the country by **emergency decrees**. The war, hunger riots and other domestic problems led France into a civil war. In order to defend and save the country Robespierre called all Frenchmen to take up arms ("levée en masse"). On their way to the front the

M 1 **Maximilien Robespierre**

Biography

Maximilien Robespierre (1758–1794)

He was born in Arras. When he was six his mother died. By 1780 he had become a lawyer, specializing in the defence of the poor. In 1789 he was elected a deputy for the Third Estate in the Estates-General. Soon after he joined the Jacobin Club and gave public speeches in the Assembly. By 1791 he had won a reputation among the radicals. He opposed the death penalty and was against the war: "Nobody welcomes armed liberators". In 1791 he did not become a member of the Legislative Assembly, because the law made him unable to serve, but he was elected to the National Convention in 1792. A year later he voted for the execution of the king: "Louis must die". In 1793 he rose to power in the Committee of Public Safety, the new government. The "Law of Suspects" marked the beginning of the Reign of Terror. In 1794 he stayed at home most of the time and did not go to meetings anymore: "The revolution is frozen". When he demanded that more *suspect* deputies should be killed in 1794 he was arrested himself and executed in July 1794.

new soldiers sang a song called the "Marseillaise", which is now the French national anthem.

The Reign of Terror

Robespierre was interested in the idea of *virtue*. Marat called him "the *Incorruptible*" in order to show his most important *character trait*. But now Robespierre introduced terror as a principle of government. Guided by "reason" he wanted to develop the revolutionary ideas of liberty, equality and fraternity further. Opponents of the new system were sentenced to death by revolutionary tribunals and executed immediately. More than 12,000 were officially guillotined, but many more died in other ways. The Convention even decreed the destruction of a whole city and set up a memorial to it with the inscription: "Lyons made war on liberty; Lyons no longer exists".

In addition Robespierre introduced a new calendar with 1792 being the year one of the revolution. In order to create an entirely new society, he invented a new cult replacing religion. In an attempt to cut off all tradition he changed the names of 6,000 towns, of animals and plants.

But he had become too powerful. When the military crisis was over in July 1794 and terror was no longer needed, the deputies of the Convention feared for their lives. They voted to arrest Robespierre and had him guillotined. The official number of people who were killed in the Reign of Terror is 16,594, the inofficial total is more than half a million.

Info

1793 Law of Suspects

"Watch committees" were allowed to search for people who might possibly speak against the new government or liberty in general or who might defend monarchy.

Everybody could report their neighbours or long-term enemies to the authorities now. There was not much of an investigation afterwards. Being mentioned was often enough to be sentenced to death.

1794 Law of the 22nd *Prairial*

Accused persons were no longer allowed to have a lawyer, witnesses were no longer needed to support accusations.

M 2 **Victims of the Reign of Terror. The last journey of the executed**

Painting, 1793

The Reign of Terror – a contemporary British cartoon

M 3 **"The *Zenith* of French Glory – The *Pinnacle* of Liberty, Religion, Justice, Loyalty and all the *Bugbears* of Unenlighten'd Minds – Farewell"**

Cartoon by James Gillray, 1793. The banner on top of the guillotine says "Vive l'Egalité" ("Long live Equality").

The Reign of Terror – contemporary French sources

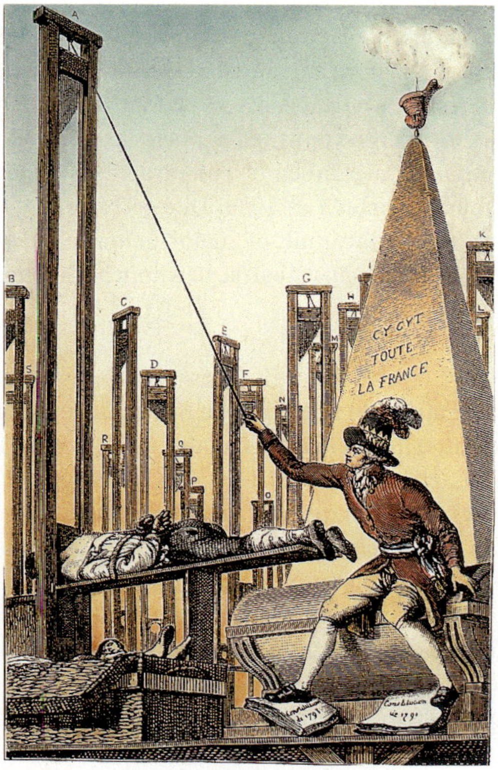

M 4 **"Here Rests all France"**
Satirical leaflet, 1793

Vocabulary

zenith: (here) highlight
pinnacle: the most successful part
bugbear: sth. that keeps annoying you

M 5 Virtue and Terror

Robespierre explained the nature of his philosophy of terror:

a) "We want a country in which the government looks after the welfare of every individual. One's duty is to punish traitors, to help the needy, respect the weak, defend the oppressed, do good to one's neighbour and behave justly."

Quoted from: Colin Shephard, Societies in Change, John Murray: London 1992, p. 144.

b) "If the *spring* of popular government in time of peace is virtue, the springs of popular government in revolution are at once virtue and terror: virtue, without which terror is fatal; terror, without which virtue is powerless. Terror is nothing other than justice, prompt, severe, inflexible; it is therefore an *emanation* of virtue; it is not so much a special principle as it is a consequence of the general principle of democracy applied to our country's most urgent needs [...]. Let the despot govern by terror his brutalized subjects; he is right, as a despot. *Subdue* by terror the enemies of liberty, and you will be right, as founders of the Republic. The government of the revolution is liberty's despotism against tyranny."

https://sourcebooks.fordham.edu/halsall/mod/robespierre-terror.asp [Oct. 2017].

Vocabulary

spring: (here) source or origin of sth.
emanation: origin, beginning, outpour
to subdue: to bring sth. under control by force
to devour: to eat, to consume very eagerly

Tasks

1. **Robespierre**
   a) Explain Robespierre's role in the course of the French Revolution (text).
   b) Find out from the Internet in which way Robespierre's political role corresponds with his private life.
   c) Assess Robespierre's ideas on government and explain why he was not successful in the end (text).
2. **The Committee of Public Safety**
   a) Explain the role the Committee played (text).
   b) Comment on the name of the Committee.
   c) Define the attitude of the radical Jacobins to the people (text).
3. **The Cartoons**
   a) Describe the cartoons (M3, M4).
   b) Explain how the artists see the French situation in this phase of the revolution.
   c) In 1793 Jacques Mallet du Pan wrote: "The revolution *devours* its children". Compare this statement with the cartoons.
4. **Virtue and Violence**
   a) Can you introduce freedom by force? Make up your mind (M5).
   b) Explain the difference between "virtue" and "violence".
   c) Discuss in class whether they go together.

CODE CIVIL
DES
FRANÇAIS.
ÉDITION ORIGINALE ET SEULE OFFICIELLE.
GRAND JUGE ET MINISTRE DE LA JUSTICE.
À PARIS,
DE L'IMPRIMERIE DE LA RÉPUBLIQUE.
AN XII. 1804.

M 1 **"Code Civil"**

Front page of the first edition, 1804

Historical Terms

coup d'état: Staatsstreich

concordat: Konkordat

Code Civil, also: Code Napoleon: Code Civil

Info

Some laws from the Code Civil:

All people are equal before the law

All feudal rights and privileges do not exist any longer

Guarantee of religious freedom

Husbands owe protection to their wives, wives must be obedient to their husbands

Wives can only own property with their husband's written permission

A wife may only divorce if her husband's mistress lives in the family's household

Fathers are allowed to imprison their children for up to one month

There is freedom of thought

Napoleon – Hero or Tyrant?

First Steps to Power – in the army

Napoleon Bonaparte went to military schools from the age of nine. At 24 he was made a general because his talent was obvious and he acted cleverly in the days of the revolution. In 1793 Napoleon suppressed a royalist revolt for the Convention. After Robespierre's death the wealthy citizens returned to power and gave France a new constitution with a government of five directors. They ordered Napoleon to put down a demonstration of hungry people in 1795. Due to his energy and *decisiveness* he was soon promoted to the rank of major general and given command of the French troops in the war against Austria, to whom he dictated the peace treaty of Campo Formio in 1797.

Military Commander – a genius

While he was on his next military campaign to Egypt, the British fleet under the command of Admiral Nelson defeated the French fleet at Aboukir in August 1798. It was not the only time that the French lost a sea battle. In 1805 Napoleon suffered a final and disastrous defeat at Trafalgar which ended all attempts to win against the British at sea. Admiral Nelson lost his life in the battle, but became a national hero. Apart from losing sea battles Napoleon was highly successful on land, including the victorious battle of Marengo against the Austrians and the ensuing peace treaty of Lunéville. He also made peace with Britain and the Russian tsar withdrew his troops from western Europe. Then he reorganized the territories of the Holy Roman Empire. Within a few years Napoleon changed the map of Europe permanently.

Domestic Policies – a success story

In 1799 Napoleon left his soldiers secretly to return to Paris where he organized a **coup d'état**. He *overthrew* the weak directors and made himself First Consul in November of the same year. As a military dictator he officially declared the revolution to be over.

Four years later he risked a referendum to be elected First Consul for Life. The risk was not very great because Napoleon had had a lot of military and political success before he had become the *undisputed* leader of his country. The signing of a **concordat** with the pope brought the Catholic Church back to France. However, it put the church under the control of the state.

A second referendum in 1804 made Napoleon Emperor of the French. He was then crowned by the pope at Notre Dame in Paris. France was a monarchy again, but the country had changed. Under Napoleon noble emigrants came back to France and the wounds from the revolution slowly healed. He set out to make dramatic reforms. The government was organized under a new centralized prefect system. *Prefects* ran the 83 departments, making sure that Napoleon's commands were obeyed in each of these regions. The education system was reorganized, giving more boys an opportunity to learn. State schools were set up which were not controlled by the church. A currency reform solved the financial problems. The most important step was the introduction of the "**Code Civil**", a complete change of the legal system. The new laws were simple and ensured many of the rights that citizens had gained during the revolution. But Napoleon also returned censorship of the press.

Napoleon in Pictures

M 2 **The First Consul, 1799**
Painting by Jean-A.-Dominique Ingres, 1804

M 3 **The General, 1796**
Painting by Antoine-Jean Gros

Vocabulary

decisiveness: ability to decide
to overthrow: to get rid of a government by force
undisputed: sth. that cannot be questioned
prefect: a public official
to crush: to get rid of sth., to wipe it out
gravedigger: sb. who digs a grave for the dead
consummator: sb. who finishes a job

Biography

Napoleon Bonaparte (1769–1821) was born in Ajaccio, Corsica. From 1779–85 he was a student at the military academies of Brienne and Paris, where he became a lieutenant of the artillery. After occupying Toulon in 1793 he became a brigadier general. From 1796 to 1815 he was the military commander of the French army in seven Coalition wars. He entered domestic politics after *crushing* a royalist revolt in Paris in 1795. In 1799 he led a coup d'état and became First Consul and from 1802 First Consul for Life. He crowned himself Emperor in 1804. His only son was born in 1811. When he lost the war against nearly all the Europeen powers in 1814, he had to abdicate and was exiled to the island of Elba. From there he returned to military power for 100 days in 1815, but lost the Battle of Waterloo at the hands of Prussia and Britain. He was sent into exile again, this time to St. Helena in the South Atlantic, where he died in 1821.

Tasks

1. **Napoleon the Politician**
   a) Say what role religion and the church played in Napoleonic France (text).
   b) Describe the images Napoleon wanted people to have of himself (M2, M3).
   c) List the changes Napoleon introduced in France.
   d) *Gravedigger* or *consummator* of the revolution. Make up your mind as to Napoleon's role, giving reasons for your choice.
2. **Napoleon the Officer**
   a) Describe Napoleon's military career (text, biography).
   b) Find out from the Internet what made Napoleon so successful with his army.

Vocabulary

principality: a country ruled by a prince

conquest: the act of taking control of a country or a city

to mediatize: to join a smaller state to a larger one

to compensate: to provide sth. good in order to balance a loss

to secularize: to take sth. away from religious control and put it under civil authority

to inflict: to cause sth. unpleasant to happen

shortcoming: a fault in a plan or system

impetus: push

M 1 Karl August von Hardenberg (1750–1822)

Info

The Prussian Reforms (1806–1816)

These things were modernized:

tax and customs, town administration, police, army, military service, emancipation of Jews, freeing of farmers, agriculture, industry, school system, universities

The Revolution and Europe

Opposition to the Revolution – Napoleon's answer

At the beginning of the revolution many French nobles fled to one of the German *principalities* on the right bank of the Rhine. From there they influenced the German princes to start a war against revolutionary France. But after Napoleon took power, the tide quickly turned. He won battles and seemed unbeatable due to his strategic talent. Even the renewed alliance of Russia, Prussia and Britain could not hinder his *conquests* from Spain to the river Elbe. After the defeat of Prussia in 1806 he began to reorganize central and eastern Europe. His ally, the king of Saxony, ruled the Grand Duchy of Warsaw (formerly Poland). Prussia was occupied by French troops.

The Principal Decree of the Imperial Deputation – end of the Empire

Napoleon wanted to crush Austrian influence in the German principalities to gain hegemony over Europe. The three southern principalities of Baden, Württemberg and Bavaria which had helped him against the Austrians became kingdoms or grand duchies and were given much more land. He "*mediatized*" forty-five free cities and the lands of 1500 imperial knights into forty medium-sized states. Sixteen of these states were joined in the Confederation of the Rhine (1806) and made French allies. In order to *compensate* the German princes who had lost land to France on the west bank of the Rhine he "*secularized*" church lands on the east bank and distributed it among the Protestant princes. All these measures meant the end of the Holy Roman Empire. When the Habsburg emperor realized that he had lost his empire, he set aside the crown but retained the title of Emperor of Austria because he wanted to keep the same rank as Napoleon.

A New Europe – and reforms in Prussia

After his defeat in the sea Battle of Trafalgar in 1805 Napoleon dropped his plan to attack Britain directly. He turned east, winning the Battles of Jena and Auerstedt, thus *inflicting* a devastating defeat on Prussia. Poland was renamed the Grand Duchy of Warsaw and ruled by Napoleon's ally, the king of Saxony. Napoleon secured his reign in Europe by marrying some of his family members to members of the leading aristocratic families. His brother Jerome was made king of the newly founded Westphalia, formed from Prussian and other territory. He wanted it to be a model state for the results of the French Revolution. So he also introduced the Code Napoleon. The leading politicians in Prussia, however, saw that reforms were necessary. Some of them began to modernize the country and unite the people behind the king, giving every citizen the feeling that they were needed. Their main targets were the military, the administration, the economy and education, but they were also willing to change the living conditions of the people in the country.

Historical Terms

The Holy Roman Empire (of German Origin): Heiliges Römisches Reich deutscher Nation (800/962–1806)

In 800 the pope crowned Charlemagne emperor. After the coronation of Otto I in 962 the HREGO came into existence. Its territory extended from the river Eider to the Vatican State in Italy and included many European states of today. The emperor was elected by a fixed number of electors. In the course of time his power became more and more limited by the growing influence of the princes of the various territories.

The Changing Face of Germany

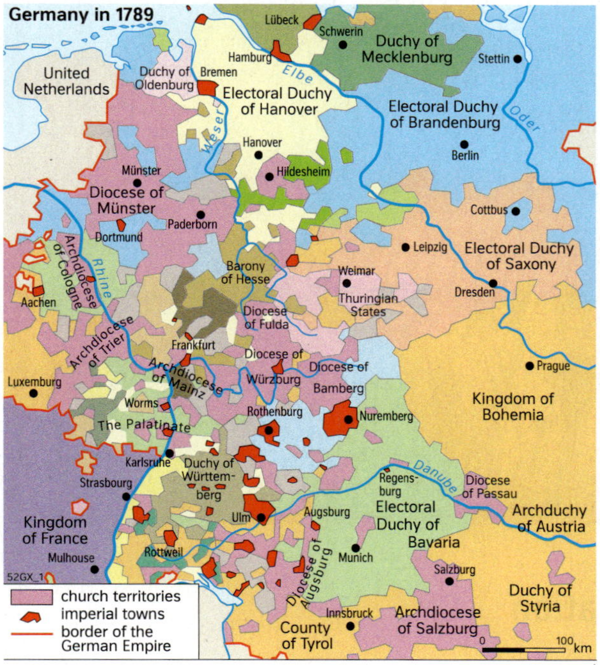

M 2

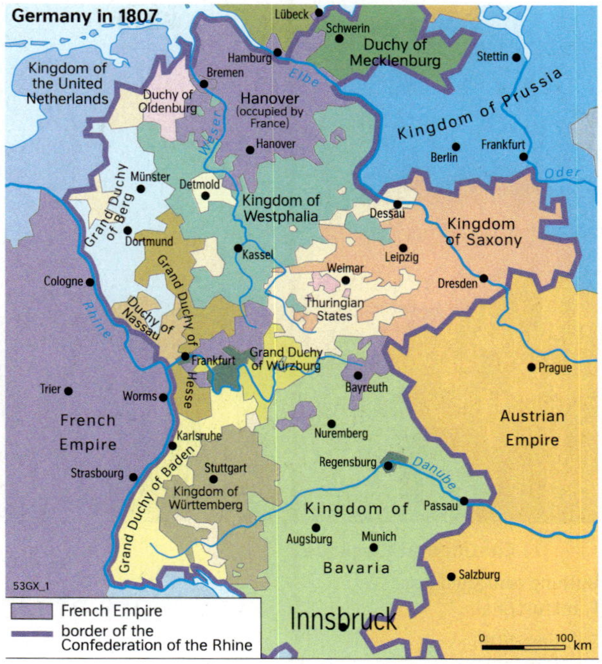

M 3

M 4 Reorganization of the Prussian State

Karl August of Hardenberg (1812):

"Despite its many *shortcomings* the French Revolution has given the French a new *impetus*. All the sleeping power has been awakened, the bad things have been destroyed, alongside with many good things. [...] The misunderstanding that the revolution could be held up by strict persecution has promoted it, so that it has spread. The power of the ideas of the revolution is so big and has been accepted so widely that the states which don't accept them will either die or be forced to introduce them. It is our aim to carry out a revolution led by the wisdom of the government, a revolution that allows people to become better. The pure form of democracy will possibly be invented in the year 2440, but it is our guiding principle to introduce democratic elements in a monarchical society by means of a good revolution."

Quoted from: Walter Demel/Uwe Puschner (eds.), Deutsche Geschichte in Quellen und Darstellung Bd. 6: Von der Französischen Revolution bis zum Wiener Kongress 1789–1815, Reclam: Stuttgart 1995, p. 87f. (transl. by Rolf J. Kröger).

Tasks

1. **The Former Holy Roman Empire (of German Origin)**
   a) Work out why Napoleon changed the face of Central Europe (text).
   b) Explain the words mediatization and secularization in detail (text).
   c) Find out who profited from the Confederation of the Rhine and who didn't (text).
   d) Germany still has to pay compensation to the Church for Napoleon's secularization. Find out why (text).
2. **The Changing Face of Germany**
   a) Show what happened to the German Empire (M2, M3).
   b) Find out who the rulers of the countries of the Confederation of the Rhine were (Internet).
3. **Reorganization of the Prussian State**
   a) Find out why Prussian politicians wanted to reform their country (text).
   b) Choose three of the reforms and find out what changed (text).
   c) Were the Prussian reforms a result or by-product of the French Revolution? Comment.
   d) Say in your own words what Hardenberg thought of the French revolution (M4).

M 1 **Continental Blockade**

Burning smuggled goods in Frankfurt/Main.

Painting, 1810

The Wars of Liberation

The Continental Blockade

Despite his military success on land Napoleon lost to the British in sea battles. So he changed his tactics. Napoleon dropped his plans to conquer Britain from the sea and turned to other methods instead.

From 1806 on he tried to weaken Britain by a trade war. The ports of Europe were closed for British goods. A year later even Russia joined in. However, people

M 2 **"The Third of May, 1808"**

The shooting of the rebels at Madrid.

Painting by Francisco José de Goya, 1814

needed British goods like cloth, coffee or tea. In order to close the European harbours completely Napoleon attacked Spain and Portugal but he was unable to get them under control. In the north Hamburg became the gateway for British goods, despite the fact that it was under French control. If they got hold of these goods the French publicly burnt them. The coastline of Europe, however, proved to be too long for Napoleon's strategy.

Historical Terms

Battle of the Nations:
Völkerschlacht

Opposition

In many parts of Europe people disliked Napoleon's reign. When he tried to make his brother Joseph king of Spain in 1808, the Spanish resisted and began to fight for their freedom. They did not do it in the usual way but invented "guerrilla" warfare. This meant that no Spanish army attacked the French openly, but partisans attacked anywhere at any time. In a number of areas farmers' uprisings took place like the one in Southern Tyrol led by Andreas Hofer. The French reaction was violent throughout.

The End

Napoleon soon seemed to have gone too far. The turning point came in 1812 when he tried to occupy Russia with an army of 600,000. He lost most of his soldiers there due to the weather and the Russian strategy. They even burnt their capital in order to keep Napoleon from benefiting from its conquest. Only 5,000 soldiers got out of Russia safely at the end of the campaign.

Prussia and Austria now started the Wars of Liberation and were supported by the tsar, who did not stop fighting after he had defeated Napoleon and driven him out of Russia. In the **Battle of the Nations** at Leipzig the allies beat Napoleon in 1813 and occupied Paris in 1814. He had to vacate his throne. From exile on the island of Elba, he returned for another 100 days as emperor. After losing the Battle of Waterloo he was banned to St. Helena in the South Atlantic where he died in 1821.

The ideas of the revolution, however, had spread all over Europe. The "Code Napoleon" had become the law in many places and many peoples had discovered their wish to form nations of their own.

M 3 Moscow Burning 1812

Painting by Johann Lorenz Rugendas, 1813

M 4 Napoleon's Grand Army on its Retreat from Russia 1812

Contemporary painting

The Continental Blockade

M5 A French View

On 21 November 1806, "At [his] Imperial Camp in Berlin", Napoleon signed the famous Berlin Decree which marked the start of a harsh economic war with Britain:

"We have placed the British Isles under blockade and have *reluctantly* ordered measures to be taken against her. It pained us to make the interests of private individuals depend upon a quarrel of kings and to return, after so many years of civilization, to principles which were characteristic of barbarism in the earliest ages of Nations. But we have been compelled, for the good of our peoples and our allies, to combat the common enemy with the same arms as he uses against us. These resolutions which were imposed by a *legitimate sentiment of retaliation* were inspired neither by passion nor by hate. What we offered after the dissolution of three coalitions which has contributed so much to the glory of my nation, we offer again today now that our arms have obtained new triumphs. We are prepared to make peace with England, we are ready to do so with Russia, with Prussia. But it can only be concluded on the basis that no one may claim any right of supremacy with regards to us [...]."

www.napoleonicsociety.com/english/chap28a.htm [Oct. 2017].

M6 A British View

In a speech he made in the House of Commons, in December 1812, Lord Liverpool declared:

"In this circumstance, Russia has *restituted* a market of thirty-six million customers to England. She has raised the price of our colonial productions, and brought activity back to our factories. It's a distinguished service for which we must be eternally grateful."

http://www.napoleonicsociety.com/english/chap28a.htm [Oct. 2017].

M7 The Blockade in Schleswig-Holstein

The Historian Eli F. Heckscher (1922):

"As a matter of fact, Schleswig-Holstein during the whole of the preceding period, had been an obstacle in the way of Napoleon's measures south of the Elbe. When the Elbe and the Weser were barred, Tönning in particular, but also Husum on the west coast of Schleswig had largely replaced the Hanse towns during the years 1803–1806 as importers of English and colonial goods; and their trade had flourished. All attempts to prevent the passing of goods to the south from Holstein territory through the town of Altona, which was practically Hamburg, met with great difficulties, all the more as the local Holstein authorities never failed to certify the neutral origin of the goods. It was, therefore, of very great importance that the ruler of Denmark [...] placed himself at the service of the Continental System, with almost unique loyalty, and as early as September 1807 ordered the seizure of all forbidden goods in Holstein."

Eli F. Heckscher/Harald Westergaard (ed.), The Continental System: An Economic Interpretation, Clarendon Press: Oxford 1922, p. 168. https://archive.org/stream/continentalsyste00heckuoft#page/168/mode/2up [Oct. 2017].

Vocabulary

reluctant: unwilling, not wanting to do sth.

legitimate sentiment of retaliation: rightful feeling of paying sb. back for doing sth. wrong

to restitute: to establish again or to restore

Tasks

1. **Napoleon's Russian Campaign**
   a) Examine the sources for information on Napoleon's Russian campaign (text, M3, M4).
   b) Find reasons for Napoleon's defeat (text, M3, M4).
   c) Comment on the role Russia played for Europe during Napoleon's reign (text, M3, M4).

2. **The Continental Blockade**
   a) Find out why Napoleon set up the Continental Blockade (text, M1).
   b) Analyse the effect of the Continental Blockade on Europe. Take the map into account as well (text, M8).
   c) Comment on Napoleon's chances of winning this economic war.
   d) Say in your own words what role Schleswig-Holstein played in the Continental Blockade (M7).

Analysing Maps

Historical maps may show a state of affairs at a certain time and the development of a historical process, giving information about space and time. Such maps contain lots of information. But be careful: Mapmakers may add or leave out data. Then the map can mislead users or not give them enough information to understand a historical process. Sometimes mapmakers simplify things to make the information clear. But even an objective map can only hint at why things happened.

M 8 **Europe at the Time of Napoleon 1812**

Historical Workshop

Analysing Maps

1. Description

a. Give the map a title.

b. Describe what exactly is shown on the map.

c. Say what time span is covered on the map.

d. Find the scale of the map and write it down.

e. Explain the legend of the map.

f. Describe all symbols, lines and coloured areas. Can they be distinguished? Is the map clear?

2. Working with the Map

a. Explain what kind of map it is – a political, social, military or an economic map. Prove your argument.

b. Decide whether the map shows a state of affairs or a development.

c. Examine if any important information is missing.

d. Explain the message of the map.

3. Interpreting Maps

a. List all of Napoleon's allies in 1812.

b. Examine the development of the French Empire in Europe.

c. Comment on Napoleon's success as a military and political leader. Point out the evidence the map shows.

1770 1775 1780 1785 1790

The Enlightenment

The Estates-General called

14 July
Storming of the Bastille

26 August
The Rights of Man and the Citizen

The Reign of Terror

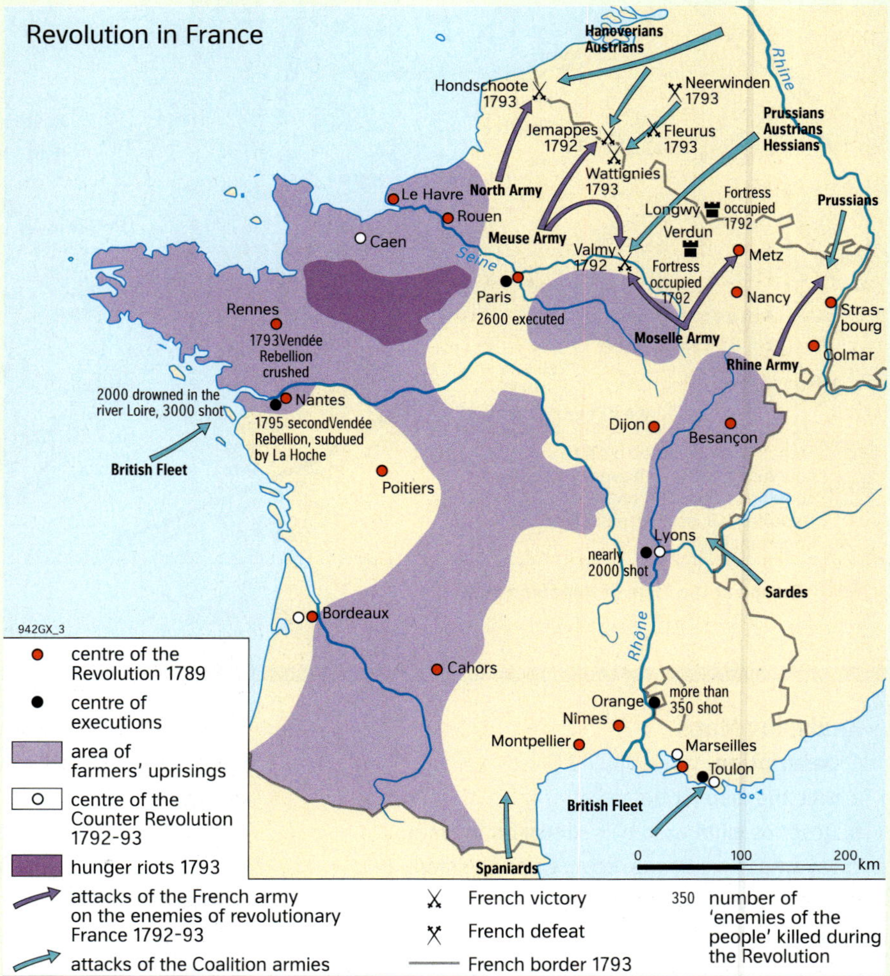

The French Revolution – the historical map

1800	1805	1810	1815	1820

Napoleon takes over power

Napoleon becomes emperor

End of Holy Roman Empire

Battle of the Nations, Leipzig

Congress of Vienna

The Continental System

Summary

Some people still say today that the French Revolution changed the direction of human history completely. Some have even said that it finally ended the Middle Ages as it marks the fall of the clergy and nobility and the rise of the bourgeoisie.

After the absolute kings of the 18th century made France bankrupt, Louis XVI called on the Estates-General in order to raise taxes. In the course of the three revolutionary acts which took place in 1789, major political changes took place, among them the "Declaration of the Rights of Man". The king did not really accept the new role that the first constitution gave him and tried to flee with his family. A war broke out between France and some European monarchies, which wanted to help the French king get back into his old position. Another new constitution was written and soon after the king and his wife were tried for treason and executed. The ideas of the revolution proved so powerful that they gave the French soldiers a lot of motivation. France was not conquered by her enemies – on the contrary.

But the revolution became more and more radical. After the Reign of Terror ended, the system changed again. One of the military leaders – Napoleon – got more political influence, officially ended the revolution in 1799, and was crowned emperor in 1804. His most important achievement was the introduction of a new code of law, the Code Civil. When he conquered most of Europe he spread the ideas of the revolution to a lot of countries. But Napoleon could not keep his empire for long and had to leave France forever after being beaten in battle by a coalition of European countries. In France the old royal family came back to power, but the monarchy was no longer absolute.

As a consequence of Napoleon's aggression there were national rebellions in some parts of Europe. In Prussia the state organized reforms from above which were influenced by the Age of Enlightenment

DATES

1789:
French Revolution

1804:
Napoleon becomes emperor

1807:
Prussian Reform Edict

1815:
Battle of Waterloo

HISTORICAL TERMS

monarchy
absolute monarchy
constitutional monarchy
republic
dictatorship
treason
demagogue
emergency decree
coup d'état
concordat
Code Civil, also:
Code Napoleon
The Holy Roman Empire
(of German Origin)
Battle of the Nations

PERSONS

Louis XVI
Robespierre
Olympe de Gouges
Napoleon
Hardenberg

HISTORY WORKSHOP

Analysing Maps

M 1 **Child Labour: Children Working in a Coal Mine**

M 2 **Banner of the Social Democratic Party of Germany**

M 3 **Factory Accident, painting by Johann Bahr, 1889**

M 4 **Diesel Engine, about 1900**

M 5 **Bottle of Aspirin, 1909**

M 6 **The Late Bed Lodger, drawing by Heinrich Zille, 1902**

04 INDUSTRIALIZATION

Curse or Blessing?

Historical Terms

industrialization:
Industrialisierung
urbanization:
Urbanisierung, Verstädterung
infrastructure:
Infrastruktur; Aufbau des Verkehrsnetzes
emissions:
Emissionen, Ausstoß (von Gasen, etc.)
the Social Question:
die Soziale Frage
insurance:
Versicherung
German Customs Union:
Deutscher Zollverein

Vocabulary

issue: a topic that is talked about

The time of **industrialization** is often called the Industrial Revolution, because the life and living conditions of everyone changed quickly. There is no exact year in which these drastic changes happened. Historians agree that 1750 can be assumed as the starting point. It all started in Great Britain and then spread to the rest of the world.

The changes happened in different forms with different effects. The doubling of the population led to **urbanization**, which again led to crowded living space and health problems. With inventions such as the steam engine improvements began in many areas, for example, in **infrastructure.** Trains and steamships made it possible to transport more in a much shorter time. But these improvements often proved to be bad not only for the individual workers and their families. The environment also suffered as the **emissions** of factories polluted the air or the waste was put into the rivers.

Because of the drastic changes many aspects (working conditions, child labour, education, etc.) became political *issues*. Theories were developed such as communism that wanted to help better the lives of workers. Once the workers started to fight for better conditions, political parties took over these ideas and it came to confrontations with the government. In the end many people, groups, organizations, the Church, as well as the government tried to find ways to solve these social problems, known as the **Social Question**. Some positive changes resulted from the political struggles such as health, unemployment and other kinds of **insurance**. The insurance system introduced by Bismarck still exists today.

However, not all aspects of industrialization led to struggle. The improvements in infrastructure also helped to unify Germany. The **German Customs Union** profited not only from new roads and railways but also from standardization of measurements. “Made in Germany” became a label of quality in the world.

This chapter deals with many questions such as:

- What changed so that industrialization started?
- Why and how was the textile industry the driving force in England?
- Why did industrialization take so long to take off in Germany?
- What was “German” about industrialization?
- Did anybody care about the environment?
- How can statistics help to understand industrialization?
- What was it like to live in such fast changing times?
- Who did what to better the living conditions?
- Were the social laws only a by-product?
- Was the Industrial Revolution a curse or blessing?

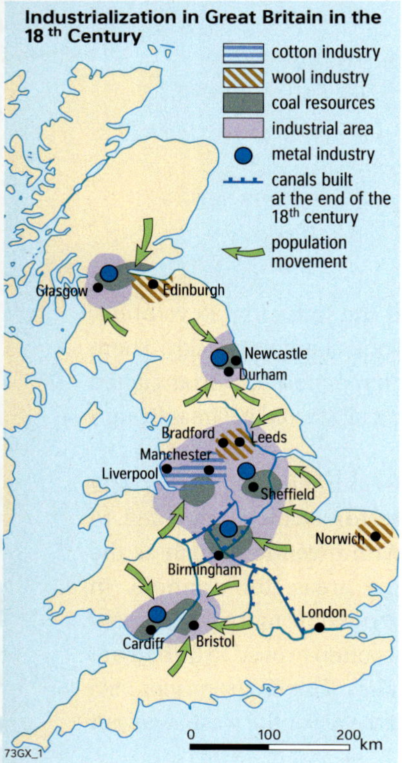

M 1

Vocabulary

invention: production of sth. new that has not existed before

improvement: sth. made better

loom: a machine to weave cloth

to exceed: to be greater than ...

contemporaries: people living at that time

cradle: (here) beginning

vaccination: medicine that is given to immunize a person or animal against diseases

famine: little or no food for a long time

supply: an amount of sth. that is provided or available

fertilizer: substance added to soil to make plants grow better

fallow: not used for growing crops

to breed (bred, bred): to mate, to couple

The Industrial Revolution

Drastic Changes – too fast?

From 1750 to 1850 the population almost doubled. Technical *inventions* like the **steam engine** or the spinning jenny and later *improvements* of the *loom* sped up production processes and increased production.

The steam engine, which did not depend on location or climate, brought about the most significant change. Its power *exceeded* human muscle power many times. Therefore, handicrafts (**cottage industry** as well as **manufactory production**) and man's relationship to nature and the environment changed drastically.

A new era dominated by machines had begun – industrialization. The changes were so dramatic and fast that *contemporaries* spoke of a "revolution".

England – the *cradle* of industrialization

There is no clear explanation why the Industrial Revolution started in England and not anywhere else in Europe. Here are some factors that led to industrialization:

- Population:
  Not only improvements in medical treatment, such as *vaccination* and hygiene, but also the fact that more people married and had children (there had been restrictions on marriage in the Middle Ages and Early Modern Times) led to population growth.
  More people moved into towns and cities to find work, so there were more workers for the newly developing industries after 1750. However, this also caused major changes in agriculture, because people living in urban areas could not grow their own food.
  The clergyman and mathematician Thomas Malthus wrote in "Essay on The Principle of Population" (1798) that there were natural limits to the number of people which caused by epidemics, war or *famine*. Accordingly, nature kept a balance between food *supply* and population.
- Agriculture:
  Traditionally farmers worked on open fields. They changed the crops they grew yearly to keep the land productive. This was necessary, because they did not have any chemical *fertilizers*. A village usually had three large fields plus a **common**, where every local farmer could bring a number of animals to graze. This type of farming was problematic for several reasons: Little fodder for the animals could be produced, so they had to be killed before the winter. Land was wasted when it lay *fallow*. Hardly any surplus could be produced, which could have been sold or traded. All the farmers' animals grazed on the common, so diseases spread easily and high-quality animals *bred* with those

Historical Terms

steam engine: Dampfmaschine
cottage industry: (System der) Heimarbeit
manufactory production: Herstellung in einer Manufaktur (vorindustriell)
common: Gemeindeland
seed drill: Drill-/Sähmaschine

of poor quality. Therefore, the richer landowners did much better outside the open fields. They fenced in their land, so that only their animals of good quality could reproduce and were protected from diseases. In addition, they could afford to experiment. The good results did not come overnight. It took more than 200 years to see improvement in agriculture. Farmers learnt by experience how to end the *inefficient* production of open field farming. Sir Richard Weston discovered that planting turnips and clover helped the *soil* recover its fertility. So over four years a different crop was planted on each field. This system was known as the Four Year Rotation or Norfolk Rotation. Traditional farmers resisted this new system, so it took quite a while to become widespread.

- Inventions and Animal *Breeding*:
  Things kept changing: In 1701 John Tull invented a **seed drill** to sow straight lines of seed in the soil instead of *broadcasting* it on top. *Threshing*, *winnowing* and *reaping* machines were invented in 1826. In 1856 John Fowler of Leeds invented a steam plough.
  Machinery and new methods in growing crops were not the only factors which led to the “agricultural revolution”. Animal breeding also improved. One pioneer, Robert Bakewell, produced larger sheep on his Leicestershire farm. Earlier, sheep had been bred mainly for wool. Bakewell bred big, fat sheep for food. He was less successful in breeding better cattle. But his ideas influenced others who produced such cattle and later bigger pigs and stronger horses.

Vocabulary

inefficient: not effective
soil: the earth on the fields
breeding: the controlled reproduction of animals
to broadcast: (here) to throw by hand
to thresh: to separate grain from the rest of the plant
to winnow: to blow air through grain in order to remove its outer covering
to reap: to cut and collect a crop from a field

M 2 **Industrial Development in Europe until 1850**

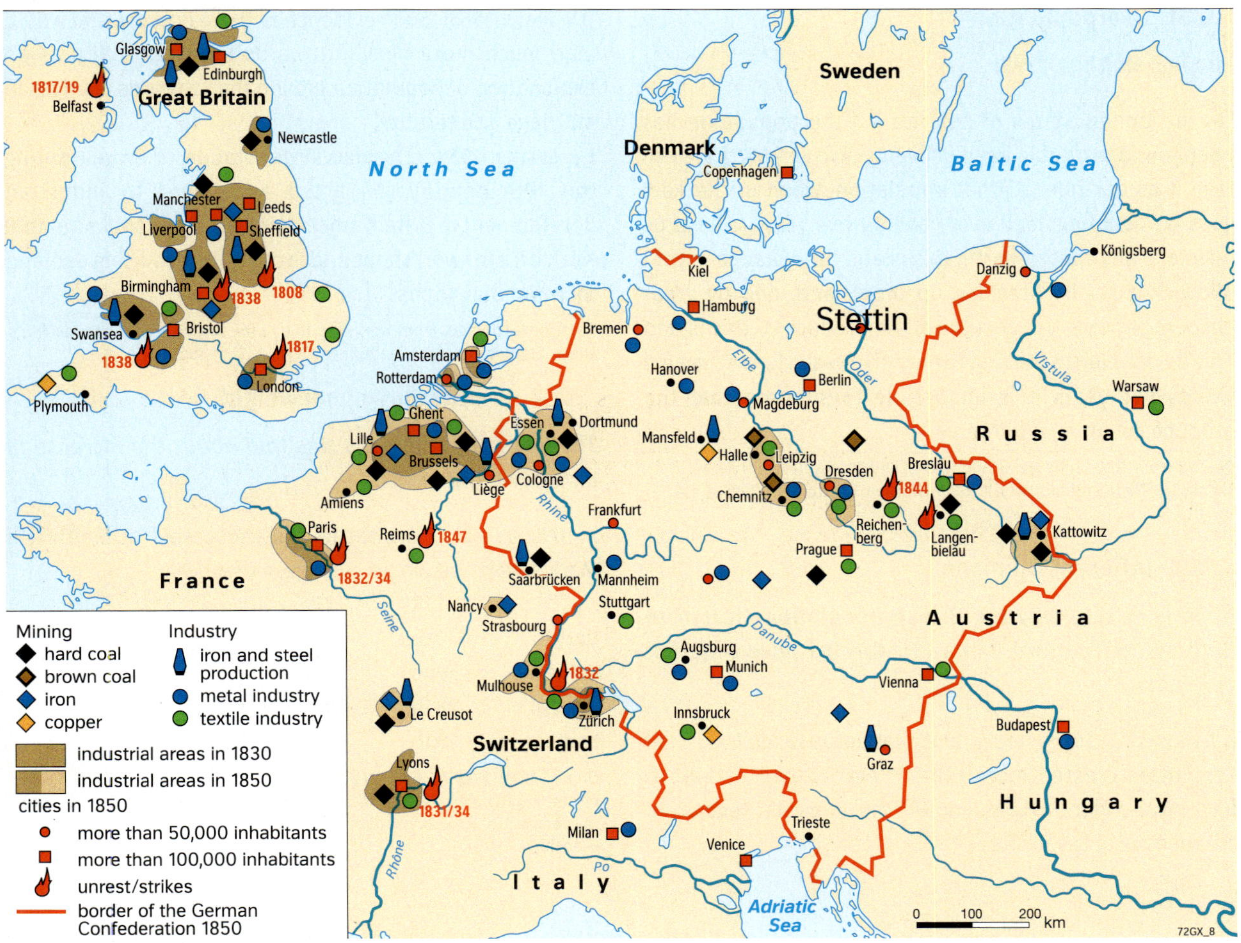

The Industrial Revolution

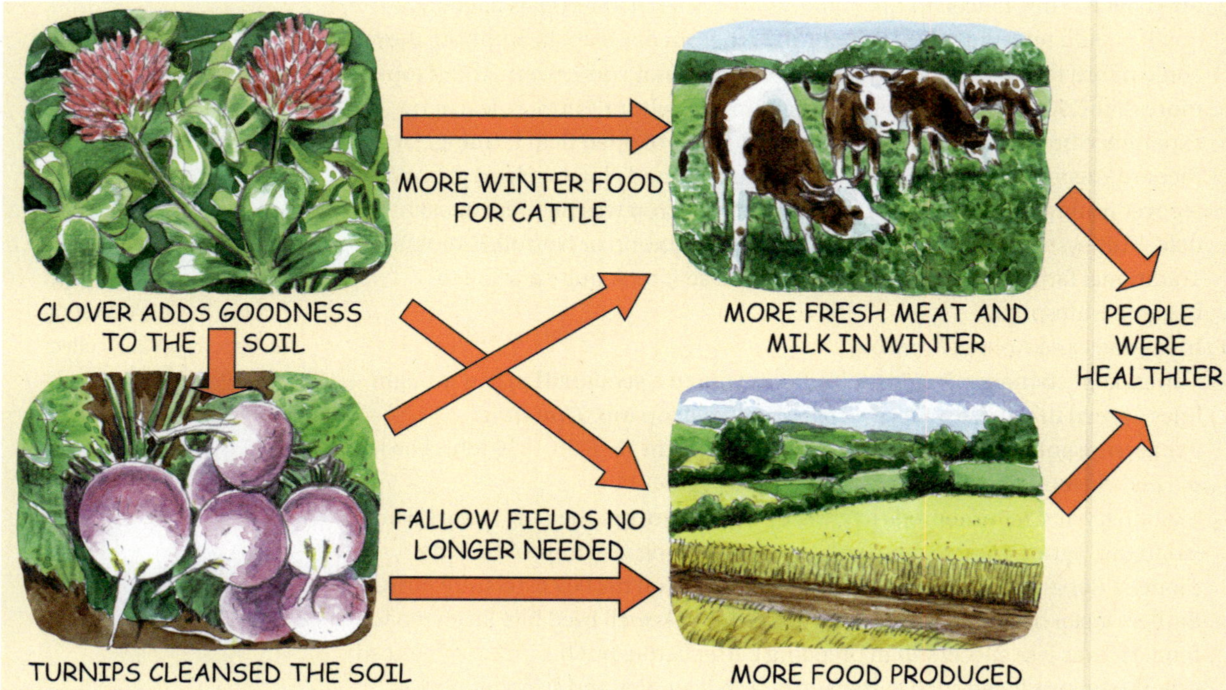

M 3 **Improvements in Agriculture**

M 4 Overpopulation

Thomas Malthus, 1798:

"In the United States of America [...] the population has been found to double itself in twenty-five years [...]. We will take it as our rule [...] that population, when unchecked, goes on doubling itself every twenty-five years [...]. Let us now take any spot of earth, this island for instance [...]. If I allow that [...] by breaking up more land, and by great *encouragements* to agriculture, the produce of this island may be doubled in the first twenty-five years, [...] in the next twenty-five years it is impossible to suppose that the produce could be *quadrupled*."

Quoted from: R. J. Cootes/L. E. Snellgrove, Key Stages in History – Expansion Trade and Industry, Nelson Thornes: Cheltenham 1999, p. 44.

M 5 Different Opinions

Nobody is sure why the British population started to outgrow its "natural limits". Historians have different opinions:

H.J. Habakkuk suggested in 1958 that because the Industrial Revolution created more jobs, it encouraged people to have more children. He asked: "Did the Industrial Revolution create its own labour force?"

D.V. Glass, 1965: "Such evidence as there is at present would lean much more heavily towards lower *mortality* as an explanation of population growth than towards changes in marriage and fertility."

E.J. Ewans, 1983: "The rise in population of Britain during the 18th century [...] acted as a *spur* to industrial development in Britain since it provided not only potential workforce for workshops and factory but also rising demand for industrial goods."

Hamish Macdonald, From workshop to empire: Britain 1750–1900. Teacher's guide, Stanley Thornes: Cheltenham 1995, p. 57. (adapted)

M 6 Increase in Animal Weight

The House of Commons was told about the increase in animal weight in 1795:

In 1710 and 1795 the cattle and sheep sold at Smithfield Market weighed, on an average, as follows:

	1710	1795
Cattle:	370 lb.	800 lb.
Calves:	50 lb.	143 lb.
Sheep:	28 lb.	80 lb.
Lambs:	18 lb.	50 lb.

Quoted from: Deanna Nebert/Dieter Krisching/Wulf Lutz (eds.), Materialien zum bilingualen Unterricht Bd. 7, Geschichte (9. Jahrgang Gymnasium), Landesinstitut Schleswig-Holstein für Praxis und Theorie der Schule: Kronshagen 1998, p. 7.

M 7 Industrial Revolution

The historian Carlo Cipolla writes about the importance of the Industrial Revolution:

"I said before that the only event historically comparable to the Industrial Revolution is the Neolithic Revolution. But apart from every other *consideration*, the Neolithic Revolution developed in the course of thousands of years. It took more than 5,000 years to move from the Middle East to Scandinavia and about 2,500 years to pass through from Mexico to the source of the Ohio River. Man had time to adapt gradually. The Industrial Revolution has invaded the world, turned our very existence upside down and overthrown the structures of all existing human societies in the course of only eight generations. And today it is beginning to press with great *urgency* new problems of such enormity that the human mind can harldy *grasp* them – the uncontrolled increase in population; the hydrogen bomb [Wasserstoffbombe]; the pollution of the atmosphere; the destruction of the natural surroundings by industrial waste; the demand for further mass education; the presence of an ever-increasing number of old people kept alive but rejected by the rest of society; the breaking up of the traditional state; the scientific organisation of uncontrolled centres of power; the unlimited possibilities held out by *geneticists* and biologists of influencing nature and the behaviour of man. Under the weight of these problems the old structures crumble. The conservatives complain that they do not understand what is happening and they *deceive themselves* by trying to keep alive a past which is already dead. Those who understand what is happening do not know of and cannot *conceive* adequate solutions to these pressing and *formidable* problems. The young people protest when they realise the inadequacy of the old institutions and the older generation, but they too have no better diagnoses and no better cures, and they *give vent* to their frustration in surges of violent anarchy and curious hatred against their inheritance, or try to escape reality either by destroying their consciousness or by a desperate search for new religions. Everyone has been taken by surprise. It is the story of the 'Sorcerer's Apprentice' [Zauberlehrling] which would be funny if it were not tragic."

Carlo M. Cipolla (ed.), The Fontana Economic History of Europe Vol. 3: The Industrial Revolution, Collins: London/Glasgow 1973, p. 20f.

Vocabulary

encouragement: giving support or hope to sb.
to quadruple: to multiply by four
mortality: the number of deaths in a period of time
spur: (here) motivation
consideration: thinking carefully about sth.
urgency: need to deal with sth. quickly
to grasp: to understand sth. completely
geneticist: a scientist who studies genetics (Vererbungslehre)
to deceive oneself: to refuse to admit to yourself that sth. unpleasant is true
to conceive: to form an idea, plan, etc. in your mind, to imagine
formidable: sth. impressive or powerful, because it is very difficult/complicated
to give vent to: to express a feeling, esp. anger, strongly
surge: sudden increase

Tasks

1. **Industrialization on the Map**
   a) List the factors that led to industrialization in England (M1, text).
   b) Explain the relationship between natural resources and industrial centres (M1, M2).
   c) Show which factors supported sea trade (M1, M2).
   d) Compare the industrial development in Europe to Great Britain (M1, M2, text).
2. **What Factors Led to Industrialization?**
   a) What does Malthus fear? Explain Malthus' warning in your own words (M4).
   b) Look at the diagram and explain the advantages of the Four Year Rotation (M3).
   c) Analyse the development of animal weight (M6).
   d) Read the opinions of the different historians who wrote about industrialization at different times (M5). Compare the historians' ideas.
   e) Even today, the number of workers on farms is getting smaller. Explain why.
3. **Industrialization – curse or blessing?**
   a) Analyse Cipolla's statement about the role of industrialization (M7).
   b) Assess the problems caused by industrialization. Take Cipolla's opinion into consideration (M7).
   c) Discuss "the new problems" considering the fact that Cipolla wrote this in 1973 (M7).

Driving Force – Textile Industry

M 1 **Spinning Wheel**
Thread is made by spinning fibres into yarn.

Cottage Industry – good old times?

In 1700 most people lived in the country as farmers. Not only did they work on the fields and breed animals, they also did other work at home (cottage industry). Very often the entire family was involved. The kind of work varied from place to place but one major field was the weaving of wool. This cottage industry could be found all over Britain.

Usually the families did not own the machines they used. They were given by a *merchant clothier* who paid the families only for the cloth produced. They were harsh employers, because they had invested their money in the machines and therefore expected as much profit as possible in return.

British wool was of excellent quality and therefore was an important export product. This explains why the textile industry moved first and fastest from the cottage to the factory. Cotton was also an important factor in the growth of the British economy. In the 1600s, cheaply produced cotton was imported from the American colonies. In Lancashire the cotton industry developed more quickly than anywhere else, because the ships from the colonies arrived there.

Spinning Jenny – a breakthrough

The invention of the flying *shuttle* by John Kay in 1733 made weaving twice as fast as before. In consequence, four workers using spinning wheels could no longer produce enough *thread* for a single weaver. In 1761 the Royal Society of Arts set up a contest for a spinning wheel that could produce several threads at once. In 1764 James Hargreaves won with his spinning jenny, a machine that spun sixteen threads at a time. Richard Arkwright invented an even better spinning machine in 1769 and the development in spinning machines continued after that.

In 1785, Edmund Cartwright invented the power loom, powered by a steam engine. Many people laughed at him in the beginning, but after technical improvements the power loom forced many workers out of work. More than 800,000 weavers in the first half of the 19th century worked in textile production. But between 1820 and 1830 the number of power looms increased from 1,400 to 55,000. More and more workers lost their jobs. By 1812 one factory worker operating a machine could produce as much as 200 cottage workers had fifty years earlier.

M 2 **"Spinning Jenny"**
In 1764 the Briton James Hargreaves invented the first spinning machine, the "spinning jenny".

Poor Working Conditions

Working conditions in most factories were terrible. Factory owners often did not care much about the well-being of their workers, but only about mill profits. The workers – many of them women and children – had to work at the *pace* set by the machines, not by themselves. A 14-hour working day which included a one-hour break for meals was the average. The room temperature could reach up to 30°C and the *wages* were low. Even worse for the workers, the factories had strict rules. If a worker broke a rule, he was punished according to a list of *fines*.

M 3 Working Conditions

Samuel Coulson of Leeds: Coulson's children worked in a mill. Here, he answers questions about the work his children did in the "brisk" times:

"At what time in the morning, in the *brisk* time, did these girls go to the mills? – In the brisk time, for about six weeks, they have gone at 3 o'clock in the morning, and ended at 10, or nearly half past, at night.
What breaks were allowed for the rest during those nineteen hours of work? – Breakfast a quarter of an hour, and dinner half an hour, and drinking a quarter of an hour.
What was the length of time they could be in bed during those long hours? – It was near 11 o'clock before we could get them into bed after getting a little food, [then] me or my mistress got up at 2 o'clock to dress them.
Were the children excessively tired by this work? – Many a time; we have cried often when we have given them the little food we had to give them; we had to shake them and they have fallen to sleep with the food in their mouth."

Evidence given to the Commission of Parliament (1831–32), adapted from: John D. Clare, The Age of Expansion 1750–1914, Nelson Thornes: Cheltenham 1996, p. 56.

Vocabulary

merchant clothier: a person who sells clothes or cloth
shuttle: a wooden stick that pulls the thread back and forth in a loom
thread: a long thin string for weaving and sewing
pace: the speed at which sb. walks, moves, runs, etc.
wage: payment for work done
fine: a sum of money that must be paid as punishment
brisk: busy

M 4 Women Spinning and Their Clothier, about 1810

Tasks

1. What is New?
a) List the most important inventions at the beginning of industrialization (text).
b) Assess the general effects of the steam engine on population, agriculture and other industries (text).

2. Textile Industry
a) Describe the development from cottage industry to factory industry in textile production (M1–M4, text).
b) Explain why the working conditions were especially hard for children (M3).

Vocabulary

to trigger sth.: to make sth. happen suddenly

engineering works/factory: a factory that produces machines, etc.

policies: principles for political decisions

to stall: to stop sth. from happening until a later date

hard coal: coal found in the ground

charcoal: coal made from burnt wood

blast furnace: a large structure like an oven in which iron ore is melted in order to take out the metal

to exploit: to use sth. in order to gain as much from it as possible

cart: a vehicle pulled by a horse for carrying loads

stagecoach: a large carriage pulled by horses for carrying people

Industrialization in Germany

Late Start in Germany

Most of the pioneering inventions came from England. Watt's steam engine, for example, is the invention that *triggered* industrialization. In 1798, thirty years later, its patent ended. Only then was the first steam engine exported to Germany. It was used in the Ruhr area to mine salt. When this new technology was used to drain water from coal mines, the engine failed. After many efforts Franz Dinnendahl managed to get the engine working. This gave him so much insight into this technology that he founded an *engineering factory* of his own.

It was difficult to start a new business, because **guilds** still limited businesses. Therefore, many new developments were held back. Often the king or the government of a state would not allow the use of a new invention. These limitations and the protective *policies* of Great Britain regarding new inventions *stalled* the start of industrialization in Germany.

When *hard coal* replaced *charcoal*, which set much less energy free and had limited availability, it was finally possible to build a *blast furnace* at the Friedrich-Wilhelm-Mill in Muelheim in 1848/49. This was the start of the mass production of raw iron, and led to the rise of the technologically advanced Ruhr area. More improvements in steel production followed. Some were especially successful after the Franco-Prussian war when Germany was able to *exploit* iron ore resources in Lorraine.

Roads – a step towards unity

Almost all of Germany was rural. There were few roads and even fewer paved roads. Most goods were transported by horse *carts* or carried by people on their backs, because roads were either wet and soft in summer, or snowed in and icy in winter.

Additionally, roads and transport connections in Germany suffered from the lack of unity. Road networks were based on each state's individual needs. The connection from one centre of commerce to the next was not necessarily the shortest, often because merchants wanted to avoid customs stations. Before 1834 there were about 1,800 customs stations, Prussia alone had 67 on her borders: All hindered the flow of trade and commerce. Even after the introduction of the Customs Union in 1834 there were still 38 customs stations left on the borders.

M 1 **The first German railway line from Nuremberg to Fuerth was opened on 7 December 1835.**

Railways – industrialization on the fast track

Stephenson's invention of "The Rocket" in 1814 started the age of railways in England. In 1830 the first tracks were built south of Essen, but the Prussian king did not permit the use of a locomotive. So the train had to be pulled by horses. Despite opposition the advantages of railways became evident: Goods were transported faster, safer and arrived more reliably than by traditional means.

On 7 December 1835, ten years after the first English railway line, the first German railway line was opened between Nuremberg and Fuerth. It was only 6.5 kilometres long. The steam locomotive "Adler" was imported from England. Many new lines followed. By the end of the 19th century the distance from Berlin to Hamburg took only five hours by train compared to three days by *stagecoach*.

The Leipzig-Dresden line was a real challenge. There was no company within the Customs Union that could provide the necessary machinery and material. So

M 2 **One of Harkort's Plants at Wetter Castle, 1834**
Contemporary painting

Historical Terms

guild: Gilde/Zunft
child labour: Kinderarbeit
stock exchange: Börse

the business went to Darby & Cort in England. To avoid such a situation in future, investments in the German industry increased. Within only thirteen years, these investments ensured iron of English quality.

The construction of new railway lines required an enormous amount of iron and a larger labour force in many new fields (e.g. stationmasters, people for signal boxes, etc.). Some of these workers came from far away, because there were not enough local workers. The German economy boomed.

The German Boom – a way to "made in Germany"

It became clear that individuals could not afford to invest the large sums of capital necessary, so the ownership of railway lines had to be taken on by more investors. The solution was found in *joint stock companies*, in which individuals or companies could invest money in return for *shares*. After 1850 the **stock exchange** backed the German coal and steel industry which took the lead over the *obsolete* English *plants*.

Now the Ruhr area with its vast coal resources became the most important industrial area in Germany. Hamburg and Bremen became Ruhr customers, too, when ships were made from steel rather than wood after 1870.

Vocabulary

joint stock company: a company that is owned by all the people who have shares in it

shares: units of equal value sold by a company to raise money

obsolete: no longer used because sth. new has been invented

plant: factory

predecessor: a person or thing that came/was there before

Biography

Friedrich Harkort (1793–1880)

He is called "the father of the Ruhr area", because his plants (the *predecessor* of DEMAG – Deutsche Maschinenbau Aktiengesellschaft) and his pumps powered by steam made deep mining for coal possible; as a politician and factory owner he tried to improve the working conditions for his workers and especially the fight against **child labour** was one of his goals. In his political career he supported education as well as social laws for workers (and their children).

M 3 **Friedrich Harkort (1793–1880)**
Contemporary painting

Industrialization in Germany

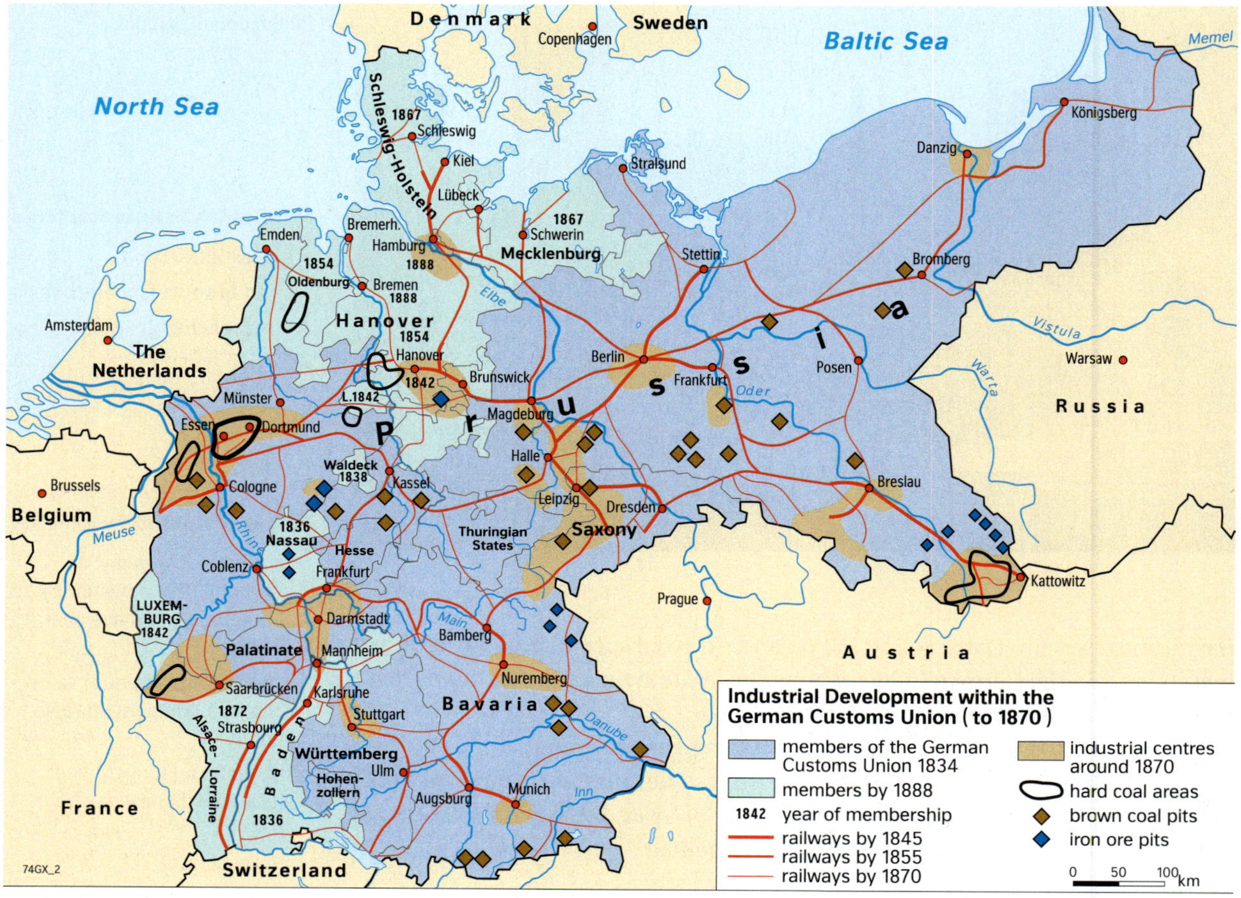

M 4

M 5 Travelling by Train

a) An English statement from 1857:

“It was declared that the railway would prevent cows grazing and hens laying. The poisoned air from the locomotive would kill birds as they flew over them. Houses next to the line would be burnt up from the fire thrown from the engine chimneys. The air would be polluted by clouds of smoke. There would no longer be any use for horses, and there would be no use for oats and hay.”

b) A traveller reported in 1830:

“You cannot imagine how strange it seemed to be journeying on without any visible cause of progress other than the magical machine with its flying white breath. The engine was set off at its utmost speed, 35 miles an hour, swifter than a bird flies. The motion is as smooth as possible, too; I could have either read or written. When I closed my eyes the sensation was quite delightful. Yet strange as it was, I had not the slightest sense of fear.”

c) A report on a trip on the Liverpool-Manchester Line:

“Today I had the satisfaction, for I can’t call it a pleasure, of taking a trip of five miles – and we did it in just a quarter of an hour – that is twenty miles an hour. The quickest motion is to me frightful. It is like flying and it is impossible to get rid of the idea of death if the slightest accident happens. It gave me a bad *headache*. There is not much smoke, but there were *sparks* in the air. One burned Miss De Ross’s cheek and another burned a hole in Lady Marian’s silk dress. I am glad to have seen this miracle, and to have travelled in it, but this first journey will also be my last.”

Quoted from: Scott and Hilary Harrison, The Industrial Age. Questioning History 4, MacMillan: London 1990, p. 79, 84. (adapted).

Vocabulary

headache: pain in the head
spark: a piece flying out of a fire

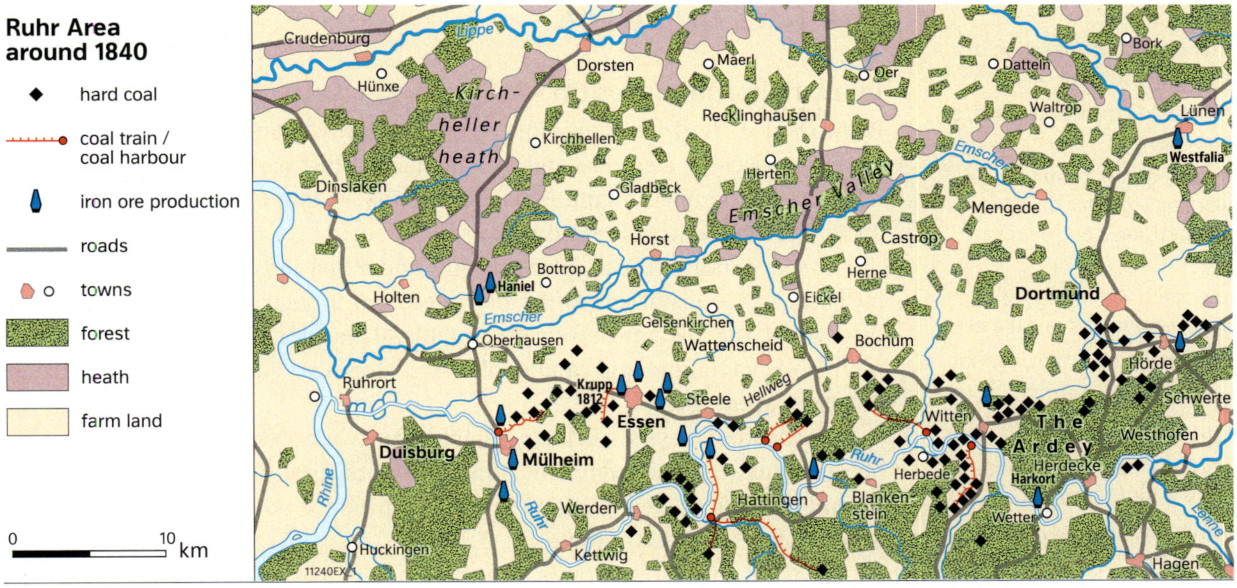

M 6

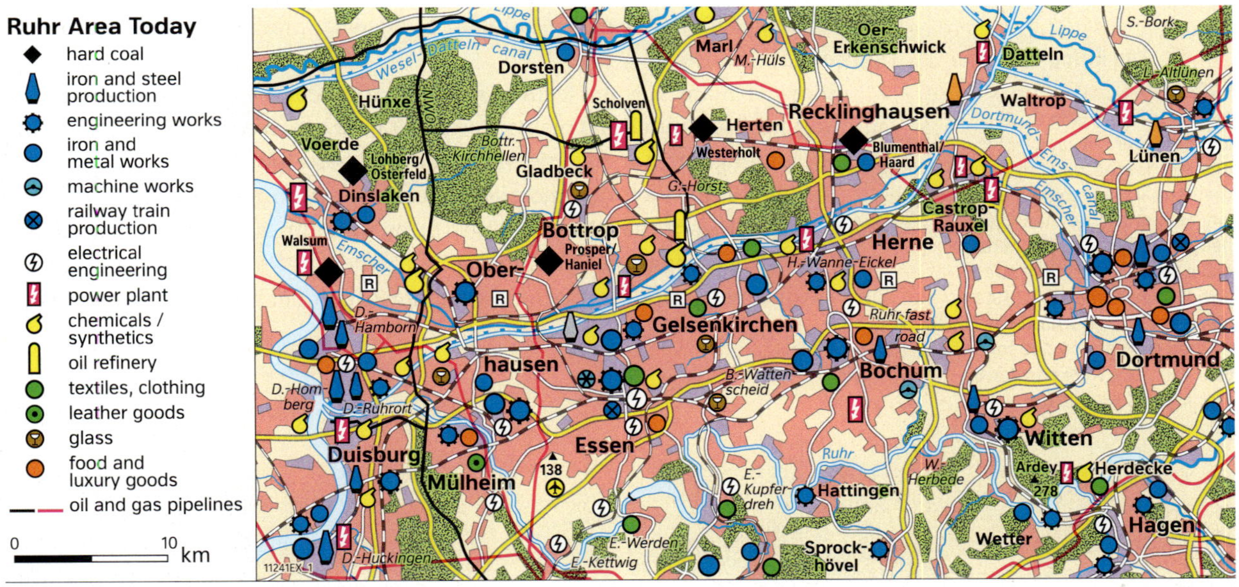

M 7

1. **Development of Railways**
   a) Compare the different statements on travelling by train. You may add your own experience of a train ride (M5).
   b) Assess the importance of railways for industrialization (text).
   c) Prepare a short talk on the development of trains based on pictures. Do your research carefully (museums, Internet, books, etc.) (M3).

2. **Industrialization in Germany**
   a) Find out more about Friedrich Harkort. Use different sources (Internet, encyclopaedia, etc.) (M3).
   b) Compare the two maps closely. List the changes (M6, M7).
   c) Explain why joint stock companies became necessary (text).

Vocabulary

branch: a special section or department

tar: a dark, thick liquid with a strong smell

trust: a group of companies working together to reduce competition, control prices, etc.

seamless: with no spaces between one part and the next

core: most important, central

muck: dirt or mud

brass: here: money

brick: a kind of stone made to build walls/houses

navigable: easy for a ship to travel on

furnace: a kind of oven

The Take-off Period

Industrialization Takes Off – bigger, faster, better?

Railways were the driving force for economic growth, but new *branches* of industry soon followed: the electrical and the chemical industries. The German economy relied more and more on industrial production, so that Germany stopped being an agricultural country around 1900.

The invention of the telephone by Alexander Bell and of the electric light bulb by Thomas A. Edison led to the new electrical industry. Werner von Siemens discovered the dynamo-electric principle. This pioneering invention made petroleum, gas lamps, and candles obsolete. Moreover, electrical energy replaced mechanical energy.

Smaller businesses such as engineering works relied on electric power, because steam engines were only profitable for big industrial plants. First, it took several hours for a steam engine to actually produce power and, second, it was only efficient when it was large.

A similar development was also seen in chemistry. Chemists examined the nature of different chemical elements and substances. They produced new substances from oil and *tar*: paint, gasoline, chemical fertilizer, as well as medicine. Theoretical scientists worked hand in hand with practical engineers, a very successful alliance.

Soon Germany was the leading nation in this sector with its inventions and innovations. New industrial plants were built near big rivers, because they could provide cooling water and get rid of waste of all kinds, too.

During this era factories and plants grew to an enormous size. Many became *trusts*, which meant that the combined firms sometimes had more than 10,000 employees. One company could invest in another or the other way round. This process of concentration led to the elimination of competition. So these new trusts dictated prices.

M 1 The Krupp Works, about 1884

The entire plant with its 73 kilometers of railways, living quarters for the workers and their families was bigger than the city of Essen. More than 15,000 people worked in shifts here to make sure the 21 rolling streets (Produktionsstraßen), 92 steam hammers and 1,195 *furnaces*, which needed more than 2,500 tons of coal each day, were constantly running and producing.

Krupp and Thyssen

Some people became very rich and successful businessmen, for example, Alfred Krupp and August Thyssen.

Friedrich Krupp had founded a **cast iron** factory, but he never managed to make it a profitable business during his lifetime. His son Alfred Krupp took over the business (it had seven employees at that time) at the age of 14 – he dropped out of school – although his mother owned the business. For several years the business was not very successful. This changed dramatically when around 1830 the development in railways sped up and more cast iron was needed in Germany and in Europe.

In 1852/53 Krupp invented a *seamless* wheel, which became the *core* product of his business, especially because most American railways used these wheels. In addition, Krupp invented and produced different weapons, mostly cannon so the business had about 1,000 employees in the 1850s.

August Thyssen was born the third son of a wealthy Catholic family which owned steel mills. In contrast to Alfred Krupp, Thyssen was well educated and trained. In 1883 he bought a neighbouring factory which specialized in machine production. This was the basis for the Machine Factory Thyssen & Co.

In 2000 the companies of Krupp and Thyssen joined together. Today ThyssenKrupp AG is one of the biggest companies in Germany and operates worldwide. It has many different branches, which still include steel production, but it also produces elevators and escalators, automobile parts and high technology products such as monorail trains (Transrapid) and marine vessels.

M 2 **Alfred Krupp (1812 – 1887)**

He created a global company, whose social institutions were role models for others.

Contemporary painting

Historical Terms

cast iron: Gusseisen

acid rain: saurer Regen

Environmental Pollution – who cared?

The British saying "Where there is *muck*, there is *brass*" shows how little the protection of the environment and how much money mattered. This saying is not only true for England but also for Germany and other countries at the beginning of industrialization. Robert Angus Smith (1817 – 1884) was a Scottish chemist who noticed that *bricks* in Great Britain did not last as long as in other countries. Therefore he started to examine the air in 1852 and found out that there was a lot of CO^2. This caused **acid rain**. Acid rain affects not only the quality of bricks but even more so the growth of plants and therefore also the breeding of animals.

In Germany, there was a first political dispute in Bamberg as early as 1802. The emissions of iron, metal or copper mills caused the people of Bamberg to fight against a new mill. The reason they gave in their petition to the officials was the protection of the beautiful landscape. But the destruction of the environment was not only caused by plants, factories and other industries polluting the air and rivers. Also river beds were changed to make them more *navigable* for ships, mountains and hills were lowered through mining or by cutting down forests in order to power *furnaces* or steam engines. In 1800 more than 30% of the land was untouched, by 1900 only about 5% of land was untouched.

In 1877 the first club was founded in Cologne ("Internationaler Verein gegen die Verunreinigung von Flüssen, des Bodens und der Luft") to protect the environment. It took until 1906 for Prussia to pass the first law and until 1919 for the Weimar Constitution to include the protection of the environment (Article 150).

M 3 **August Thyssen (1842 – 1926)**

In 1871 he founded the Thyssen company.

Contemporary painting

The Take-off Period – visions of the future

M 4 **"Learning in School"**

Many drawings like these were made for a series of collector's cards in 1899. They show the ideas of the artist for the year 2000.

M 5 **"The Make-Up Machine"**

M 6 **"The Dictation Machine"**

Vocabulary

Useful words and phrases

The pupils have/use ...
headphones – Kopfhörer
mill – Mühle
to grind sth. up in a mill

to push a button
a broom/brush to clean sth.
to apply face powder with a powder puff
to comb/brush one's hair
to have a pedicure/manicure
automatic arms
mirrors
to move/throw a lever

to speak into a microphone
loudspeaker
a roller prints the words ...
to dictate sth.

Environmental Pollution – who cared?

M 7 **The Krupp Works with "not too much smoke". Photo from 1867**

M 8 Environmental Pollution

Alfred Krupp wrote in Nice on 12 January 1867:

"For the exhibition in Paris and as presents to high-ranking personalities we need to take new photographs in May when everything is green and there is no wind. You see, in general, I think that small photographs are good enough, still I wish two larger-scale views or even better two views including decoration and life in the squares, yards and railways. I suggest using a Sunday, because there is too much smoke, steam and activities during the week, and the loss of work is also too great.
Whether 500 or 1000 men are necessary, I do not care. It is disadvantageous if too much steam fogs the environment, but it will be beautiful if a little steam comes from as many places as possible. The steam engines and trains are also very impressive just as are the big transport wagons for casting."

Historisches Archiv Krupp (ed.), Alfred Krupps Briefe und Niederschriften B. 9: 1866–1879, Bl. 108f. (adapted and transl. by Barbara Nerlich).

Tasks

1. Visions of the Future
   a) Describe each picture in detail (M4, M5, M6, useful phrases box).
   b) Assess what ideas of the future have become true by now (M4, M5, M6).

2. Environmental Pollution – who cared?
   a) List the different forms of environmental destruction (text, M8, M1).
   b) Show what Krupp's instructions on how to take pictures tell you about environmental pollution in the 19th century (M8).
   c) Explain how acid rain affected and still affects agriculture. What is the situation today (text, Internet research)?
   d) Examine how the population explosion led to environmental pollution (Internet research).
   e) Find out what and when clubs or groups were founded in your area/home town that wanted to protect the landscape and/or the environment. Was there an incident that triggered the founding (Internet research, local archives)?

Development of Steam Power in Europe 1840 to 1896

a) **Capacity of all Steam Engines** [in 1000 horsepower (hp)]

	GB	G	F	A	B
1840	620	40	90	20	40
1850	1 290	260	270	100	70
1860	2 450	850	1 120	330	160
1870	4 040	2 480	1 850	800	350
1880	7 600	5 120	3 070	1 560	610
1888	9 200	6 200	4 520	2 150	810
1896	13 700	8 080	5 920	2 520	1180

b) **Capacity of all Steam Engines** (in 1000 hp)

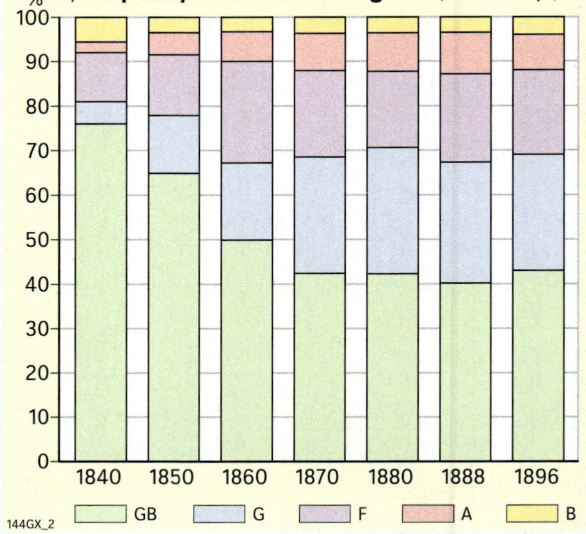

c) **Capacity of all Steam Engines 1840** (in 1000 hp)

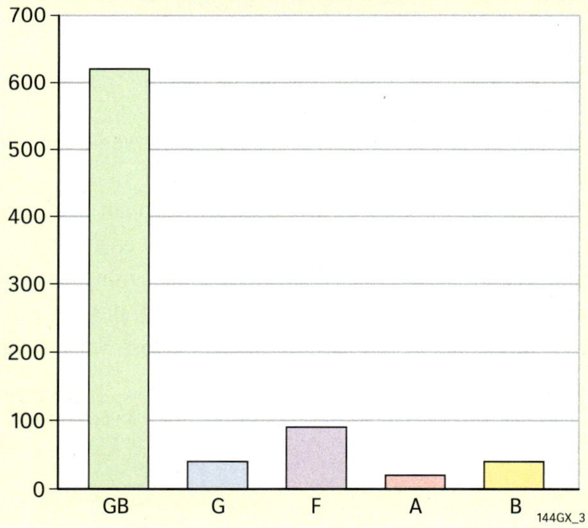

d) **Capacity of all Steam Engines in Germany** (in 1000 hp)

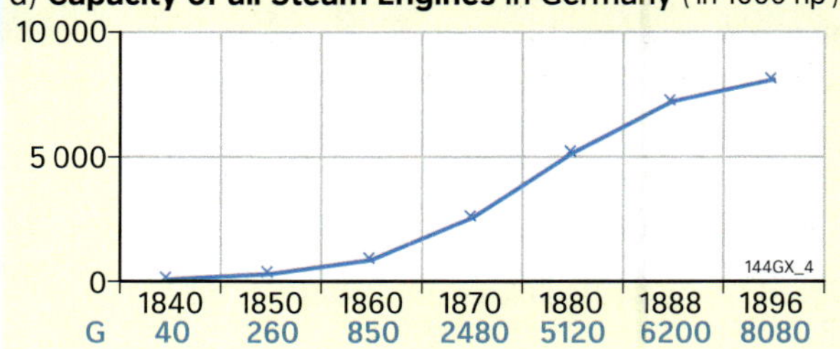

e) **Capacity of all Steam Engines in 1896** (in 1000 hp)

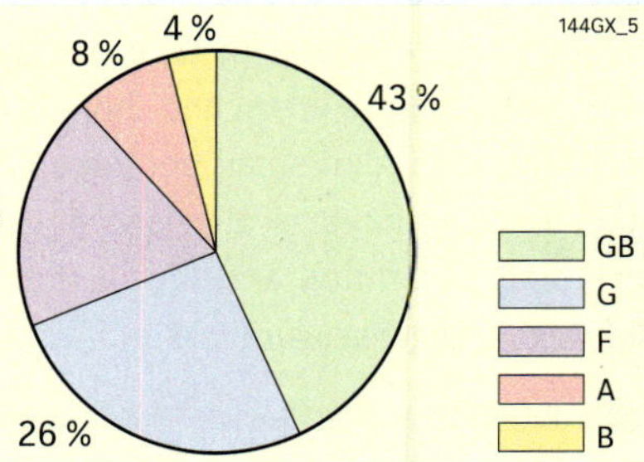

Vocabulary

Technical terms

pie chart: Tortendiagramm/Kreisdiagramm

bar chart: Säulendiagramm

graph: Graphik (mit Verlaufslinien)

Vocabulary

Useful phrases

Look at ...

Take for example ... / For instance ...

Let me give you an example

It is important to mention that ...

The percentage of ... is higher/lower than/the same as ...

The number of ... rises/falls/stays the same/is level with ...

Analysing Statistics

Statistics, whether in form of tables, diagrams or graphs, are part of everyday life. They give very complex information in a very *concise* form, often according to a specific point of view.

Statistics are numbers listed in a particular order. Diagrams and graphs often help to show how these numbers are *interrelated*. A pie chart, for example, shows how big one factor is in comparison to the whole, whereas a bar chart is often used to compare the same thing at different times. In contrast to this, a graph has the advantage of showing a process of development over time.

In former times people did not write everything down. That is why the analysis of statistics is a rather young science. To make statistics about something in earlier centuries historians often have to guess or *laboriously* collect the needed information from many different sources.

There is very little reliable statistical material from the 19th century. Still, statistics are especially helpful to understand the phenomenon of industrialization. Even more helpful are numbers that show the differences in development in various European countries. Looking at the data of the power of steam engines, for example, is one way to compare the times when industrialization began and to allow conclusions about where development was faster, earlier, or later.

However useful statistics are, they can also be misleading. A number of famous quotations hint at this fact. Sir Winston Churchill said: "[…] The first lesson that you must learn is, when I call for statistics about the rate of *infant mortality*, what I want is proof that fewer babies died when I was Prime Minister than when anyone else was Prime Minister. That is a political statistic." Josef Stalin stated at the Potsdam Conference in 1945: "The death of one man is a tragedy. The death of millions is a statistic." Benjamin Disraeli claimed: "There are three kinds of lies: lies, damned lies, and statistics."

Vocabulary

concise: clear and short, focused

interrelated: closely connected and affecting each other

laborious (adj.): taking a lot of time and effort

infant mortality: deaths of small children and babies

Historical Workshop

Analysing Statistics

1. Description

a. Name the topic of the given statistics.
b. How is the topic presented?
c. Show the differences in the statistics.

2. Interpretation

a. Compare absolute numbers and per cent in M1 a) and M1b).
b. Explain what additional or more specific information is given in M1c), M1d) and M1e).
c. Analyse whether any information is lost.

3. Conclusion

a. Assess the advantages and disadvantages of each form of presentation.
b. Imagine you have to give a report about the economy in Germany. Argue which of the diagrams you would choose to use.
c. Discuss the statements made by Churchill, Stalin and Disraeli (text).

Living Conditions in the Early Days of Industrialization

Vocabulary

flat: room to live in

toll: (here) price

disability: the state of not being able to use body or mind fully

to contribute: to give sth., esp. money or goods

pregnancy: the state of a woman with a child inside her body

Industrial Centres – why were cities more attractive?

Many people left the countryside to find work in urban areas. Therefore, many small towns quickly became industrial centres within a few years. New factories were built, new businesses started. Around 1830 there were only two major cities with a population of more than 100,000 inhabitants in Germany (Hamburg and Berlin), by 1850 there were three (plus Munich) and by 1880 there were thirteen. Berlin's population had even increased to more than one million. Never before was there a more rapid growth of cities than during industrialization.

The myth of a happier life in the city started. People thought they could make more money and assumed that there was more entertainment for them. Unfortunately, reality did not live up to the dream.

Life of the Working Class – a living hell?

In the course of industrialization very few people became rich. The majority remained poor or became even poorer than before. Wages were low and *flats* were expensive, so many people often shared one room. In addition, working conditions were bad. Big factories could only grow if the production of goods stayed cheap. Therefore, most factory owners did not care about the safety of their workers. Long working hours and dirty work took its *toll*. But not only dirty work and long working hours helped diseases to spread. During urbanization too many people moved to the cities in too short a time. Therefore the flats were very crowded and the hygienic conditions extremely bad. Most of the waste landed in the streets. There were many rats and the air was polluted because of the many factories.

M 1 Daily Working Hours in Handicraft Workshops and Industrial Factories in the 19th Century

1800–1820: 10–13 hours
1820–1840: 11–15 hours
1840–1860: 12–16 hours
1869–1870: 12–14 hours
1870–1890: 11–13 hours
1890–1910: 10–11 hours
1910–1914: 10 hours

M 2 The Flats of the Poor in London

Unknown Artist, 1875

Things had changed a great deal, not only the living but also the working conditions. Instead of being paid for the piece of work produced, the basis for wages now was time. Therefore, at the beginning of industrialization, people worked at least fourteen hours (sometimes up to seventeen hours) a day. In addition to their working hours, some people had a two-hour walk to the factory (one way).

Wages were low. Alfred Krupp, for example, paid his workers 1.25 marks a day in 1850. In 1873 he paid 3.74 marks. Skilled workers in an industrial factory earned about double what a craftsman earned. Women and children earned least of all and were the cheapest **labour** available. In many factories workers had to pay fines if they were late, for example, or something broke. Sometimes even the repair cost of machines was taken out of a worker's wage.

Exhaustion was not the only aspect that made work dangerous. Space in the factories was limited and air conditioning still unknown. Heat, cold, damp, noise and poisonous gases or dust often made the working environment unbearable. Also, workplaces were not primarily designed for people, but for the product being made there. Designing better workplaces would have cost money, which factory owners invested in new machines rather than their workers. These machines had few safety precautions, so there were many serious accidents as well. Poor working conditions caused *disabilities*. Since there was no health care system, a family then had to feed one more person who could not *contribute* to the family income. This made it necessary for the children of a family to start working as early as possible.

Historical Terms

act: Gesetz
labour: Arbeitskraft

Child Labour – cheap and easily replaced

Children were more of a burden to their families than a blessing. On farms in the countryside, women and children helped in cottage industry. There they played an important role and could work at home. In the industrial centres children meant problems, starting with the mother's *pregnancy*. Because of the working conditions, about 9% of all children were dead at birth. Those who lived started working at the age of about six years. Because of their small hands they were preferred workers in the textile industry. But the mining industry, too, liked child labourers, because they could crawl or walk through very narrow tunnels. In the cities they were also often employed as chimney sweeps , because they could crawl into the chimneys. All these jobs were extremely dangerous, especially because there were hardly any safety precautions. Children had long working hours, very low pay, and many died of exhaustion or in accidents.

Because these children had to work all day, there was no time for school. This meant that the children did not learn to read or write, and therefore could not get a better job in their later life. This fact and the bad treatment of children made many people want to change things. In England, for example, a Commission of Parliament interviewed hundreds of people who worked in mills between 1831 and 1832. The results were horrible and reforms were put in a Factory **Act**, which was passed in 1833. It said that children had to be at least nine years old to work, but who could tell how old the children were? The working hours were also limited (between nine to twelve hours a day). This act also included education. But after seven hours of work, two hours of lessons seemed like a welcome break for the children, so that effective learning was hardly possible. This problem still exists in many parts of the world today.

M 3 Child in a Carolina Cotton Mill

A 12-year-old girl in a spinning mill. Photograph by Lewis Hine, 1908

Working Conditions

RULES
TO BE OBSERVED
By the Hands Employed in
THIS MILL.

RULE 1. All the Overlookers shall be on the premises first and last.
2. Any Person coming too late shall be fined as follows:—for 5 minutes 2d, 10 minutes 4d, and 15 minutes 6d, &c.
3. For any Bobbins found on the floor 1d for each Bobbin.
4. For single Drawing, Slubbing, or Roving 2d for each single end.
5. For Waste on the floor 2d.
6. For any Oil wasted or spilled on the floor 2d each offence, besides paying for the value of the Oil.
7. For any broken Bobbins, they shall be paid for according to their value, and if there is any difficulty in ascertaining the guilty party, the same shall be paid for by the whole using such Bobbins.
8. Any person neglecting to Oil at the proper times shall be fined 2d.
9. Any person leaving their Work and found Talking with any of the other workpeople shall be fined 2d for each offence.
10. For every Oath or insolent language, 3d for the first offence, and if repeated they shall be dismissed.
11. The Machinery shall be swept and cleaned down every meal time.
12. All persons in our employ shall serve Four Weeks' Notice before leaving their employ; but L.WHITAKER & SONS, shall and will turn any person off without notice being given.
13. If two persons are known to be in one Necessary together they shall be fined 3d each; and if any Man or Boy go into the Women's Necessary he shall be instantly dismissed.
14. Any person wilfully or negligently breaking the Machinery, damaging the Brushes, making too much Waste, &c., they shall pay for the same to its full value.
15. Any person hanging anything on the Gas Pendants will be fined 2d.
16. The Masters would recommend that all their workpeople Wash themselves every morning, but they shall Wash themselves at least twice every week, Monday Morning and Thursday morning; and any found not washed will be fined 3d for each offence.
17. The Grinders, Drawers, Slubbers and Rovers shall sweep at least eight times in the day as follows, in the Morning at $7^{1}/_{2}$, $9^{1}/_{2}$, 11 and 12; and in the Afternoon at $1^{1}/_{2}$, $2^{1}/_{2}$, $3^{1}/_{2}$, $4^{1}/_{2}$ and $5^{1}/_{2}$ o'clock; and to notice the Board hung up, when the black side is turned that is the time to sweep, and only quarter of an hour will be allowed for sweeping. The Spinners shall sweep as follows, in the Morning at $7^{1}/_{2}$, 10 and 12; in the Afternoon at 3 and $5^{1}/_{2}$ o'clock. Any neglecting to sweep at the time will be fined 2d for each offence.
18. Any persons found Smoking on the premises will be instantly dismissed.
19. Any person found away from their usual place of work, except for necessary purposes, or Talking with any one out of their own Alley will be fined 2d for each offence.
20. Any person bringing dirty Bobbins will be fined 1d for each Bobbin.
21. Any person wilfully damaging this Notice will be dismissed.

The Overlookers are strictly enjoined to attend to these Rules, and they will be responsible to the Masters for the Workpeople observing them.

WATER-FOOT MILL, NEAR HASLINGDEN,
SEPTEMBER, 1851.

J. Read, Printer, and Bookbinder, Haslingden

M 4 **Rules from Water-Foot Mill near Haslingden in Lancashire, 1851**

M 5 Working Conditions

Conrad Alberti describes the "perfect" worker:

"I want workers who work like machines from dusk till dawn, who do their rather mechanical job in a mechanical way, who eat and sleep as if it was a mechanical process, who drop like dead from their chairs to the straw and who do not get up a minute too early to be on the job at eight sharp. Only this makes a profitable and lasting business. The individual has to become a wheel in the machinery of the business just like a soldier in the army."

Conrad Alberti, Maschinen, Luckhardt: Leipzig 1895. (adapted and transl. by Barbara Nerlich).

M 6 A Child Labourer Reports

Anna Perthen, a worker in the textile industry, tells about her youth around 1880:

"The wages of Father were low, so that Mother always had to go back to work right after having given birth and despite nine children. As the way to the factory was too far for us, we worked at home sewing on buttons. Of the nine brothers and sisters only three survived. Mother's exhaustion and malnutrition might have been the cause of their deaths.
When I was twelve years old, I had to work in the textile factory, where the working hours lasted from 5 a.m. to 7 p.m. in those days. In the afternoons from 4 to 6 we went to the factory school, which took place in an inn next to the factory. Learning was hardly possible, we looked at these two hours more as rest. Work was rather mentally tiring. When I went home to sleep, I had to get up at 3.30 am, because the way to the factory was very long. At times I lodged with somebody and went home only on Saturdays. In the town where the factory was we slept in an attic, where there were so-called long plank beds and straw mattresses next to each other. We were lucky, because older women, who looked after us, were there, too.
I was glad that I earned money, but often the disappointment was bitter. The wages were low. The two hours of schooling were of course taken off our money. When I had paid for lodging only very little was left, and on Saturdays Father was already waiting to take the rest of my money.
When I was fourteen, I went to a factory together with my parents, but we still had to work at home on Sundays and at night. When a six-week strike began to achieve shorter working hours I was sent to a different factory. Father, who was active in the strike, was fired and did not find any more work anywhere. So Mother and I were left to worry about the other siblings. I stayed in that factory long after I was married; because as was the case for most poor girls, after the wedding more grief and problems started. They did for me, too."

Quoted from: Richard Klucsarits/Friedrich G. Kürbisch (eds.), Arbeiterinnen kämpfen um ihr Recht. Autobiographische Texte rechtloser und entrechteter „Frauenspersonen" in Deutschland, Österreich und der Schweiz im 19. und 20. Jh., Peter Hammer Verlag: Wuppertal 1975, p. 84f. (adapted and transl. by Barbara Nerlich).

Tasks

1. **Living Conditions in the Early Days of Industrialization**
   a) Chose one of the pictures in M2. Describe the living conditions shown in your picture.
   b) Compare your results with your classmates' pictures.
2. **Everyday Working Life**
   a) Analyse the working hours. What do they tell you about the development of industrialization (M1, text)?
   b) Find three punishments for breaking rules (M4).
   c) Explain what Conrad Alberti wants to say when he describes the "perfect" worker (M5).
   d) Discuss Alberti's opinion (M5).
   e) Based on Alberti's definition of a "perfect" worker, explain what it tells you about the status of workers during industrialization.
3. **Child Labour**
   a) Describe the girl's day (M6).
   b) Compare Anna Perthen's day to your own (M6).
   c) Describe the picture of the little girl (M3).
   d) Imagine what she is thinking. Make a short speech for Anna to give (M3).
   e) Find out about child labor today (Internet).

Vocabulary

exploitation: overuse of a person or a thing

Silesian: schlesisch

threat: danger that is about to come/happen

Attempts to Solve Social Problems

Workers Unite

Karl Marx and Friedrich Engels, who had a **middle class** background, started a new movement called communism after having seen the suffering of workers in England and Germany. The two men claimed that the only thing workers could sell to earn a living was their working power. They did not have any money or own any productive means (such as machines, raw material or land). Those who did were **capitalists**, who determined wages. In order to earn as much profit as possible they always underpaid their workers, so working power was never valued enough.

Marx's theory states that there is a predetermined order of societies in the history of mankind. First there is a primitive society, then one based on slavery, followed by a feudal system, which in turn is replaced by a capitalistic **bourgeois society**. A revolution to overthrow the capitalistic society by a communist one would lead to a free society without a class system, a ruler, subjects, owners (capitalists) or poor people.

The idea was a revolution of all workers against all capitalists. Many leaders of **trade unions**, socialist groups and parties were influenced by these ideas. In 1847 the Communist League was founded to oppose workers' *exploitation*. The revolution of 1848 with its goal of more democratic structures supported these new ideas, too. Ferdinand Lassalle founded the **General Association of German Workers** in 1863. Six years later the **Social Democratic Workers' Party** was

M 1 **The Strike**

Painting by Robert Koehler from Hamburg, 1886.

M 2 **"The New Relationship Between Workers and Industrialists"**
Cartoon from "Neuen Postillon", Switzerland, 1896

founded. These two parties joined in 1875 to become the **Social Democratic Party of Germany**.

Factory Owners – only interested in profit?

After the uprising of the *Silesian* weavers in 1844, factory owners felt an immediate *threat* and realized that something had to be done. In order to limit the damage, many came up with concepts of their own to deal with workers' problems.

Some turned to paying for health insurance. They started to grant their workers money in case of sickness, some even set up pension systems. Others paid a bonus at the end of the year or for a short holiday.

Alfred Krupp, for example, built houses for his workers and tried to secure a basic school education. But in return he expected his workers to refrain from strikes or other political activities. He, like others, would only grant help to "good" workers.

Historical Terms

middle class: Mittelkasse, Bürgertum

communism: Kommunismus

capitalists: Kapitalisten

bourgeois society: bürgerliche Gesellschaft

trade union: Gewerkschaft

General Association of German Workers: Allgemeiner Deutscher Arbeiterverein

Social Democratic Workers' Party: Sozialdemokratische Arbeiterpartei

Social Democratic Party of Germany: SPD

socialism: Sozialismus

Tasks

1. The Strike
a) Describe the painting as exactly as possible. Pay special attention to clothes, action, positions, etc. (M1).
b) Discuss the atmosphere of the picture.
c) Striking led to great conflicts for workers and their families. How does the painting show these conflicts (M1)?

2. Capitalism – working with a cartoon
a) Describe the cartoon (M2).
b) Explain the message (M2).
c) Assess how the situation of employer and employee has changed today (M2).

Attempts to Solve Social Problems

M 3 **Pyramid of Capitalist System**

Published by Nedeljkovich, Brashick and Kuharich, 1911

M 4 The Cummunist Manifesto (1848)

In the Manifesto of the Communist Party (the English version was published in 1888) Karl Marx wrote:

"A spectre is haunting Europe – the spectre of Communism. [...]

The immediate aim of the Communists is the same as that of all the other proletarian parties: formation of the proletariat into a class, overthrow of the bourgeois supremacy, conquest of political power by the proletariat. [...]

The working men have no country. We cannot take from them what they have not got. [...]

Nevertheless in the most advanced countries, the following will be pretty generally applicable:

1. Abolition of property in land and application of all rents of land to public purposes. [...]

6. Centralization of the means of communication and transport in the hands of the State.

7. Extension of factories and instruments of production owned by the State [...]

10. Free education for all children in public schools. Abolition of children's factory labour in its present form. [...]

Let the ruling classes tremble at a Communistic revolution. The proletarians have nothing to lose but their chains. They have a world to win.

WORKING MEN OF ALL COUNTRIES, UNITE!"

Manifesto of the Communist Party (1888 translation), in: MECW – Marx/ Engels Collected Works Volume 6, International Publishers: New York 1976, p. 476–519. www.hartford-hwp.com/archives/26/176.html [Oct. 2017].

Biography

Karl Marx (1818 – 1883)

He was a philosopher and economist, whose ideas made him the father of the workers' movement. Even today his theories are controversial.

When Karl Marx saw the negative effects of industrialization he developed (together with Friedrich Engels) his ideas of communism. He said that the only capital a worker had was his working power. Without this working power factory owners could not make a profit. This led to the workers' movement and then to many organized strikes. These strikes helped to better the working conditions and the wages of the workers.

Because of his childhood experiences his father had converted from Judaism to Protestantism shortly before Marx' birth so he could keep his job as an attorney. Karl Marx himself despised religion. He did not make a difference between faith and church. In his theory of communism he said that "religion is the opium for the masses".

M 5 **Karl Marx (1818 – 1883)**

Tasks

1. Rich and Poor – society during industrialization

a) Describe the cartoon (M3).

b) Explain the structure of society as shown in the cartoon (M3).

c) Show whose side the caricaturist was on (M3).

2. Communism

a) List the aims of communism (M4).

b) Explain why there were arguments over these aims among the workers (M4).

c) Discuss the ideas you find appealing and which you find unacceptable (M4).

d) Find out about Friedrich Engels' life and present your findings to the class (research, Internet).

Vocabulary

donation: money given by people in order to help

journeymen: a person who learnt a handicraft and travels to find work or works for a master

board and lodging: a place to stay and get food

to abolish: to end a law officially

Church and Government React

The Church and the Poor

Traditionally the church took care of the poor, sick, old, widows and orphans. *Donations* were used to give money, food or board to people in need. The help was mainly directed to individual cases; there were hardly any organized projects. In the face of mass poverty in the 19th century a different approach was needed.

The Protestant teacher Johann Hinrich Wichern (1808–1881) wanted to help neglected children in Hamburg. He founded a boarding school (Rauhes Haus) for the children where they were trained for different jobs. It still exists today. In this way, Wichern started a new kind of clerical charity – called the "inner mission".

The Catholic priest Adolph Kolping (1813–1865) was a trained shoemaker. He realized that craftsmen and *journeymen* on their travels had problems finding *board and lodgings* as well as work. He founded the "Catholic Journeymen's Club", which provided unmarried men a heated room with newspapers and books. The clubs gave them general as well as specific job information to improve their training. Since this was a church institution, religious questions were important, too. When Kolping died, 60,000 members were organized in 420 clubs. Kolping houses still exist in many cities today.

Besides these individual attempts to solve social problems the Bishop of Mainz, Wilhelm Emmanuel Ketteler (1811–1877), wanted the Catholic Church as well as the German people to see how much rich and poor were drifting apart. For him it was more important to close this gap by means of Christian faith than to attack the material problems with money. His approach influenced many Christian workers' associations and helped to form Christian trade unions.

Government – social reforms only a by-product?

The government tried to attack the problem from two different sides: a Socialist Law and social laws. In order to win back the trust of workers Bismarck worked to pass some social laws. Among them were a health insurance and a social security system which still exist today. Additionally, he appointed inspectors in factories to ensure minimum safety precautions and to prevent child labour. But Bismarck's hope that workers would leave the different workers' parties was disappointed.

In 1890 the Socialist Law was *abolished* and the SPD became a mass party. In 1912 the parliament had 110 Social Democrats (34.8%), the strongest party in the Reichstag. By 1914 it had more than one million members.

Biography

Johann Hinrich Wichern (1808–1881)

He was a theologian and social pedagogue, who studied at the University of Goettingen and founded organizations such as Diakonie or the Inner Mission. He also reformed prisons.

Biography

Adolph Kolping (1813–1865)

As a shoemaker he saw and to some degree experienced the living and working conditions of many journeymen. He went back to school and later studied in Munich and Bonn to become a priest. In order to better the situation for journeymen he founded the "Catholic Journeymen's Club". The "Kolpingwerk" still exists today.

M 1 Rerum Novarum

Encyclical of Pope Leo XIII on Capital and Labour (1891):

"In any case we clearly see, [...], that some opportune remedy must be found quickly for the misery and wretchedness pressing so unjustly on the majority of the working class: [...] Public institutions and the laws set aside the ancient religion. Hence, by degrees it has come to pass that working men have been surrendered, isolated and helpless, to the hardheartedness of employers and the greed of unchecked competition. [...]
[...] Working for gain is creditable, not shameful, to a man, since it enables him to earn an honorable livelihood, but to misuse men as though they were things in the pursuit of gain, or to value them solely for their physical powers – this is truly shameful and inhuman. [...] Hence, the employer is bound to see that the worker has time for his religious duties; that he be not exposed to corrupting influences and dangerous occasions; and that he be not led away to neglect his home and family, or to squander his earnings. Furthermore, the employer must never tax his work people beyond their strength, or employ them in work unsuited to their sex and age. [...]"

http://w2.vatican.va/content/leo-xiii/en/encyclicals/documents/hf_l-xiii_enc_15051891_rerum-novarum.html [Oct. 2017].

M 2 Advertisement of the German Government to Promote Social Security
about 1890

1883 Health Insurance
benefits: free consultation of doctors, medication and treatment in hospital, sick-pay 50% of wages for 26 weeks
premium: 2–3% of wages, 2/3 employee, 1/3 employer

1884 Accident Insurance
benefits: (in case of accident) doctor's treatment and 2/3 of wages as pension, (in case of death) 20% of wages as pension for the widow
premium: 100% employer

1889 Disability and Old Age Insurance
benefits: disability pension in case of inability to work, old age pension after the age of 70
premium: 1–3% of wages, 50% employee, 50% employer

Vocabulary

encyclical: an official announcement by the pope in form of a letter

premium: amount of money paid regulary for insurance

Tasks

1. The Church Reacts
a) Discuss the role of the church in the attempts to solve the social problems (text).
b) Explain Leo XIII's ideas (M1).
c) Assess whether Leo XIII's aims were achieved (M1, text).
d) Find out about Hinrich Wichern and his work (Biography, Internet).

2. The Government Reacts
a) Analyse the government's effectiveness in solving social problems (text).
b) Assess the 19th century health and social security system and what is missing (M2).
c) Compare the insurance system established by Bismarck with today's insurance system (M2, Internet).

1765 | 1780 | 1795 | 1810 | 1825

1764: Invention of the spinning jenny

1769: Invention of the steam engine

1829: "The Rocket"

1835: Nuremberg-Fuerth railway line

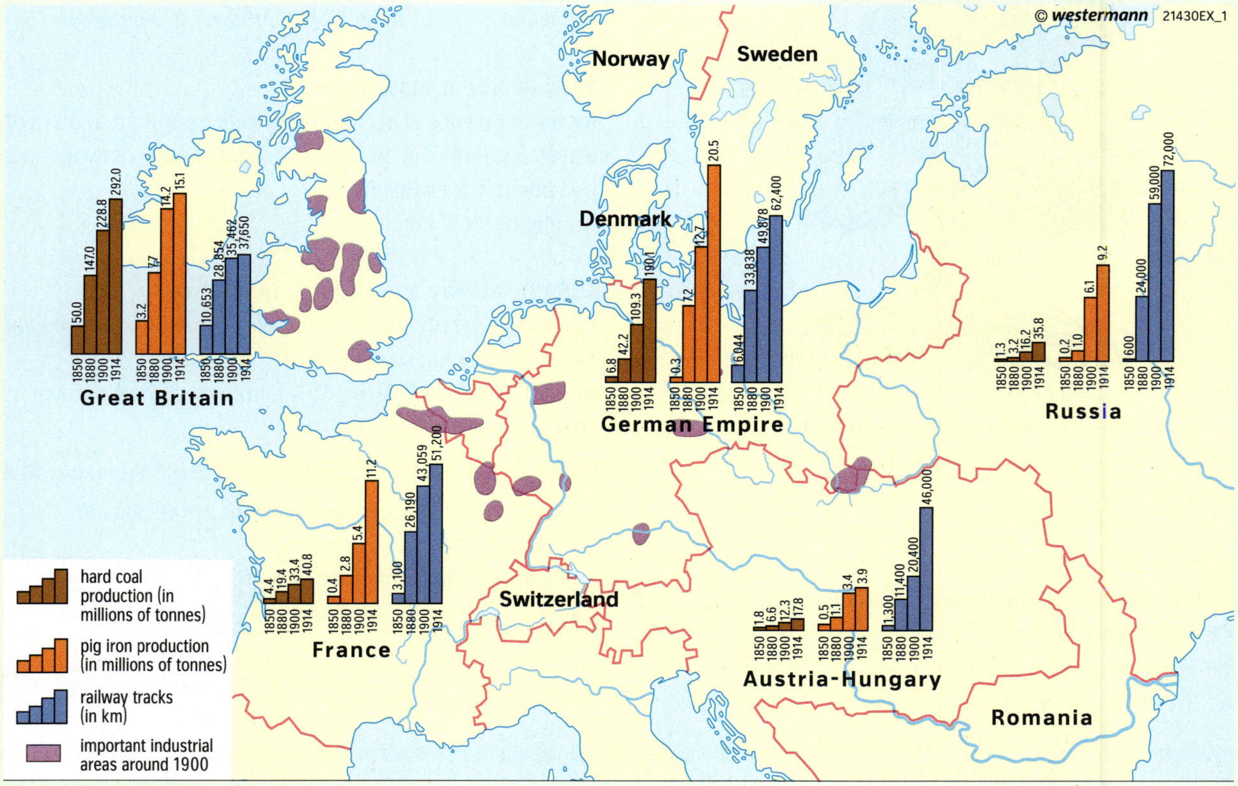

Industrialization – the historical map

1855 1870 1885 1900 1915

4: Prussian ...toms Union

1848: Karl Marx's Communist Manifesto

1871: Founding of the German Empire

1875: Founding of the SPD

1878–1890: Socialist Law in effect

1914–1918: First World War

Summary

For many people the changes during industrialization were so big and happened so fast that they had the feeling they could not follow. Therefore, many felt as if their lives had turned up-side down. The changes in agriculture were fast and drastic. But also the production of goods from rather slow cottage industry to a 14-hour working day in front of a machine took its toll on people. Especially, the factory owners – called capitalists by Karl Marx – were only interested in profit. They did not want to invest money in improvements of machines and working places to make them safer. Their only interest was to make them faster and more efficient. There were enough workers, because there were so many people unemployed. Poverty ensured that also small children had to work to support their families. Misery made people ask for reforms. These reforms took the form of different laws. By 1837 in Britain children had to have two hours of (ineffective) lessons every day.

The Social Question led to the workers' movement and quickly became a political issue. Many different organizations and parties tried to better the situation. Communism supported the workers, and so did the SPD. The socialist groups and parties threatened the government. As a result laws were passed to make the life of the workers, especially children safer. In Germany Bismarck introduced an insurance system including health insurance and disability insurance to give workers more security. The church helped in different ways, for example by setting up clubs and houses for poor children and orphans. Still the gap between rich and poor became greater rather than smaller.

However, focussing only on the negative effects on the people does not do justice to industrialization. Many inventions and improvements led to positive changes. The development of infrastructure in Germany, for example, helped further German unity.

DATES

About 1750:
Industrialization begins in Britain

1835:
First German railway

1848:
Communist Manifesto

HISTORICAL TERMS

industrialization
urbanization
infrastructure
the Social Question
German Customs Union
guild
child labour
act
middle class
trade union
Social Democratic Party of Germany
socialism

PERSONS

James Watt

Karl Marx

Friedrich Engels

Alfred Krupp

Johann Hinrich Wichern

Adolph Kolping

HISTORY WORKSHOP

Analysing Statistics

M 1 "The Hambach Festival" on 27 May 1832

M 2 Barricades on the Breite Strasse, Berlin, 1848

05 EUROPE IN REVOLT – THE STRUGGLE FOR UNITY AND LIBERTY (1815 – 1849)

Unity and Liberty Are Hard to Win

It was hard to form democratic governments in Europe. From 1815 to 1849 there were moments of progress and also harsh set-backs. This unit takes a closer look at these ups and downs.

After Napoleon lost, the rulers of Europe wanted to organize a settlement for the continent to keep the peace. Because most of the rulers were monarchs, they tried to restore the European system as it had been before the French Revolution. Between 1814 and 1815 they met at the Congress of Vienna for talks. Their agreement affected all of Europe for many years.

No matter how hard they tried, the monarchs were not able to stop ideas from the French Revolution about democracy and liberty. Also, the idea of national unity, which had become popular as different countries fought against France, grew stronger during this period. In many European countries people opposed the principles set up in Vienna and showed this clearly in public when they could. The monarchs used force to put down any unrest as quickly as possible. They censored books and the press to keep public discussion about politics closed. Still, popular unrest could not be stopped. In 1848 revolution broke out all over Europe. In Germany, a national assembly met to write a national constitution. However, by 1849 the German monarchs regained the control they had lost. The revolution ended in failure, but that was not the end of the story …

This chapter deals with many questions such as:

- What did the Congress of Vienna agree on?
- How was the agreement put into practice and how did people feel about it?
- How did unrest grow in all of Europe?
- How did the German Customs Union ("Zollverein") play a role in uniting Germany?
- How did Germans show their support of personal liberty and national unity?
- How did the Revolution of 1848 break out in Germany and how did the monarchs deal with the revolutionary situation?
- How did the German National Assembly meet and write the first German national constitution?
- Why did the revolution fail and what happened to the popular demands for liberty and unity in Germany?

M 1 **Prince Metternich (1773–1859)**

Klemens von Metternich was an Austrian diplomat and minister of foreign affairs. He was the leading statesman at the Congress of Vienna. Contemporary painting

The Congress of Vienna 1815

Restoring the Old Order: Old wine in old bottles?

For more than twenty years (from 1792 until 1814) the countries of Europe fought wars against France. After Napoleon was finally defeated in 1815, representatives of the European powers came together in Vienna. They wanted to keep the countries of Europe at peace with one another. No one power should become too powerful. No power should be able to have **hegemony** over the others. Instead, a **pentarchy** of five major powers (Great Britain, France, Austria, Russia, and Prussia) were to stay in balance with each other so that no country alone could go to war against the other powers (**balance of power**). The statesmen in Vienna hoped this balance of power would bring lasting peace and keep Europe calm in future.

The leading statesman at the Congress of Vienna was Klemens von Metternich, chancellor of Austria. During the French Revolution, people had demanded the equality of all citizens, civil rights (especially freedom of religion, of assembly, of the press, and the right to vote) and **popular sovereignty**. Metternich believed that these ideas were dangerous and had led to war, so he aimed to keep them under control.

The Congress of Vienna: Looking forward or turning back?

The main principles of the Congress of Vienna were:

- **restoration**: Europe should return to the political situation of 1792
- **legitimacy**: the sovereigns, the heads of the states (who had been removed by Napoleon) were still seen as the rightful and legitimate leaders of these countries, received their thrones back
- *compensation*: territory which had been taken away was given back or paid for
- solidarity: the leaders would work together.

Also, at Vienna the European countries agreed to work together to keep any one of the powers from becoming more powerful than the others. The **Holy Alliance**, a personal alliance among the leaders of Russia, Prussia, and Austria, was set up so that any democratic tendencies could quickly be put down with the help of the three rulers.

Eight powers signed the final act of the Congress of Vienna on 8 June 1815. It was the most *comprehensive* treaty that Europe had seen. Of course, those people who had hoped for national unity and those who liked the ideas of the French Revolution were deeply disappointed. They considered the Vienna settlement completely *reactionary*. But the peace organized in Vienna lasted for nearly forty years.

Territorial Reorganization: Can we change the map any way we like?

The territory that Napoleon won was to be given back to the country it had been taken from. If this was not possible, then the countries had to be compensated by Napoleon's allies. Denmark lost control over Norway to Sweden. The Austrian Netherlands (Belgium) went to Holland. On the new map, a ring of states around France protected Europe in case of a future French attack. Austria was compensated for her loss in the Netherlands and gained control of Parma, Modena, and Tuscany. Poland was divided among Russia, Austria and Prussia. Britain gained territory in the Mediterranean, the West Indies, and South Africa.

Historical Terms

hegemony: Vorherrschaft, Hegemonie

pentarchy: Pentarchie

balance of power: Gleichgewicht der Mächte

popular sovereignty: Volkssouveränität

restoration: Restauration

legitimacy: Legitimität

Holy Alliance: Heilige Allianz

Vocabulary

compensation: payment, making up for sth.

comprehensive: broad, thorough

reactionary: strongly opposed to any political or social changes; the opposite of progressive

M 2 The Congress of Vienna

Caricature by Josef Zutz, 1815: 1. Emperor Francis I (Austria), 2. Tsar Alexander I (Russia), 3. King Frederick William III (Prussia), 4. Duke of Wellington (Britain), 5. King of Denmark, 6. King of Bavaria, 7. King of Württemberg, 8. Elector of Hesse, 9. Duke of Brunswick, 10. Talleyrand (France), 11. mediatized princes and statesmen.

M 3 Two Opinions on the Congress

a) Metternich to an American observer:

"It is true that I do not like democracies. Democracy is in every case a principle of *dissolution*, of *decomposition*. It tends to separate men, it loosens society. I am opposed to this because I am by nature and by habit constructive. That is why monarchy is the only government that suits my way of thinking [...].

Monarchy alone tends to bring men together, to unite them in compact, efficient masses, and to make them capable by their combined efforts of the highest degree of culture and civilization."

b) Speech by Sir James Mackintosh on the Congress of Vienna in the House of Commons (1815):

"The object of the new system is to crush the weak by the combination of the strong; *to subject* Europe in the first place to an *oligarchy of sovereigns*, and *ultimately* to swallow it up in the *gulp* of universal monarchy; where civilization has always *perished*, with freedom of thought, with controlled power, with national character and spirit, with patriotism and *emulation*, in a word, with all its characteristic *attributes*, and with all its *guardian* principles."

Quoted from: Eric Wilmot, The Great Powers 1814–1914, Thomas Nelson Publishers: Watson-on-Thames 1992, p. 45, 15.

Vocabulary

dissolution, decomposition: falling apart, rotting
to subject: to put sth. under the control of sb.
oligarchy of sovereigns: a small group of rulers
ultimately (adv.): finally
gulp: a quick swallow of a large amount of a drink
to perish: to die
emulation: competition
attributes: features
guardian: protecting

Tasks

1. **Prince Metternich**
   a) Find out more about Klemens von Metternich on the Internet.
   b) Make a short report on him to your class.
   c) List Metternich's reasons for not liking democracy (text, M1, M3a).
2. **The Congress of Vienna**
   a) List the main principles of the Congress of Vienna.
   b) Show reasons why nationalists and supporters of ideas from the French Revolution were disappointed by the Congress of Vienna (text, M3b).
   c) Make a table listing reasons to support the principles of the Congress of Vienna and to oppose them.
   d) Look at the picture (M2). What does it tell about the delegates to the Congress?

Historical Terms

German Confederation: Deutscher Bund
Holy Roman Empire: Heiliges Römisches Reich
confederation: Staatenbund
citizen: Staatsbürger/in
subject: Untertan
constitutional monarchy: konstitutionelle Monarchie
republic: Republik

The German Confederation: Not a Popular Institution

Even after France was defeated, ideas from the French Revolution stayed popular. Many who had opposed French rule still wanted to live by some of the principles which the revolution had supported. Nationalism and liberalism were two examples of these principles.

A New Structure, but still divided

In the German states Napoleon dissolved the old **Holy Roman Empire** in 1806 and set up an *efficient* government under French control. In place of this, the Congress founded a new **confederation** of thirty-nine states, mostly monarchies, with a central assembly in Frankfurt am Main. The delegates to the assembly were sent by the governments of the states, which stayed in control of their own affairs. Austria played the leading role in the **German Confederation** and the Austrian delegate was the chairman of the assembly. The confederation did not have an elected parliament or an economic system with common finances, taxation, laws, or systems of weights and measures. It did not function as a German national state. Instead, the confederation reflected the interest of the Great Powers in a divided Germany.

Prussia took on a new role among the German states after 1815. She had joined the pentarchy as a power for the first time at the Congress of Vienna. She also was given territory in the Rhineland and Westphalia as compensation for her participation in the wars against Napoleon. This new territory lay in the west of the country, so uniting the country became a goal. As time went on, Prussia and Austria began to compete for the leading role in the confederation.

Nationalism and Liberalism

Many Germans fought in the wars against France. During these wars they had seen how strong national unity in France was. This was something they wanted for all Germans, too, in form of a German national state. This was not a goal at the Congress of Vienna or within the German Confederation, because the Great Powers' interest in a divided Germany was stronger. However, many Germans still hoped for a constitution and a parliament for all Germans.

Of course, nationalists had different ideas about the nation state they wanted. Some expected all national groups living in the same territory to become part of a German state, even if they were Polish, Danish, Austrian, or French. Others felt that only Germans should be a part of the German state and other national groups should have their own nation states. These nationalists supported other groups which fought for their independence, such as the Greeks during their war of liberation against the Turks (1821–29) and the Poles who revolted against the Russian Empire in 1830. Neither of these wars of independence was supported by the principles of the Congress of Vienna.

Liberalism was based on the ideas of the Enlightenment and the French Revolution. Liberals wanted personal freedom. People should be free **citizens** of their countries, not **subjects** ruled by a monarch. Liberals believed that their rights could be guaranteed in a written constitution. The constitution would also limit the power of the monarch in a **constitutional monarchy**. A constitution would protect civil rights (especially freedoms of the press, assembly, property, and equality before the law). Citizens could elect a parliament to take part in law-

Vocabulary

efficient: well-organized, effective

M 1

making and keep the government under control. Even though the German Confederation decided in 1815 that all the member states would give themselves new constitutions, by 1829 only fifteen of the states had done so. The two leading member states, Austria and Prussia, did not make any effort to become constitutional monarchies in this time.

The more the monarchs in the German Confederation opposed the idea of constitutional monarchy, the more another group raised demands which went farther. They wanted to do away with monarchy and replace it with a **republic**. Such a government could be elected by all (male) voters for a certain length of time. When that time had passed, a new government could be elected.

Tasks

1. The German Confederation

a) List the five largest countries in the German Confederation (M1).

b) Three countries are not entirely within the borders of the Confederation. Find them on the map.

c) Make a table to show how the German Confederation's central assembly and a democratic parliament are different.

2. Nationalism and Liberalism

a) Find two definitions of nationalism in the text.

b) Name other factors which can define a nation.

c) Compare nationalism in the 19th century with nationalism today.

d) List at least five things liberals wanted.

e) Explain which of these goals you find the most important.

Historical Terms

Ottoman Empire: Osmanisches Reich

laissez-faire (Fr.): gewähren lassen

migration: Wanderungsbewegung

emigration: Auswanderung

immigration: Einwanderung

M 1

European Unrest 1815–1848

Unrest in Many Countries

The Congress of Vienna had tried to keep Europe calm, but unrest remained on the continent.

Date	Country	Event
1820	Spain	rebellion of the liberals; triggered by part of the army
1820	Italy	the Carbonari revolt against the Austrians (Naples)
1820	Portugal	revolution led by the army
1821	Italy	revolt in Piemont against King Victor Emmanuel
1821–29	Greece	war of liberation against the Turks
1830	France	rioters fight on the barricades in Paris; king abdicates
1830	Poland	uprising in Warsaw against Tsar Nicholas I
1845–50	Ireland	great famine; terror wave by the "Young Ireland" group
1847	Italy	uprising in Messina against the Habsburgs

In countries with strong authorities, the uprisings failed. In Italy the Carbonari rebels were put down by the Austrian army. In Poland rebels were no match for the troops of the Russian *tsar*. But when the Great Powers Russia, France and Great Britain helped the Greeks in their fight against the Turkish **Ottoman Empire**, the revolutionaries were successful.

In France the king tried to restrict voting rights and introduce press censorship in 1830. He had *to abdicate* when a majority of his citizens resisted. A "citizen king", Louis Philippe, replaced him. Europeans watched events in France carefully. An uprising or revolt there could set off unrest in other countries during this period.

In Britain leaders tried to be flexible in political matters to keep unrest down at home. They passed the Reform Act of 1832 to extend voting rights. But British leaders dealt poorly with problems in Ireland (see below).

All these examples of political unrest, whether successful or not, showed that Metternich's plans to keep the old order were in danger.

M 2 **"The Greek Revolution"**
Painting by Eugéne Delacroix on the Greek uprising, about 1826

Starvation in Ireland Leads to Migration

Irish farmers had simple lives. Most farming families had no other skills. Education in Ireland was poor – most people could not read. Potatoes were the main food. The poor lived almost entirely on them. Mainly just one type of potato was planted. In 1845 a potato *blight* wiped out the whole potato harvest. A severe *famine* was the result. Landlords forced farmers who could not pay their rent to leave the land. It was more profitable to plant grain on the fields or to graze animals on them. The potato blight was a good opportunity to do so. When the famine began, the British government did not help enough. Then the British stopped all help completely and stood by as the situation grew worse and worse. There were several reasons for this. First, political leaders believed that the government should leave markets alone (**laissez-faire** economics). Second, some thought the famine showed the will of God, so God should solve the problem. Third, some worried that helping the Irish might make them depend on public assistance in future. The Irish should solve their problems themselves. Although Ireland grew plenty of grain during the famine, it was exported and sold for profit. It was too expensive for the Irish themselves, so they died of hunger.

Vocabulary

tsar: (also: czar) Russian emperor

to abdicate: to give up the throne

blight: plant disease

famine: little or no food for a long time

to emigrate: to leave one's country

coffin: box to bury a dead person in

to immigrate: to come into a country

M 3 The Irish Famine, 1845–1849
Woodcut, 1900, unknown artist

It was the worst famine that Europe has known. By 1850 nearly one million Irishmen had died from starvation or disease. About one and a half million *emigrated* to other countries. After the famine ended, the economy was ruined. Emigration continued for many years. Those who emigrated overseas went to the USA (70%), Canada (28%), or Australia (2%).

The ships to Canada and the USA were called "*coffin* ships" because of the poor conditions on board. Many passengers died of fever or other diseases, either on the ships or shortly after they arrived. Those who survived the transport were not welcome when they left the ships. Cities were not prepared for the large numbers of immigrants. Because the Irish were Catholic, religion also became a problem. Therefore, the unskilled Irish workers were hired only for the lowest paying jobs. At the same time, landlords in the cities charged high rent for flats.

The famine caused lasting bitterness towards British rule in Ireland. This led to the movement for Irish independence, which was achieved in 1922.

Migration from Germany: Looking for opportunity

Germans had many reasons *to immigrate* to the USA, where 90% of German emigrants went. Many young men decided to emigrate instead of serving in the military. Farmers who worked for landlords in Germany could get their own land in the USA cheaply, which made **immigration** very attractive. Once there, they wrote letters to friends and relatives back home telling them about their success. This led to "chain migrations".

Germans also emigrated for political reasons. Some grew tired of waiting for political reforms under the Metternich System. After the revolution of 1848 failed, many "Forty-Eighters" emigrated. Intellectuals and scholars took their "radical" ideas of land reform, workers' and women's rights, and social activism with them. Also, many Jews decided to emigrate because of anti-Semitism in Germany and Austria-Hungary.

German immigrants to the USA had more money than the Irish to move to areas where they could start farms. Germans were also skilled workers who could start their own businesses in cities, especially in the Midwest.

Between 1820 and 1920, over 5.5 million Germans immigrated to the USA. This was the largest group from any country at the time. In the same period 4.4 million immigrants from Ireland, 4.2 million from Italy, and 3.7 million from Austria-Hungary settled in the USA.

M 4 Emigration
Poster advertising a German shipping company, about 1890

Migration from Germany – working with pictures

M 5 **Emigrants at the Overseas Dock in Bremerhaven,** coloured woodcut in the style of Johannes Gehrts, ca. 1880

M 6 **German Emigrants in the Cheapest Quarters,** a passenger ship on its way to America, 1886

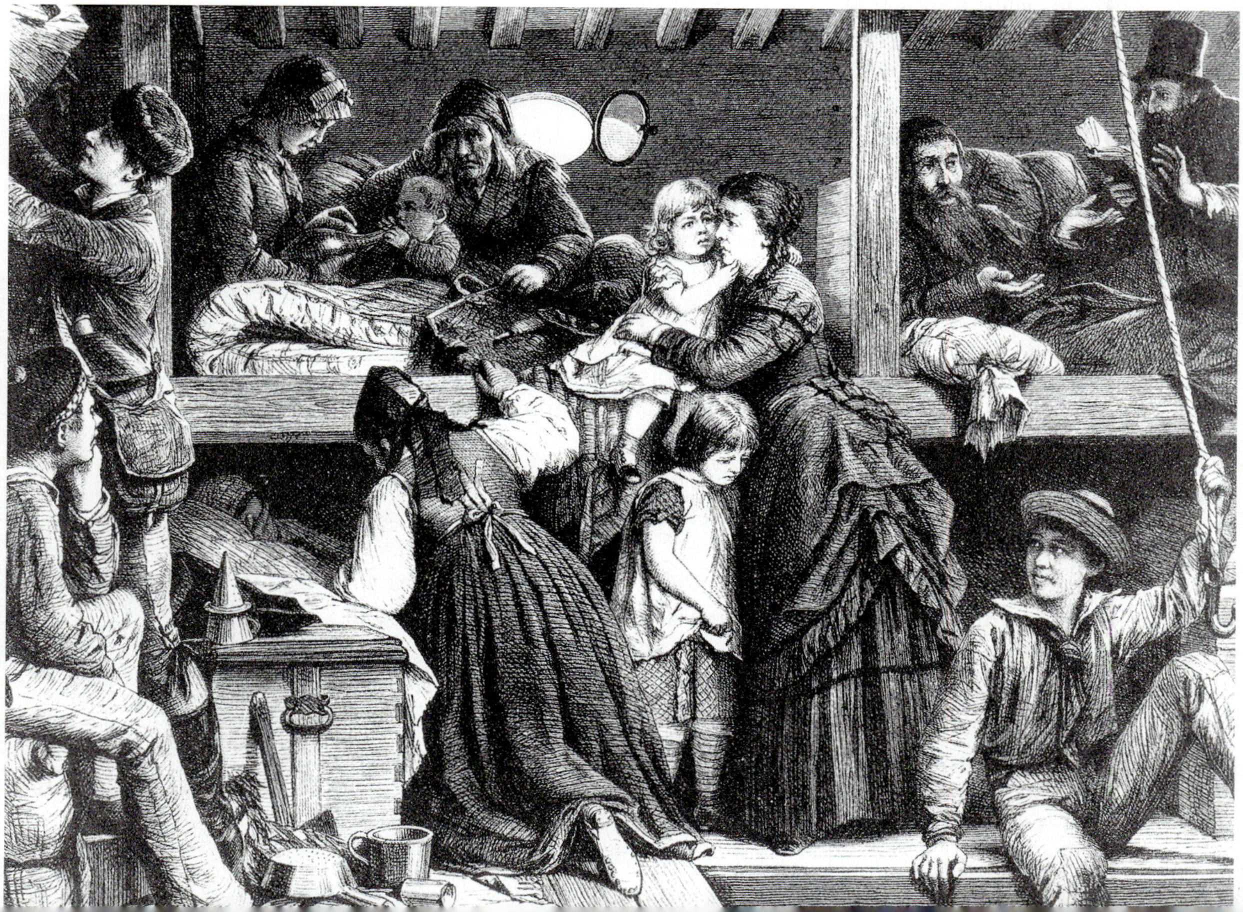

M 7 **Painting of Ship Arriving in New York City Harbour**
Unknown artist, 1887

Tasks

1. Delacroix Painting
   a) Describe the painting (M2).
   b) Explain the symbols which the artist uses.
   c) Discuss the artist's opinion of the Greek revolution.

2. European Unrest
List the factors which led to the success or failure of unrest from 1815 to 1848 (text).

3. Migration
   a) Make a table listing
      - reasons why people migrated at this time
      - what people had to give up in order to migrate
      - what happened to them when they got to where they were going (text).
   b) Compare and contrast the message in the pictures (M5, M6, and M7).
   c) Step into the picture (M6). Describe your situation.

Historical Terms

Customs Union:
Zollverein

The Customs Union: Economic Unity for Some States

One of the most important developments during this time was the founding of the "Zollverein", a German **Customs Union**. The thirty-nine states in the German Confederation were still separate countries, so customs duties had to be paid on goods passing from one state to another. These customs duties made trade expensive and difficult. Friedrich List, an economist from southern Germany, proposed that the states form a customs union within Germany. On 1 January 1834 Prussia founded a larger free trade zone: It included 26 million people, was called the German Customs Union, and was recognized as an important economic and financial structure in the confederation. By 1842 the Customs Union grew even larger and became a great success, especially in improving trade relations and building railroads within the free trade area.

In the early days of the Customs Union, Austria had refused to join. Later, when Austria wanted to join, Prussia actively prevented her from doing so. Prussian leaders saw that economic power was an important tool and could be used to work against Austria's leadership of the confederation.

The Customs Union played an important role later, when the German states became one nation state. That is why the growth of the Customs Union in the nineteenth century might be a model for the European Union today. Economic unity can be a helpful first step in reaching political unity.

M 1 The German Customs Union up to 1842

The Customs Union – analysing a cartoon

M 2 **"Border Embarrassment"**

"You see, Mr. Border Guard, that I have nothing to declare, because what is in the back of the wagon has not yet crossed the border of Lippe. There is nothing in the middle and what is at the front of the wagon is already beyond the border of Lippe." Cartoon from "Fliegenden Blättern", 1849

Vocabulary

Useful terms to discuss the cartoon

covered wagon: a wagon, drawn by horses or oxen, covered with heavy material, like canvas, to keep out wind and rain

wagon wheel: wheel attached to a cart or wagon

axle: long piece of wood or metal connecting wheels

no man's land: area between two borders which belongs to neither country

border barrier: a barricade keeping people and goods from passing a border

border sign: sign showing where the border of a country begins or ends

Lippe-Schauenburg: principality of Lippe-Schauenburg (today it is called Schaumburg-Lippe) in Westfalia; it was one of the smallest German states at this time, which is why it is often used in cartoons making fun of the many small German states

Vocabulary

customs officer: government official who checks goods at the border and collects customs duties on them

border guard: government official who protects the border and keeps people from entering the country without permission

wooden soldier: soldier made of wood
How can a wooden soldier protect the border?

team of horses: group of horses who work together to pull a load

rider: person who sits on top of a horse and leads it

customhouse: office where customs duties are collected, or where customs officers can wait

Tasks

1. **The Customs Union**
   a) Explain why economists like Friedrich List wanted a Customs Union (text).
   b) Make a list of advantages and disadvantages of the Customs Union.
2. **Economic Policy in the EU Today**
   a) Find out about the Schengen Agreement on the Internet.
   b) Name its most important features.
   c) Make a list of advantages and disadvantages of the Schengen Agreement and compare with task 1b).
3. **Analysing the Cartoon "Border Embarrassment"**
   a) Describe the cartoon (M2).
   b) Explain the problem which the cartoon shows.
   c) State the cartoonist's opinion.

Historical Terms

Carlsbad Decrees: Karlsbader Beschlüsse

absolute monarchy: absolute Monarchie

coup d'état (Fr.): Staatsstreich

Vocabulary

pigtail: hair braided together, symbolizing authority

to investigate: to find out about sth.

demagogue: a leader who misleads the people

hunt: a search for sth.

to spy: to find out secret information

fair: people's festival

Palatinate: German "Pfalz"

Examples of Unrest in Germany 1815–1847

Student Societies Discuss How to Unite a Democratic Germany

Many students disliked the Metternich System in Germany. Some had taken part in the Wars of Liberation against Napoleon. Starting in 1815 they formed patriotic groups known as "Burschenschaften". In secret meetings they discussed how to unite Germany as a democratic country. The two ideas of unity and liberty seemed to go together. Representatives of fourteen German universities met in Jena on 18 October 1818 and founded the "Allgemeine Deutsche Burschenschaft", a federation of all German students. On their clothing they wore "German colours", the same colours a famous regiment had worn in the 1813 Battle of Leipzig: black, red and gold. Metternich thought the student organizations were dangerous and looked for a way to forbid them.

From the Wartburg (1817) to Carlsbad (1819)

On 18 October 1817 about 500 students from Jena attended a festival at Wartburg Castle near Eisenach to celebrate the Battle of Leipzig (October 1813) and the start of the Reformation (October 1517).

During the meeting speakers criticized the political system and burned some of its symbols, like a policeman's *pigtail* and a copy of the German Act of Confederation. The students' demonstration seemed quite harmless, but German rulers were nervous and Metternich was alarmed.

On 23 March 1819 Carl Ludwig Sand, a theology student at Jena University, killed the journalist and playwright August von Kotzebue at his home in Mannheim. Kotzebue had made fun of the students' liberal and patriotic ideals. Sand was executed on 20 May 1820. His deed was controversial. Some called him a fanatic, others called him a martyr to German freedom. Metternich used the murder as an excuse to silence the liberal and national movement in Germany.

The frightened rulers of the Confederation agreed to the **Carlsbad Decrees** on 20 September 1819. The Decrees censored everything that was printed and had fewer than 320 pages, placed the universities under strict supervision and set up a commission at Mainz *to investigate* "revolutionary plots and demagogic connections". A "*demagogue hunt*" followed as the police *spied* on liberal students and professors. The liberal movement was unable to express its demands in public and lost support.

M 1 **"The Hambach Festival" 1832**

Hundreds of flags with the German colours were shown, in addition to national flags of other countries, including France and Poland.

The Hambach Festival 1832: A walk for democracy

After the Revolution of 1830 in France, Germans looked for a way to express their political goals in public. Such demonstrations were, of course, illegal in the Metternich System. So the public was simply invited to a "*fair*" at Hambach Castle in the *Palatinate*. On 27 May 1832 30,000 southern liberals and radicals walked in a parade to demand national unity and a republican government in Germany.

The Göttingen Seven 1837: Constitutional crisis in Hanover

Great Britain and Hanover had been ruled in personal union since 1714. This ended in 1837 when Victoria was crowned queen in Britain. Ernst August II became king in Hanover, broke with the constitution and restored **absolute monarchy**. Seven university professors in Göttingen protested the king's **coup d'état** in an open letter. The king dismissed the men, which made the scandal worse.

A Political Murder and Its Consequences – working with pictures

M 2 **The Assassination of August von Kotzebue on 23 March 1819**

Steel engraving by W. Pobuda, about 1840

M 3 **The Execution of the Assassin Carl Ludwig Sand in Mannheim on 20 May 1820**

Lithograph, 1820

Tasks

1. **The Student Societies**
   a) List the ideas of the student societies.
   b) Name arguments for and against showing the "German colours" at this time.
   c) Explain why Metternich thought the students' ideas and their societies were dangerous.
2. **Carl Ludwig Sand and the Carlsbad Decrees**
   a) Describe Sand's reasons for murdering Kotzebue.
   b) List the effects of the Carlsbad Decrees on public life in Germany.
   c) Work in pairs. Choose either M2 or M3 and describe how Sand is shown.
   d) Compare and contrast with your partner.
   e) Discuss whether Sand was an early German patriot or a fanatical murderer. Give reasons for your opinion.

Analysing "The Thinkers' Club"

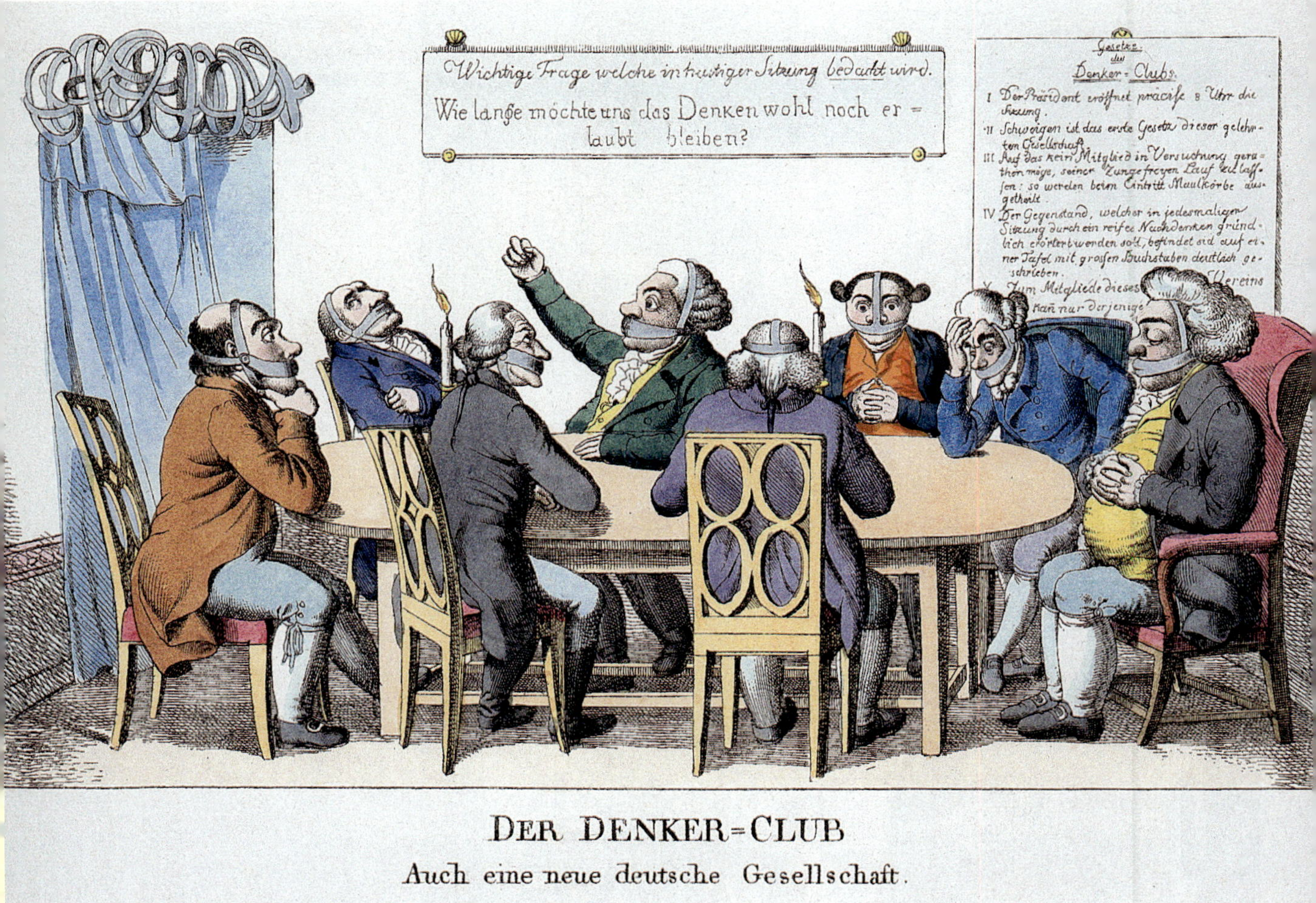

M 4 **"The Thinkers' Club. Another New German Society"**
Cartoon, about 1820.

The middle sign says:

Important question of today's meeting.

How long may we still be allowed to think?

The sign on the right side says:

Rules of the Thinker's Club:

I. The president opens the meeting at precisely 8 o'clock.

II. Silence is the first rule of this society.

III. So that no member may be tempted to let his tongue run free, muzzles will be handed out upon entry.

IV. The topic to be thought about in each meeting will be found written legibly in large letters on a sign.

V. Only someone ... [text cannot be read] can be a member of this club.

Vocabulary

Useful terms to discuss the cartoon

to sit around a table/on a chair
to wear a muzzle
to think about sth./consider a topic
to raise a hand/lean sb.'s head back
to rest sb.'s head on his hand/on his chin
to fold / lean on one's arms

The German National Anthem and State Flag

M 5 **German State Flag**

M 6 **The German National Anthem**

Third verse of "Das Lied der Deutschen" by August Heinrich Hoffmann von Fallersleben, 1841. Sung to the tune of "Kaiserlied" by Joseph Haydn, 1796–97. German text and English translation:

Einigkeit und Recht und Freiheit
für das deutsche Vaterland!
Danach lasst uns alle streben
brüderlich mit Herz und Hand!
Einigkeit und Recht und Freiheit
sind des Glückes Unterpfand;
Blüh im Glanze dieses Glückes,
blühe, deutsches Vaterland!

Unity and right and freedom
For the German fatherland!
Let us all pursue this purpose
Fraternally with heart and hand!
Unity and right and freedom
Are the pledge of happiness;
Flourish in this blessing's glory,
Flourish, German fatherland!

Translation: https://www.bundestag.de/en/parliament/symbols/anthem/anthem/197926 [Oct. 2017].

Tasks

1. **Analysing "The Thinkers' Club"**
   a) Describe the cartoon "The Thinkers' Club" and list the laws of the club briefly (M4).
   b) Interpret the artist's intention.
2. **The Hambach Festival**
   a) Describe what happened at the Hambach Festival (text, M1).
   b) Assess the importance of the festival at the time.
3. **The Göttingen Seven**
   a) Explain why the university professors protested and what happened to them as a result (text).
   b) Find out about the Göttingen Seven on the Internet. Who were they? What happened later in their careers?
4. **The German National Anthem**
   a) Find out about Hoffmann von Fallersleben on the Internet.
   b) Report to your class on his situation at the time he wrote the text for the German anthem.
5. **The Unrest in Germany, 1815-1847**
   Draw a conclusion about what events in this unit show about public opinion in Germany at this time.
6. **The German Flag**
   a) Find out about the colours on the Internet (M5).
   b) Explain the origins of the eagle as a national symbol.

M 1 **Paris 1848**

Storming the Seat of Government in Paris, February 1848.

Revolution Breaks Out in 1848

Unrest began in Italy in January, but the Paris uprising in February 1848 set off revolutionary ideas all over Europe. French citizens complained about the king's censorship of the press and using the army *to stay in charge*. Because only 250,000 citizens could vote, liberals had no seats in parliament and could not express their opinions. So reformers held *banquets* to discuss political changes. When a banquet set for 22 February 1848 was forbidden, public protests began. Troops shot at the demonstrators and people in Paris revolted. The king was forced to abdicate.

Vienna and Berlin 1848

News of the events in Paris spread – by March people in Vienna demanded freedom of the press, civil rights and a **constitution**. On 13 March 1848 a crowd came together and called for Metternich to leave office. Troops broke up the demonstration. Students, members of the city *militia* and some workers set up barricades. Metternich fled to safety in England. The Austrian government published a new constitution quickly, but unrest continued.

In 1815 Prussians hoped for a constitution, but none was written. When Frederick William IV was crowned in 1840, he insisted that no written document could come between God, the king and the people of Prussia. Nevertheless, people did not forget what they wanted. When news of the events in Vienna reached Berlin, Frederick William IV relaxed press censorship and promised a new constitution. On 18 March a crowd came together to thank the king for his last-minute changes. Suddenly, the palace guard fired shots. The crowd quickly set up barricades. The king's troops killed more than 230 people. Frederick William was upset and shocked by the tragic events. He ordered his troops to return to their barracks. He seemed to give in to public pressure. He rode through Berlin under the black-red-gold flag, the symbol of united Germany. On 22 March the king promised to ask a Prussian **national assembly** to write a constitution.

The Constitution "From Above"

The national assembly began writing a constitution for Prussia, but this group, the king's liberal cabinet and a group of conservative landowners soon disagreed. When troops put down a revolt in Vienna in October 1848, Frederick William IV called his troops back to Berlin. The Prussian national assembly moved to Brandenburg. The king's soldiers broke it up in December. The king rejected the assembly's constitution and introduced one written by his advisors. This constitution "from above" included a list of civil rights, but the king kept an **absolute veto**. From 1850 to 1918 Prussian elections were held according to a **three-class voting system** which was well-known for its unfairness.

Historical Terms

constitution: Verfassung

national assembly: Nationalversammlung

absolute veto: absolutes Veto

three-class voting system: Dreiklassenwahlrecht

Vocabulary

to stay in charge: to keep control over a situation

banquet: large, formal dinner

militia: citizen's army

M 2 "To My *Beloved* Berliners"

Message of Frederick William IV (19 March 1848):

"The shout of joy which greeted me from *innumerable faithful* hearts still resounded in my ears when a crowd of peace-breakers mixed with the loyal *throng*. As the courtyard was cleared by the cavalry, two guns went off by themselves, without, thank God, causing any injury. A band of *wicked* men, mainly foreigners, have succeeded in filling the excited minds of my faithful and beloved Berliners with thoughts of revenge for *supposed bloodshed*. My troops, your brothers and fellow countrymen, did not make use of their weapons till forced to do so by several shots fired at them.
It is now up to you, *inhabitants* of my beloved native city, *to avert* a fearful evil. Remove the barricades which are still standing. All the streets and squares shall immediately be cleared of troops. Forget the past, as I shall forget it, for the sake of the great future which is dawning upon Prussia and through Prussia upon all of Germany."

Quoted from: Tim Klein (ed.), Der Vorkampf deutscher Einheit, W. Langewiesche-Brandt: Ebenhausen bei München 1927, p. 178f. (adapted and transl. by Gernot Schikowski).

Vocabulary

beloved: dear
innumerable: uncountable
faithful: loyal
throng: crowd
wicked: evil, bad
to suppose: to imagine
bloodshed: people losing blood
inhabitants: people living in a place
to avert: to prevent

M 3 "Barricades in Berlin"
The "Königsstraße" on the night of 18 to 19 March 1848. Painting, 1848

M 4 "The King Gives In"
Frederick William IV rides through Berlin on 21 March. Painting, 1848

M 5 "From Above"
The Prussian people receive the constitution "from above". Cartoon, 1849

Tasks

1. **Outbreak of Revolution in 1848**
   a) Make a table listing the reasons why revolution broke out in France, Austria, and Germany, in 1848.
   b) Compare and contrast the reasons for revolution in the three countries.
2. **Frederick William IV**
   a) Sum up the main ideas in the king's speech (M2).
   b) Analyse the king's explanation of the revolutionary uprising.
   c) Describe the role of Prussia in the unification of Germany, according to the king.
3. **The Revolution in Berlin**
   a) Look at the pictures of the revolutionary events in Berlin (M3 – M5).
   b) Describe the events shown in the pictures.
   c) Explain the historical context of the events.

M 1 **The Preliminary Parliament**

574 members gather at St. Paul's Church in Frankfurt on 30 March 1848.

Historical Terms

suffrage (Wahlrecht): the right to vote

Suffrage is **universal** [allgemein] when everyone has the right to vote. It is **equal** [gleich] when each vote counts the same. In the nineteenth century, **universal suffrage** meant all men could vote. Today this is called **universal male suffrage**, because suffrage is not universal if women are not included.

An **election** is **direct** [direkt] when the voters themselves chose the person who is elected. It is **indirect** [indirekt] when someone else, an **elector** [Wahlmann], makes the final choice after the voters have done so.

The **secret ballot** [geheimes Stimmrecht] gives every voter the right to keep his opinion private.

Vocabulary

preliminary: coming before

constituent assembly: group which writes a constitution

sovereign: having independent power

inherited: passed from parent to child

gutter: edge of street carrying water and waste

The First German National Assembly Meets

While separate assemblies started writing constitutions for the German states, many people demanded a German national constitution. A *preliminary* parliament met in Frankfurt to prepare the elections to a *constituent assembly*.

The members were elected according to universal and equal male **suffrage**. In nearly two-thirds of the German states this was the first time such an **election** was held. However, the election was indirect. Voters chose "electors" who then elected the members of the Frankfurt Parliament – a method to keep the election results under control. On 18 May 1848 over 500 members met in St. Paul's Church in Frankfurt. They had important decisions to make.

Problems of the National Assembly: What is a united and democratic Germany?

- Sovereignty: Who should rule?
  The Frankfurt Parliament elected Heinrich von Gagern president on 19 May 1848. But the governments of the separate states were still in power. The parliament had to decide whether it was a *sovereign* institution or whether the German states had to agree with its decisions. As a compromise the parliament elected Archduke Johann of Austria its "imperial administrator", a preliminary constitutional monarch. Although the separate states accepted this change, the office had no real power. It depended on the good will of the rulers of the states. Their good will disappeared as the revolution weakened.
- Constitution:
  There was no agreement on a constitution when the parliament met in May 1848. The members had to decide whether a new emperor should be head of state, whether he should have an elected or *inherited* office, what role parliament should play, and how elections should be organized. Working out the final version of the constitution by April 1849 was a solid achievement.
- German borders:
  The territory of the new Germany was not clear. The members had to decide whether Austria, or only part of Austria, should be included in the new Germany. The parliament decided to put off this decision until late October.
- Human rights:
  The national assembly began its work discussing human rights because these had been raised by the revolution in the first place. Also, it was easier to agree on human rights than on other problems. But it took a lot of time for the parliament to decide such questions. When the constitution was finally presented, the kings were back in power of their separate states again. Still, the list of human rights from the Frankfurt Parliament was one of the few aspects which went into German constitutions later.

Crown Offered to the Prussian King

On 28 March 1849 the parliament voted to offer the German crown to Frederick William IV. A delegation traveled to Berlin to present their crown to him. The king refused to "pick up a crown from the *gutter*" – harsh terms for a crown offered by the elected representatives of the German people.

In the end both Prussia and Austria rejected the Frankfurt constitution. Most of the state governments ordered their members of the parliament to return home.

M 2 **"Refusal"**

The President of the Frankfurt Parliament von Gagern with Borussia. She asks, "Why are you crying, little boy?" He replies, "I've carved a crown for your little 'un, but 'e doesn't want it!". Cartoon, 1849

Vocabulary

Useful terms to discuss the cartoon

eagle: The eagle is a common symbol. Here there are two different eagles on each of the shields held by the woman in foreground and the statue in the background.

Germania: female symbol for Germany

Borussia: female symbol for Prussia

spiked helmet: helmet worn by Prussian soldiers

Wilhelm Heinrich von Gagern (1799–1880) elected president of the Frankfurt National Assembly

to pout: to show unhappiness, often by sticking out the lower lip

to rub one's eyes: (here) to wipe away tears when crying

bedroom slipper: soft shoe worn in the house

Frederick William IV (1795–1861), Prussian king 1840–61

bear: animal, symbol of Russia

whip: strip of leather on a handle used to make an animal move

house of cards: structure made of playing cards

top with stick: toy which spins when pushed with the stick

Tasks

1. **Problems of the National Assembly**
   a) Draw a diagram showing the problems the Frankfurt Parliament had to solve (text).
   b) State which of these problems you consider the most important.
   c) Say which of the problems you consider the most difficult to solve. Explain why.
   d) The parliament is criticized for its long debates and that it took so long to come to conclusions. Agree or disagree with this criticism. Explain your arguments.
2. **The Frankfurt Constitution**
   Evaluate the effect of the constitution of 1849, even if it never actually was put into practice (text).
3. **Analysing the cartoon "Refusal"**
   a) Describe the cartoon (M2).
   b) Decide what the figures symbolize.
   c) Interpret the artist's opinion.

M 1 **The Execution of Robert Blum**
Engraving, 1849

Vocabulary

firing squad: a group of soldiers who shoot a prisoner

rump parliament: a smaller parliament left over from a larger parliament

Historical Terms

feudal rights:
Feudalrechte

The End of the 1848 Revolution

The Reaction in Austria and Prussia Returns

By the summer of 1848, reformers put pressure on the Austrian government. National groups, such as Czechs, Slovaks, and Hungarians, wanted their own governments, too. They demanded independence from Austria. Ethnic German revolutionaries in Austria insisted on taking part in politics in future.

The emperor used his army to take control again. In June 1848 Austrian troops put down a Czech revolt in Prague and another in Italy in July. The army marched back into Vienna in October 1848 and drove out the city government within five days. General Windischgrätz, the military commander, showed no mercy. Robert Blum, a member of the Frankfurt Parliament from Saxony who had fought on the barricades in Vienna, was shot by a *firing squad*. Austrian and Russian troops put down the movement for independence in Hungary in June 1849.

In Prussia, conservatives also got back into power. The king ordered his troops to return to Berlin in September 1848. He appointed a conservative minister-president. In November the king sent the Prussian national assembly home. That ended all hopes for a democratic constitution. In its place he presented his own constitution "from above" – it was written without any input from representatives of the people. Frederick William IV now directly opposed the revolution. When members of the Frankfurt Parliament offered him their crown on 3 April 1849, he refused to take it.

What Became of the Failed Revolution?

At that point the Austrian members left the Frankfurt Parliament. The remaining members realized that no agreement with the German rulers would be possible. Most of them gave up and returned home. A "*rump parliament*" of about 100 members from democratic and republican groups met again in Stuttgart, but the Württemberg military ended their meeting. In Baden a group of revolutionaries held out longer than in other places. This was possible because the troops there took sides with the rebels and the fortress in Rastatt was easy to defend. When the fortress finally fell, fifty-one leaders of the rebellion were executed, 845 revolutionaries were put in jail. Many fled or emigrated to the United States. Others committed suicide – for example, Friedrich Daniel Bassermann in Baden.

The hopes of liberal citizens from March 1848 were completely disappointed in 1849. For years, political opposition in Germany came to a halt. However, the revolution had long-term effects. **Feudal rights** were abolished and farmers became more independent from their landlords. These changes could not be reversed. The Frankfurt Parliament's constitution had been written down. Even though the German monarchs refused to accept its ideas, it became a model for the constitution of the first German republic in 1919. A united and democratic Germany was not created, but this national ideal lived on after 1849.

M 2 **"After the Prussian Army Put Down the Revolt in Baden: The Red Monarchy"**
Frederick William IV sits on a newly designed throne. Cartoon, 1849

M 3 "Solution of All the Political Problems"

Carl Schurz (1829–1906), a 48er who emigrated to the United States and became a political leader there, explained why he became more radical during the Revolution of 1848:

"Our democratic club was *composed* in almost equal parts of students and citizens, among whom there were many of excellent character, of some *fortune* and good standing, and of moderate views, while a few others had worked themselves into a state of mind *resembling* that of the terrorists in the French Revolution. Kinkel [a professor of law in Bonn] was the recognized leader of the club, and I soon became a member of the *executive* committee. At first the establishment of a constitutional monarchy with universal suffrage and *well-secured* civil rights would have been quite satisfactory to us.

But the reaction, the *threatened* rise of which we were observing, gradually made many of us believe that there was no safety for popular liberty except in a republic. From this belief there was only one step to the further *conclusion* that in a republic, and only in a republic, all evils of the social body could be cured and the solution of all the political problems be possible."

Carl Schurz, The Reminiscences of Carl Schurz, Doubleday, Page & Co.: New York 1913, Vol.1, p. 133–137.

M 4 "Another Dance of Death"
Woodcut by Alfred Rethel, 1849

Vocabulary

to compose: to make up
fortune: success
resembling: similar to
executive: leading
well-secured: guaranteed
threatened: dangerous
conclusion: decision

Tasks

1. **The Reaction in Austria and Prussia**
   a) Make a timeline of the events in Austria and Prussia, 1848–49 (text).
   b) Explain how the monarchs regained control over their countries in 1849.
2. **Robert Blum**
   a) Describe how the artist portrays Blum in M1.
   b) Find out about Blum and how he is remembered today on the Internet.
   c) Report back to your class on your research.
   d) Imagine building a historical monument in memory of Robert Blum. Decide what kind of monument should be built, where it should be, and what it should look like.
3. **Analysing the Caricature**
   a) Describe the caricature briefly (M2).
   b) Explain the symbols used.
   c) Comment on the caricature's subtitle "The Red Monarchy".
4. **Carl Schurz**
   a) Find out more about Schurz on the Internet.
   b) Report back to your class on him.
   c) Outline Schurz's reasons for becoming a republican (M3).
5. **Analysing "Another Dance of Death"**
   a) Describe the woodcut (M4).
   b) Explain the symbols used.
   c) Interpret the woodcut.
   d) Agree or disagree with Rethel's opinion of the events in 1849.
6. **The Results of the Revolution of 1848**
   a) Make a table listing the successes and failures of the revolution in Germany, 1848–49 (text).
   b) Find out about one of the 1848 German revolutionaries on the Internet. Discuss how he is remembered in Germany today (street name, school name, monument, etc.).

M 5 **"The times are changing, and with them, customs."**

22 March 1848: "Hat off!"

26 February 1849: "Hats off!"

Cartoon in "Deutsche Reichs-Bremse: Organ für politische-satyrische Sticheleien", Beiblatt zu "Der Leuchtthurm : Monatsschrift zur Belehrung und Unterhaltung für das deutsche Volk", Leipzig 1849

Analysing Cartoons

Mainly Visual Sources

Caricatures and historical cartoons offer lots of information at one glance. Caricature comes from the Italian word "caricare", meaning *to exaggerate*. These pictures make fun of people and things by exaggerating their features and weaknesses. The artists often take a stand, either for or against their subjects.

Because caricatures are visual, rather than *merely* textual, they became a popular way of informing people who could not read about political events. Cartoons are a good source for finding out how people who lived at the time of historical events felt about these events and political figures. But, like all types of sources, we have to learn how to interpret them.

Commenting on Historical Events

The main figures, events, successes and failures of the Revolution of 1848 were popular topics for caricatures at the time. The two cartoons on the opposite page deal with Frederick William IV's reactions to revolutionary events. To analyse them you need to know that the king removed his helmet and bowed his head to the coffins of those who died in the March 1848 uprising in Berlin. On 26 February 1849, Frederick William opened the new Prussian parliament in a political situation which had completely changed. Weeks later, when representatives of the German National Assembly asked him to become the new German emperor, he refused their "crown from the gutter".

Vocabulary

to exaggerate: to overstate, overemphasize

merely: only, just

Historical Workshop

Analysing Cartoons

1. Description

a. List the objects or people you see in the cartoon.
b. Identify the cartoon caption and/or title.
c. Find the main words or phrases used by the cartoonist (Note: Here no other words appear besides the titles.)
d. Record any important dates or numbers that appear in the cartoon.

2. Assessing the Information

a. Name the objects on your list which are symbols.
b. Explain what each symbol means.
c. Explain why the words used in the cartoon are significant.
d. List adjectives that describe the emotions portrayed in the cartoon.

3. Interpreting the Cartoon

a. Describe the action taking place in the cartoon.
b. Explain how the words in the cartoon clarify the symbols.
c. Explain the message of the cartoon.
d. Name special interest groups which would agree or disagree with the cartoon's message. Explain why.

1810 1815 1820 1825 1830

1815: Congress of Vienna

1817: Wartburg Festival

1819: Assassination of Kotzebue

1820: Carlbad Decrees

1832: Hambach Festival

Europe in Revolt – the historical map

1840 1845 1850 1855 1860

37: Göttingen protest
d dismissal of seven
iversity professors

1848/49: Revolution

Summary

The principles made at the Congress of Vienna kept the peace in Europe for many years. But this peace came at a high price. European monarchs tried to stay in control of the public discussion of political ideas. However, the ideas from the French Revolution about national unity and personal liberty could not be held back.

The Metternich System restricted public life in the German Confederation. Still, Germans in the separate states were very creative in finding ways to express their opinions in public. The monarchs' methods, such as censoring the press and keeping people from coming together in public, simply did not work over a longer period of time. The rulers had to put down popular unrest again and again. Revolution finally broke out all over Europe in 1848.

The German Customs Union was a successful economic solution to problems in the German states. At first political leaders in Austria did not understand that it was important to join the Customs Union in order to keep Austrian influence in German affairs. When Austrian leaders saw their mistake, it was too late.

Parliamentary assemblies met in the separate German states to write constitutions in 1848. Also, a national assembly was elected to write a constitution for a united Germany. But time was needed for the members to come to agreements in the assemblies. By the time the constitutions were written, the monarchs were once again in charge of the separate states. They rejected the constitutions the representatives of the people had written. The Revolution of 1848 seemed to have failed.

In 1919 a new German national assembly returned to many of the solutions which had been written down in the 1849 constitution. So even though the 1849 constitution never went into effect, it did have lasting value.

DATES

1815: Congress of Vienna

1817: Wartburg Festival

1819: August von Kotzebue murdered

1820: Carlsbad Decrees

1832: Hambach Festival

1834: German Customs Union founded

1845–52: Irish Famine

1848: Revolutions of 1848

HISTORICAL TERMS

Carlsbad Decrees
German Confederation
German Customs Union
Holy Roman Empire
Ottoman Empire
absolute monarchy
citizen/subject
constitution
constitutional monarchy
republic
laissez-faire
liberalism
nationalism
migration
emigration / immigration

PERSONS

Napoleon

Klemens von Metternich

August von Kotzebue

Carl Ludwig Sand

Friedrich List

Frederick William IV

Robert Blum

Carl Schurz

HISTORY WORKSHOP

Analysing Cartoons

M 1 Proclamation of German Empire in Versailles, 18 January 1871. Painting by Anton von Werner, 1885

M 2 A working-class family in its living room-kitchen-bedroom. Photograph, 1907

M 3 Middle-class children doing their homework. Photograph, 1899

06 IMPERIAL GERMANY

The German Empire: A New Nation in Europe

From the middle of the nineteenth century the German states underwent great changes. A new German state, the German Empire, was founded under the leadership of Prussia and without Austria. The new Germany meant that European diplomacy had to be thought through once more. The old balance of power on the continent had to be reorganized. New rivalries and anger affected the way the Great Powers dealt with each other. The relationship between Germany and France was especially difficult.

Of course, life in the new German Empire had to change, too. New political structures took the place of older ones. At the same time capitalism and industrialization transformed society and the economy. Germany had a talented Chancellor, Otto von Bismarck, who served for a generation until he was dismissed in 1890. Bismarck's success often depended on his ability to influence others – either members of parliament and/or the Prussian king and German emperor. In a constitutional system, this informal way of running the government led to problems.

This chapter presents the basic problems the new German Empire had to deal with and shows how the country tried to find a secure place in Europe and the world up to 1890.

This chapter deals with many questions such as:

- How did Prussia become the leading power in the German states?
- How did two wars – between Denmark and then Austria – begin and end?
- How did the Franco-Prussian War lead to the founding of the German Empire?
- How did the German Constitution of 1871 organize the separate German states into one empire?
- How did discrimination against Catholics and Social Democrats set off political problems?
- How were ethnic minorities (Danes, Poles, and Jews) treated in the Empire?
- How did women organize to fight for their civil rights?
- How did Bismarck, the German Chancellor, organize a complex alliance system?
- How do we interpret historical monuments (in the workshop)?

M 1 **William I (1861–1888)**
Photograph

M 2 **Bismarck (1815–1898)**
Photograph, 1862

Change in Prussia Leads to Change in Germany

After the Revolution of 1848 failed, Germany had to be re-organized. The German Confederation was renewed, but it clearly needed reform. Two major powers competed with each other in the confederation: Prussia and Austria. Which would lead in the new situation?

Prussia: Military reform leads to constitutional crisis

In 1858 King Frederick William IV of Prussia became ill and was removed from office. His brother took over and became King William I in 1861. At first, many hoped that William would be more flexible than his brother – because of these hopes this period is called the "New Era". William swore his loyalty to the constitution (although Frederick William warned him not to do this) and even appointed several liberal ministers to his cabinet. But William was trained from his youth as a military officer and he was unpopular from the Berlin uprising in 1848. As he had been willing to shoot at demonstrators, he was called the "machine gun prince". He decided to reform the army when he took charge of the country's affairs.

There were good reasons for reform: the Prussian army was smaller than the French, Austrian or Russian armies. The number of soldiers had stayed the same since 1814 and more than two-thirds of the men *eligible* in Prussia did not serve in the military. This made military service unfair for those who did have to serve.

Prussian Minister of War Albrecht von Roon drew up a plan in 1860 to increase the size of the *standing army* during peacetime, to lengthen military service from two to three years, and to weaken the status of the militia (Landwehr). The liberal majority in the Prussian parliament did not approve of these plans. When William tried to put them into effect *in spite of* parliamentary opposition, the parliament refused to approve the budget. The king was at a loss and even considered abdicating. At this point Roon suggested Otto von Bismarck as the person who could help in the crisis.

Otto von Bismarck Becomes Prussian Minister-President

As the son of a landowning aristocrat, a Junker, Bismarck's conservative thinking was well known. He had served as Prussian *envoy* to the Frankfurt Parliament, as Prussian ambassador in St. Petersburg and in Paris. When he told the king in 1862 that he would support the military reform in spite of parliament's opposition, the king appointed him Prussian Minister-President. Bismarck announced that the Prussian constitution had a "gap" – the constitution did not foresee a conflict between the king and the parliament. In such a situation, according to Bismarck, only the king was responsible and had to make the final decision. Using this excuse, Bismarck led Prussia without parliamentary approval for the following several years.

Vocabulary

eligible: suitable, (here) fit for military service

standing army: army on permanent duty

in spite of: without considering

envoy: diplomat who represents his country, (here) at the Confederation in Frankfurt

Historical Terms

deed of abdication: Abdankungsurkunde

M 3 **Bismarck in the Parliament of the North German Confederation**
Cartoon, Vienna, 1870

M 4 Bismarck's Promise to the King

a) The conversation between William I and Bismarck (22 September 1862):

"Nobody knows exactly what took place at Babelsberg, but Bismarck's own over-colourful *account* is probably near enough to the truth in essence. There on the table lay the **deed of abdication,** ready for the king's signature; there, also, was a long memorandum presented by the king for Bismarck to read and *digest* as they took a walk together in the park: in it the duties and opportunities of a first minister of Prussia were [explained]. The king announced that he saw no way to reign with dignity if he were to be subject to the will of parliament. Bismarck [claimed] that he could manage parliament, that he could form a ministry and put through the army reforms, if necessary *in defiance of* a parliamentary majority. If that was really so, the king replied, then it would indeed be his own duty to fight on. It says everything both for Bismarck's charm and almost hypnotic intensity of will that William, who feared and distrusted him, who knew both from his own experience and the tales told him by Augusta [the king's wife] and his ministerial advisers just how reckless, *insolent*, and at the same time profoundly *devious* [Bismarck] could be, so easily *succumbed*. [...] William did not have to ask how Bismarck proposed to manage his *tour de force*. It was clearly a matter of will-power and drive, and his new champion had both."

Edward Crankshaw, Bismarck, Viking Press: New York 1981, p. 126f.

b) Bismarck to the budget commission of the Prussian Parliament (29 September 1862):

"We [Prussians] are too hot-blooded, we *have a preference* for putting on *armour* that is too big for our small body; and now we're actually supposed *to utilize* it. Germany is not looking to Prussia's liberalism, but to its power; Bavaria, Württemberg, Baden may *indulge* liberalism, and for that reason no one will assign them Prussia's role; Prussia has *to coalesce* and concentrate its power for the opportune moment, which has already been missed several times; Prussia's borders according to the Vienna Treaties [of 1815] are not favorable for a healthy, *vital* state; it is not by speeches and majority *resolutions* that the great questions of the time are decided – that was the big mistake of 1848 and 1849 – but by iron and blood."

Quoted from: Otto von Bismarck, Die gesammelten Werke Bd. 10: Reden 1847–1869, bearb. v. Wilhelm Schüssler, Verlag f. Politik u. Wirtschaft: Berlin 1928, p. 139f. (transl. by Jeremiah Riemer for German History in Documents and Images [http://germanhistorydocs.ghi-dc.org], which is published by the German Historical Institute, Washington, DC.).

Vocabulary

account: version
to digest: to absorb, to take sth. in
in defiance of: against
insolent: disrespectful
devious: dishonest
to succumb: to give in, to surrender
tour de force (Fr.): masterpiece, triumph
to have a preference: to like sth., to prefer
armour: covering (usually metal) to protect the body from weapons
to utilize: to use
to indulge: to enjoy, to give in to
to coalesce: to unite
vital: living
resolutions: parliamentary decisions

Tasks

1. **The Prussian Constitutional Crisis**
   a) List the military reforms planned by Minister of War Albrecht von Roon (text).
   b) Discuss why William I thought the reforms were important (text).
   c) Give reasons why the Prussian parliament did not approve of the plans (text).
   d) Interpret the king's unwillingness to govern together with parliament (text).
2. **Otto von Bismarck**
   a) Make a mind map showing why the king's appointment of Bismarck as Prussian Minister-President was controversial (text, M4).
   b) Bismarck writes about his meeting with the king on 22 September 1862 in his memoirs. Discuss in class how reliable such evidence is.
   c) Look at Crankshaw's text (M4a) and list the strengths and weaknesses of the king.
   d) Now list the strengths and weaknesses of Bismarck (M4a).
   e) Analyse Bismarck's view of the role of Prussia (M4b).
   f) Assess his opinion of the Revolution of 1848 (M4b).
3. **The political cartoon**
   a) Describe the cartoon (M3).
   b) Interpret the symbols used and the body language of the human figures.
   c) Assess the Viennese opinion of Bismarck shown in the cartoon.

M 1 **"Germany's Future"**
"Will Germany fit under one hat? I think it's going to fit under a spiked helmet." Cartoon, Vienna, 1870

The Road to German Unity

Germany was finally unified in three wars: the German-Danish War in 1864, the Austro-Prussian War in 1866, the Franco-Prussian War in 1870–71. Bismarck saw to it that none of the wars involved a conflict with more than one Great Power at a time.

The Wars with Denmark (1864) and Austria (1866)

In 1863 the new Danish king and parliament changed their constitution to include the duchy of Schleswig, which had a majority of *ethnic* Danes. This violated the London Protocol of 1852 which guaranteed that the duchies of Schleswig and Holstein (which had a majority of ethnic Germans) would stay together.

Other European powers stayed out of the conflict: Russia had to deal with the Polish uprising of 1863, and Britain had guaranteed the London Protocol. Bismarck convinced Austria to support Prussia in the German Confederation. Austrian and Prussian troops defeated Denmark and forced her to give up the duchies. In the peace treaty of Gastein (1865), both allies agreed that Austria would administer Holstein and Prussia Schleswig.

The administration of the duchies led to disagreement. Austria turned to the German Confederation to ask for help in solving the disagreement, which Prussia saw as a violation of the Treaty of Gastein. Prussia then invaded Holstein (15 June 1866) and demanded that Austria leave the German Confederation. The alliance of Austria, Hanover, Electoral Hesse and the southern German states then declared war. Prussia won the decisive battle at Königgrätz, or Sadova, on 3 July 1866; on 23 August the war ended with the Treaty of Prague. The modern Prussian military beat the traditional Austrian army quickly.

Historical Terms

reparations: Reparationen, Kriegsentschädigungen

Realpolitik: Realpolitik

Promises Kept and Broken

Before the war Bismarck seemed to promise Napoleon III payment for France to stay neutral. In April 1866 Bismarck made a deal to give Italy Venetia if she attacked Austria during the war. When the Prussian king William I wanted to hold a victory parade in Vienna, Bismarck insisted that Austria should not *be humiliated*. Prussia also did not demand **reparations**. Austria lost little territory, but Venetia returned to Italy as promised. Bismarck refused to pay France for her neutrality. He claimed that Napoleon III had misunderstood him and besides, the war was over before France could take part in it. Bismarck's policies were called **Realpolitik**.

Vocabulary

ethnic: having a common cultural background (customs, language, history, etc.)

to be humiliated: losing pride, seeming foolish

to annex: to add a territory to another state

to consolidate: to combine, to unify

Prussian Influence Grows and the Constitutional Crisis is Resolved

According to the Treaty of Prague (1866) Prussia *annexed* Schleswig and Holstein, as well as Hanover and Electoral Hesse which were on Austria's side. A new North German Confederation of twenty-two German states north of the Main River and led by Prussia ended the old German Confederation. The German states south of the Main signed a secret defensive alliance with Prussia in case of attack. In fact, Germany was divided into three parts: Prussia with the North German Confederation, the southern German states, and Austria. With no role in Germany any longer, Austria turned to *consolidating* the new Austro-Hungarian Empire and her diplomatic interests in the Balkans and southeast Europe. Public opinion in Prussia changed completely – nationalists and liberals actively supported the military budget. The Prussian parliament even approved Bismarck's actions during the constitutional crisis after the fact.

The Wars of Unification – analysing a historical painting

M 2 **"William I in the Battle of Königgrätz" 1866**

Painting by Christian Sell, 1866.

Nearly 500,000 soldiers fought in the battle. More than 5,700 Austrians were killed. There were also about 7,800 missing, 8,500 wounded, and 9,300 were taken prisoner. The Prussian losses were smaller: About 9,200 were killed and 7,200 were wounded.

Tasks

1. **The War with Denmark**
   a) Explain how an ethnic conflict between Danes and Germans led to the war (text).
   b) Assess Bismarck's diplomacy before the war with Denmark began (text).
   c) Explain the advantages and disadvantages of the Treaty of Gastein to Austria and to Prussia (text).
2. **The War with Austria**
   a) Make a list of the conflicts between Austria and Prussia before the war broke out in 1866 (text).
   b) Explain Bismarck's pre-war diplomacy (text).
   c) Analyse the reasons for Prussian success in 1866 (text).
   d) Make a table of what Austria lost and Prussia gained after the war (text).
   e) Interpret Bismarck's unwillingness to humiliate Austria in 1866 (text).
   f) Interpret the cartoon (M1).
3. **The painting "William I in the Battle of Königgrätz"**
   a) Describe the painting briefly (M2).
   b) How does the artist show the facts of the battle (M2)?
   c) Point out what the artist thinks is important to show about the battle (M2).
   d) Discuss how accurately the painting deals with historical facts of the battle (M2).
4. **Prussian Constitutional Crisis**
   a) Show what effect the two wars had on the Prussian constitutional crisis (text).
   b) Interpret the consequences of the resolution of the conflict (text).

M 1 **"Prussia Chains Alsace to Himself"**
French caricature by Cham, 1871

Vocabulary

candidacy: being a choice for an office

on a spa: at a health resort with a mineral spring

dispatch: message, official letter

to mobilize: (here) to assemble troops at the start of a military action

capture: taking sb. prisoner

utterly (in M3): (adv.) completely

ardently (in M3): (adv.) intensely

Historical Terms

ambassador: Botschafter

to ascend a throne: einen Thron besteigen

guerrilla (Sp.): Guerrilla, Untergrundkampf

The Franco-Prussian War 1870–1871

The Hohenzollern *Candidacy*

The Spanish throne was empty in 1868. A Catholic member of the Hohenzollern family, Leopold of Hohenzollern-Sigmaringen, was suggested as a candidate for the Spanish crown. Napoleon III feared France would be surrounded by a Hohenzollern Prussia and Spain. (In the 16th century Habsburg rule in Spain and Austria had endangered France.) Because of the strong opposition from France, Leopold gave up his candidacy. The Prussian king William I, head of the Hohenzollern family, agreed. That could have ended the affair, but Napoleon wanted more. He sent his **ambassador** to Prussia, Count Benedetti, to ask William to promise that no Hohenzollern would ever **ascend the** Spanish **throne**. Benedetti talked to the king on the promenade at Bad Ems, where William was resting *on a spa*. William refused the request in written form and informed Bismarck in Berlin that he could publish "all or part of" the king's reply in the press. Bismarck shortened the telegram so that the king seemed to insult the French ambassador (as well as the French emperor). Bismarck's timing was important, as the *dispatch* was published on 14 July – the French national holiday. Napoleon's hopes for a diplomatic triumph turned into a disaster. On 19 July 1870 France declared war on Prussia.

War and Peace

The southern German states went to war along with Prussia. Napoleon had hoped that they would remain neutral, but he did not know about their secret defensive alliance with Prussia from 1867. A wave of nationalism swept up the northern and southern German states. The Prussian army and its allies *mobilized* faster than the French forces. The decisive battle was won by the German forces on 2 September 1870 at Sedan, where Napoleon himself and 100,000 French soldiers were taken prisoner. But Napoleon's *capture* led to revolution in Paris – an unforeseen development.

Moderate French republicans proclaimed the Third Republic (4 September 1870) and organized resistance to the Germans. Suddenly, the war became a national struggle. That meant great difficulties for the German troops, who now faced **guerrillas**. The French National Assembly in Bordeaux did not accept defeat in a preliminary peace treaty in Versailles until 21 February 1871. The surprisingly long conflict and the Treaty of Frankfurt which ended it led to bitterness and frustration. France had to let Germany annex the provinces of Alsace and Lorraine, to pay reparations of 5 billion francs, and to accept the German occupation of eastern France until the sum was finally paid.

The German Empire

Before the war was over, the new German Empire was proclaimed in the Hall of Mirrors at Versailles on 18 January 1871 – a further humiliation for the French government and people. For Germany a new era, called the "Gründerzeit", began with the founding of the empire.

M 2

M 3 Opinions about the New Germany

a) Comment of The Times on the new German Empire (20 January 1871):

"Within living memory German nationality was *utterly* dead, and up to 1866 the country was linked with foreign and hostile communities. In 1871 Germany starts independent, *ardently* patriotic, almost purely national. She is about to have the most powerful instrument of unity, a great popular Assembly, an institution which seems in these days to have a more strongly centralizing influence than any despot can command."

Quoted from: Michael Gorman, The Unification of Germany, Cambridge University Press: Cambridge 1989, p. 98.

b) Benjamin Disraeli (British opposition leader) in the House of Commons (9 February 1871):

"This [Franco-Prussian] war represents the German Revolution, a greater political event than the French Revolution of the last century [...]. Not a single principle in the management of our foreign affairs [...] any longer exists. There is not a diplomatic tradition which has not been swept away [...]. The balance of power has been entirely destroyed, and the country which suffers most, and feels the effects of this great change most, is England."

Hansard, Parliamentary Debates, Series 3, Vol. 204, London 1871, Col. 81–82. www.hansard-archive.parliament.uk [Oct. 2017].

Tasks

1. The War with France
   a) Describe the problem of the candidacy for Spain and France (text).
   b) Assess Bismarck's decision to publish part of the king's telegram (text).
   c) List the reasons for the German victory over France (text).
   d) Assess the consequences of the Franco-Prussian War on German-French relations later.

2. Opinions about the New Germany
   a) Work as partners. One of you sums up text M3a, the other text M3b.
   b) Compare your summary with your partner's.
   c) Interpret the British opinions on the new Germany.

M 1 **The new German Flag**
With the colours of Prussia (white and black) and the former Imperial cities (red)

M 2 **The Imperial War Flag**
The Imperial eagle with Prussian shield and crown of the Holy Roman Empire was the official symbol of the German Empire.

Vocabulary

to dissolve: to dismiss a parliamentary body

to initiate: to begin the process of passing laws

Historical Terms

suffrage: Wahlrecht

Prussian Chamber of Deputies: Preussisches Abgeordnetenhaus

Federal Council: Bundesrat

M 3 **The Victory Column**
Erected in Berlin on 2 September 1873 to commemorate the wars of 1864, 1866 and 1870–71.

Politics in the New Germany

Germany After 1871: Authoritarian or democratic state?

The new German constitution was based on the Constitution of the North German Confederation of 1867. It included a mixture of authoritarian and parliamentary features.

The German Empire unified twenty-five separate countries. Their rights and privileges were guaranteed by the Federal Council, the assembly of the individual states. Without the council's approval, no law could be passed.

Prussia, with two-thirds of the population and territory of the new Germany, played a hegemonial role. But Prussia had only seventeen out of fifty-eight seats – not a majority – in the Federal Council. However, one-fourth of the seats in the council (fourteen votes) were enough to stop a law from passing. Prussia's special role was clear in other ways: the Prussian King was automatically German Emperor, the Prussian Minister-President was automatically Chancellor.

Problems with the Parliaments

The Reichstag was the popular assembly. Its members were elected by equal, direct, and secret ballot. All men over the age of twenty-five could vote (universal male **suffrage**). The candidate who received a majority of votes in his district was elected. Members of the Reichstag received no payment for their parliamentary duties, so they had to earn an income by other means. The Reichstag had no influence on the government, as the chancellor was appointed by the emperor and was only responsible to him. The chancellor appointed the state secretaries, the officials who were in charge of the administration. The emperor could *dissolve* the Reichstag and call for new elections. However, the Reichstag had the right *to initiate* new laws, to ask questions and demand answers from the government. In order to pass a law, including the budget, the Reichstag had to approve of it. The chancellor had to find a majority in every Reichstag that was elected so that laws could be passed.

In Prussia (as in many of the separate states) the three-class electoral system for the **Prussian Chamber of Deputies** was indirect, unequal, and oral. Not surprisingly, this system led to more conservative results than the electoral system for the Reichstag. With time this structural problem – the differences in parliamentary majorities in the Reichstag and the Prussian Chamber of Deputies – made finding coalitions in both parliaments a problem. As long as Bismarck stayed in office he tried to manipulate the assemblies according to his needs. But over the years this became more difficult.

In 1871 it was unclear which of the constitutional organs would be most powerful – the emperor and his government, the **Federal Council**, or the Reichstag. The constitution seemed to favour the Federal Council and through it the rulers of the twenty-five separate states. In later years the role of the Reichstag increased as the press reported and discussed its debates. Public opinion could even put pressure on the emperor – a fact which William II discovered rather late.

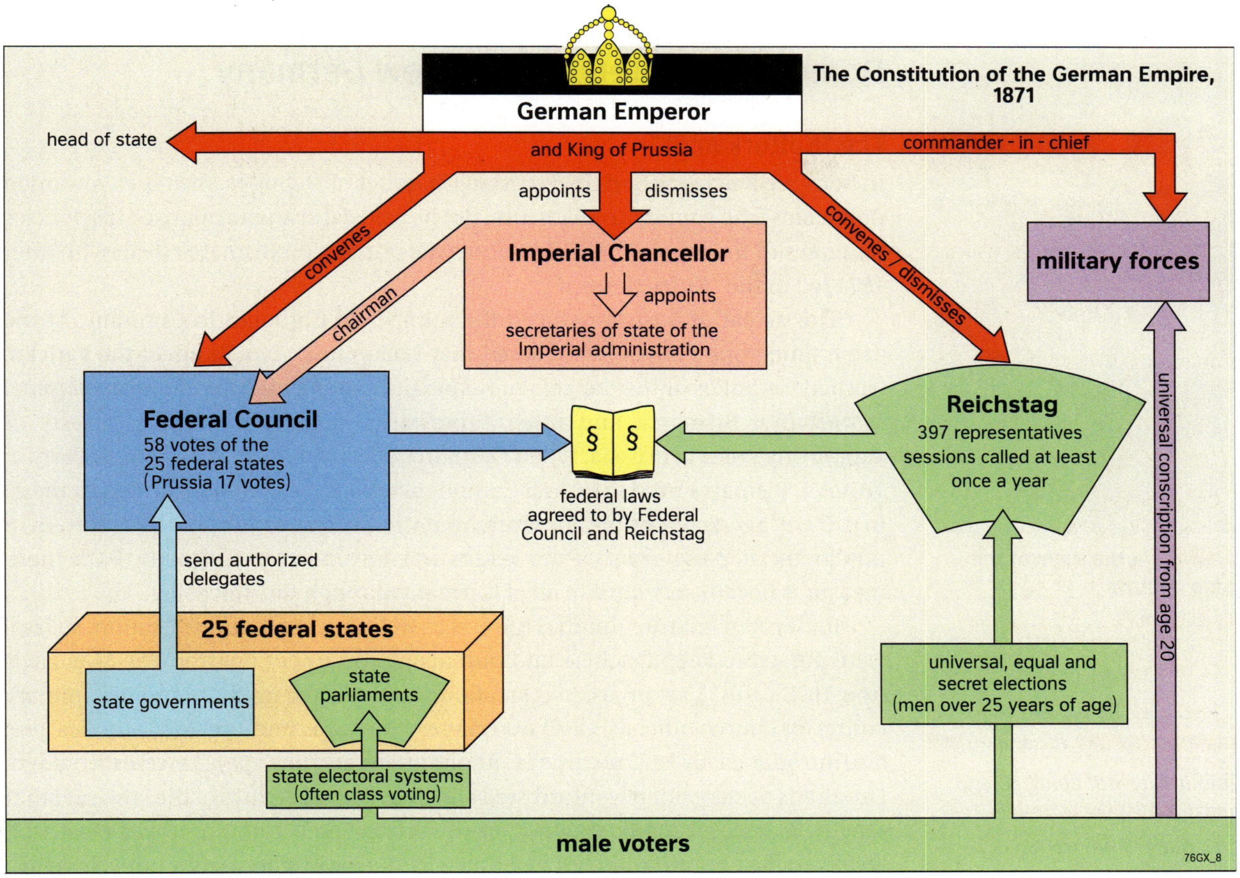

M 4 **The Constitution of the German Empire**

M 5 "So-called Freedom"

Jacob Burckhardt, Swiss historian, in a letter to a friend, on the lack of real freedom in Germany (1872):

"Our Berlin *masters* are, I believe, full of anxiety, not *on account of* foreign countries but on account of their basically false position *in face of* the nation. The *external apparatus* of so-called freedom has been allowed to come into existence, but they are secretly *resolved* to act for all time according to their own will."

Quoted from: Helmut Böhme (ed.), The foundation of the German Empire. Select documents, translated from German by Agatha Ramm, Oxford University Press: Oxford 1971, p. 35–39.

Vocabulary

masters: leaders (ironical)
on account of: because of
in face of: regarding
external apparatus: outside machinery
resolved: determined, firmly decided

Tasks

1. **The Victory Column**
   a) Describe the statue briefly (M2).
   b) Explain the symbols used.
   c) Ask someone in your class who has visited the Victory Column in Berlin about his or her impression of it.
2. **The German Constitution of 1871**
   a) Look at the diagram (M4).
   b) Make a list of features which are authoritarian and which are democratic.
   c) Assess which of the constitutional organs seems most powerful. Explain your thinking.
   d) Critics of the constitution called it "only a constitution in form, not in substance". Give reasons for such an opinion.
3. **Jacob Burckhardt's Comment**
   a) Sum up Burckhardt's opinion (M5).
   b) Do you agree or disagree with his opinion? State your reasons.

M 1 **At the Helm of the Ship of State**

Cartoon, 1879

Domestic Problems in the New Germany

The "Kulturkampf"

In both the Reichstag and the Prussian Chamber of Deputies, Bismarck rewarded politicians who cooperated with him. But he called those who opposed his policies "enemies of the empire." The first domestic opposition Bismarck dealt with after 1871 led to the "**Kulturkampf**".

The defeat of Austria reduced the number of Catholics in Germany. At the same time Pope Pius IX, who feared that Italian unity would affect the Vatican, warned Catholics of the dangers of nationalism and stated the doctrine of papal *infallibility*. Bismarck and other Protestants suspected Catholic priests of supporting Poles in Prussia. When German Catholics founded the Centre Party in 1870-71, Bismarck tried to restrict Catholic activities by passing laws against them. In 1871 it became a crime for churchmen to comment on political matters in public. In 1872 the order of the Jesuits was forbidden in Germany. Both these measures became effective in all of Germany through the Reichstag.

In German "culture" implies the arts as well as schools and education, so laws were passed to keep teachers and public opinion under control. The May Laws from1873 to 1875 set Prussian education standards for teachers and disciplinary courts for church officials. **Civil marriage**, which was immoral for Catholics, was also introduced. By 1875 nearly all Catholic orders and newspapers were forbidden. Hundreds of clergymen were arrested and imprisoned. Critics of the laws said that they *violated* civil rights. As the Centre Party gained strength, it was clear that loyalty to the church could not be broken by the laws. When a new pope, Leo XIII, was elected, Bismarck found a compromise with the church and ended the dispute in 1878. But the integration of Catholics in the new empire was slow.

Vocabulary

infallibility: not being able to make a mistake in beliefs

to violate: to injure

assassination: murder, killing

Historical Terms

Kulturkampf: Kulturkampf (English uses the same word)

civil marriage: Zivilehe

Socialist Law: Sozialistengesetz

The Socialist Law

Bismarck used two *assassination* attempts on William I in 1878 as an excuse to fight another "enemy of the empire" – the Social Democrats. The Reichstag was disbanded, new elections were held and the **Socialist Law** forbidding the Social Democratic Party organization, treasury, meetings, and publishing house was passed. Candidates could still stand for election, so the Reichstag became the centre of public Social Democratic activities from 1878 until 1890.

The measures against the party failed, just as those against Catholics during the Kulturkampf did. By 1890 the party won three times more votes than in 1878. Disagreement with the new emperor William II about renewing the law led to Bismarck's dismissal in 1890.

M 2 **"Between Berlin and Rome"**

Cartoon from "Kladderadatsch", 1875.

"The last move was unpleasant for me, but the match is still not lost. I have another good move in reserve." "That will be your last, and you will soon be checkmated – at least in Germany."

M 3 The Socialist Jack-in-the-box

Cartoon from "Punch", 28 September 1878

M 4 Socialist Law

American Historian Vernon L. Lidtke on Bismarck's reasons for the Socialist Law (1966):

[T]here were four fundamental reasons for [Bismarck's] desire to crush the Social Democrats: in constitutional-political outlook, they were republicans, and therefore a threat to the monarchy; in foreign affairs, they were internationalists, which implied to Bismarck that they would be the friends of Germany's enemies; in domestic affairs, they sought a fundamental transformation of the existing social and economic order, opposed to the Junker foundation of the society; and, in religious matters, they were atheists, and thus undermined the religious and moral norms of Christian society.

For Bismarck's part, the political goals were the most dangerous aspect of the Social Democratic program, not the attack on the principles of capitalism or economic liberalism. The tactics of the Chancellor in the 1880's show that he assumed that he could suppress the political danger of Social Democracy without at the same time denying that the workers had legitimate complaints against the existing economic structure. [...] In true Junker fashion, Bismarck chose *to apply the whip before offering the carrot.* But, because the whip was so *indiscriminately* applied against almost all workers' organizations, Bismarck's distinction between the political and economic goals was *blurred*, and the carrot could not achieve the purposes for which it was intended.

Vernon L. Lidtke, The Outlawed Party: Social Democracy in Germany 1878–1890, Princeton University Press: Princeton 1966, p. 71.

Vocabulary

to apply the whip before offering the carrot: to punish first and then reward sb. [Zuckerbrot und Peitsche]
indiscriminately: without any purpose, randomly
to blur: to make sth. unclear

Tasks

1. **The "Kulturkampf"**
   a) Describe the cartoon "At the Helm of the Ship of State" (M1).
   b) Point out symbols and terms which the artist uses.
   c) Assess the artist's opinion of Bismarck's leadership.
   d) Describe the cartoon "Between Berlin and Rome" (M2).
   e) Point out symbols and terms which the artist uses.
   f) Interpret the cartoon (M2).
   g) Discuss which cartoon (M1 or M2) is more optimistic about Bismarck's ability to keep his political opponents under control.
   h) Explain Bismarck's motives for opposing Catholics in Germany (text).
   i) Give reasons for Bismarck's change in policy by the end of the 1870s (text).
2. **The Socialist Law**
   a) Explain why Bismarck regarded the Social Democrats as "enemies of the empire" (text, M4).
   b) Assess the long-term effect of the German government's opposition to Catholics and to Social Democrats.
3. **"Socialist Jack-in-the-Box"**
   a) Describe the caricature briefly (M3).
   b) Point out symbols, terms, and figures used.
   c) Interpret the caricature.

Historical Terms

anti-Semitism: Antisemitismus

stock market crash: Börsenkrach

reserve officer: Reserveoffizier

Social Structure in the New Germany

Ethnic Minorities

Two and one-half million Poles made up the largest ethnic minority in the new empire. From 1871 on Poles were to be "*Germanized*" to keep them from leaving Germany or founding a separate Polish state. Different laws were passed to make certain that German was the only language used in schools and in public places. Also, laws passed during the "Kulturkampf" discriminated against Catholics – the largest religious group in Poland. The measures *backfired* and strengthened Polish nationalism instead of weakening it.

The Danish population of North Schleswig faced similar treatment. However, opponents of "Germanization", including young men who wanted to avoid Prussian military service, simply emigrated to nearby Denmark.

In Alsace-Lorraine the integration of the French also caused problems. German officials in the annexed territory distrusted the local people. Thus, many members of ethnic minorities felt like only second-class citizens in Germany.

Anti-Semitism in Germany

Beginning in the early 19th century, the different German states began to accept Jews as citizens. By 1871 Jews in Germany had full civil rights. But they still had to deal with social and professional discrimination. They were often denied work in public service or membership in social clubs. In time many became well educated and moved up in society. Then others *envied* them for their professional and social success.

When the new German Empire was founded, a new wave of **anti-Semitism** began. After the **stock market crash** of 1873 many tried to make Jews *scapegoats*

M 1 "Jews are not tolerated here!"
An anti-Semitic postcard from the island Borkum, 1901

for the rapid changes of modern life in an industrial society. This new form of prejudice against Jews did not rely on the religious intolerance of earlier anti-Semitism. Instead, this "modern" form took a racist viewpoint. It argued that Jews were racial outsiders who could not be ethnic Germans.

Adolf Stoecker, pastor at the court in Berlin, warned in 1879 that Jews would always be foreign to Germany and would ruin the country. The historian Heinrich von Treitschke, whose phrase "the Jews are our misfortune" became a slogan of the movement, made anti-Semitism acceptable in the middle class, especially among students at German universities.

By the end of the 1870s different political parties and organizations adopted anti-Semitic programmes. They demanded that Jews should not have the same civil rights as Germans, that immigration of Jews from Eastern Europe should be forbidden, and that Jews should not be allowed to take up certain professions. Politically, these parties were not successful and they were not important by the end of the 1890s. But they kept the idea of a "Jewish question" alive in popular opinion. Although Jewish civil rights in the German Empire were never in danger, Jews were discriminated against in many ways. The situation in the military was especially harsh. In the Prussian army not a single officer was Jewish – Jews were not allowed to become **reserve officers** from the 1880s on.

Vocabulary

to „Germanize": to make sb. more German

to backfire: to have the opposite effect

to envy: to be jealous of sb., to hate sb. or sth.

scapegoat: a person who is blamed unjustly

meticulousness: paying attention to details

punctuality: always being on time

incorruptibility: never doing sth. illegal or immoral

diligence: working hard

to take a toll: to pay a high price

monotonous: one-sided, boring

Social Differences in the New Germany

In Germany industrialization weakened the aristocracy, which earned its living from its large farms. Although this group lost its economic power, it kept a prominent role in society, mainly through contacts to Imperial court circles. But the middle class formed the economic backbone of German society.

The middle class was made up of different groups. Wealthy businessmen, bankers and industrialists – the upper middle class – were the most prominent. Few of the very wealthy accepted noble titles – most were confident enough of their own achievements. Well-educated professionals, such as doctors, lawyers, upper secondary teachers and professors had to pay for expensive homes, clothing, and children's educations to stay prominent. These families might also marry their children into aristocratic families. Their sons often became reserve officers (which only aristocrats had been before the 19th century) by volunteering for one year and passing the examinations.

A reserve officer could wear an officer's uniform in public, serve in military campaigns, and had to follow a military code of behaviour. "The officers are the highest social class", reported a Norwegian observer in 1907. It wasn't a surprising development. Three wars had unified the country and the military guaranteed Germany's well-being. Men in uniform were often seen in the streets, medals were desirable decorations, and the military was admired in all of Germany. Military discipline was a model for civilian life.

The largest group within the middle class – artisans, shop owners, small businessmen, lower civil servants, employees in business, in trade and industry – was the lower middle class. This group showed pride in a legendary work ethic of *meticulousness*, *punctuality*, loyalty, *incorruptibility* and *diligence*.

The lower class was made up of unskilled workers who had left farming jobs to find work in industry. The hard work *took its toll* – by the age of fifty, workers faced unemployment, poverty and social decline. With daily lives characterized as *monotonous*, hopeless and empty, this group often felt like third-class citizens in Germany.

M 2 The Authoritarian State

An East-Elbian Junker speaks to his villagers after the election: „A liberal vote was counted. From today on the local teacher doesn't get any more potatoes." Contemporary cartoon by Eduard Thöny (1866–1950)

Social Structure in the New Germany

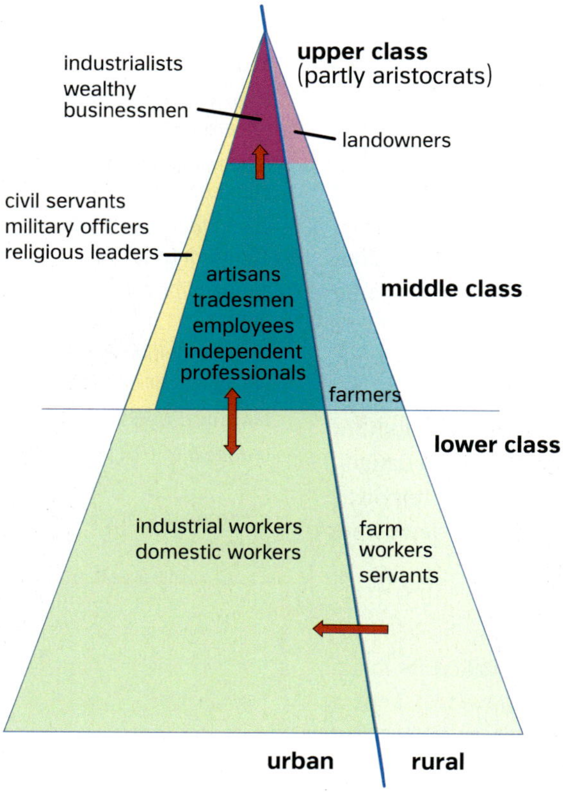

Source: Gerhard A. Ritter, Klaus Teufelde, Arbeiter im deutschen Keiserreich 1871 bis 1914, Bonn 1992, S. 130.

1376GX_1

M 3 **Social Structure in the New Germany**, diagram

M 4 **Ferdinand Baron von Stumm. Member of the Reichstag for the Free Conservative Party.** Painting, 1888

M 5 **Technical Employee in an Office for the Development of "Cooling Machines".** Photograph, Augsburg, about 1900

M 6 **August Bebel and Family. The member of the Reichstag and later leader of the German Social Democratic Party with his family.** Photograph, about 1884

M 7 **Locomotive and Carriage Wheel Factory in the Friedrich Krupp Steel Factory in Essen.** Photograph, about 1900

Cartoons Dealing with the Military in German Society

M 8 "Standing at Attention"

"...and then you must remember that you come here as civilians and leave as human beings."

Cartoon by Olaf Gulbransson, in "Simplicissimus", 1910

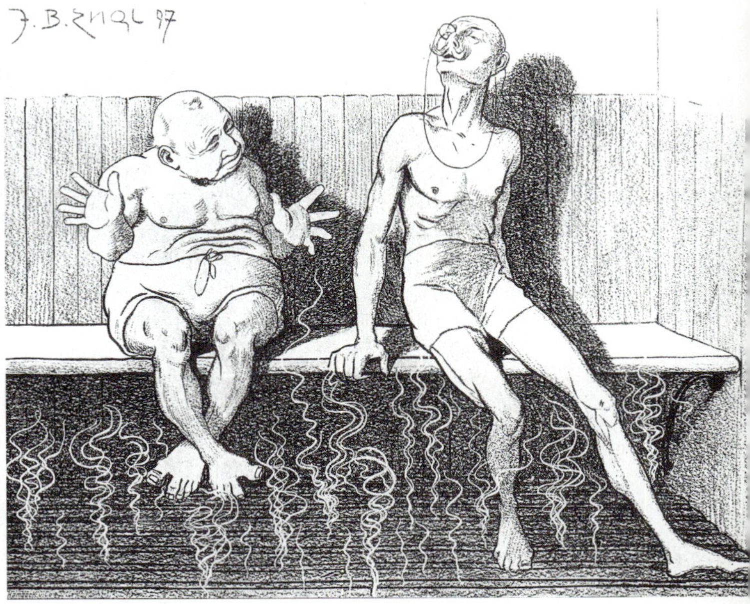

M 9 "In the Sauna"

"You, lieutenant, wear your monocle in the sauna?"

"Eh, otherwise I worry about being taken for a civilian."

Cartoon in "Simplicissimus", 1897

Tasks

1. Anti-Semitism

a) Point out the differences between religious and racial anti-Semitism (text).

b) Make a list of how Jews were discriminated against (text).

c) Show the difference between political and social discrimination (text).

d) Walther Rathenau, then chief executive of AEG and later Foreign Minister in Germany, said in 1911 that every German Jew could always remember a painful moment in his youth when he first realized that he was born into this world as a second-class citizen and nothing he could do would free him from it. Discuss how society can find solutions to this problem today.

2. Social Differences in the New Germany

a) Analyse the diagram (M3).

b) Look at the pictures in M5– M8.

c) Decide which social classes are shown in the pictures.

3. Militarism in German Society

a) Show why the military played such an important role in German society (text).

b) Explain the role of reserve officers in civilian society (text).

c) Describe the cartoons briefly (M8, M9).

d) Explain the symbols and the people portrayed.

e) Interpret the artists' intentions.

4. The Authoritarian State

a) Describe the picture briefly (M2).

b) Explain the symbols and the people portrayed.

c) Interpret the artist's intention.

M 1 **Helene Lange (1848–1930)**
Photograph

M 2 **Clara Zetkin (1857–1933)**
Photograph

Liberty – For Women, Too?

Women fought on the barricades and died during street battles in 1848, they took part in the meetings to demand reforms from German rulers. But when the German National Assembly was elected, no woman could vote or stand for election. Most people could not imagine German women taking part in political affairs – they were limited to family life. Nevertheless, some women insisted on their right to be included in political life.

Class Differences Among Women

German women had no political rights in the 19th century. They could not even belong to political clubs or organizations legally until 1908. Working-class women had to earn money because working men's wages did not support a family. They worked as servants, *nursemaids*, cleaning women, *laundresses*, factory workers, and in cottage industry.

It was socially unacceptable for middle-class women to earn money. They depended on their families to survive. Most moved from their fathers' authority to their husbands' when they married. "*Old maids*" or widows could not support themselves because they did not have the proper training. Women's education was poor: girls attended schools with lower standards than boys' schools, they could not get proper school-leaving certificates or study at a university. The only acceptable work for an unmarried middle-class woman was as a *governess, social companion*, or teacher.

These class differences led women to seek their rights differently. Middle-class women tried to improve their situation through education and better job opportunities. Louise Otto, for example, helped to found the General German Women's Organization in 1865 to support such goals. Helene Lange (1848–1930) demanded good schools for women and, in 1905, "equal pay for equal work". The writer Hedwig Dohm (1831–1919) insisted on the right to vote, saying in 1876, "Classes which do not have voting rights are in the power of those which do." Her arguments went too far for most men and women. Some felt that the time had not yet come for women to vote, others thought that women's rights were of minor importance in the new Germany.

Some Social Democrats Take the Lead

Some but not all Social Democrats agreed that women should be able to vote. Clara Zetkin (1857–1933), publisher of the magazine "Equality", considered women's voting rights necessary to free the entire working class. August Bebel and Wilhelm Liebknecht supported this goal as early as 1875, claiming, "A party which writes equality on its banner insults itself by refusing political rights to half of humanity." Still, the SPD did not include women's voting rights in its party program until 1891.

Slow Progress for Women's Rights

Many in the 19th century believed that the right to vote should only be given to citizens who had proved – by the property they owned or the taxes they paid – that they had earned it. When voting rights were extended to men who did not own property or pay taxes in the 1871 constitution, those men who felt they had earned their right to vote even tried to abolish universal male suffrage. When some men could deny other men the right to vote, it was *ridiculous* to consider it for women. The importance of the military in German life also worked against women's right to vote. All men had to serve in the German military, women did not. The argument that military service and voting rights were connected was repeated throughout the 19th century. Politics was for men alone.

Women's rights made only slow progress. In 1892 girls were allowed to finish upper-level school examinations at boys' schools in Prussia. By 1900 women were allowed to listen to lectures in Prussian universities, if university *trustees* and professors agreed. Women were not permitted to take state examinations. In 1908 they could become members of political clubs and organizations, but they could not vote or stand for election. Women's right to vote was granted in 1918 after the fall of Imperial Germany only because the SPD, then the largest political party in the Reichstag, had supported it.

Vocabulary

nursemaid: woman hired to care for children in a household

laundress: woman who does the washing and ironing in a household

old maids: women who did not marry (alte Jungfer)

governess: woman employed in a private home to train and teach children

social companion: person employed to live or travel with sb.

ridiculous: laughable, silly

trustee: supervisor

M 3 "On the Women's Movement: Women's Dreams of Marriage in the Future"

Cartoon, ca. 1908

Liberty for Women, Too? – Louise Otto

M 4 "I am not a ... liberated woman"

Louise Otto explained her principles in the first edition of her newspaper (1849):

"In the *midst* of the great *upheavals* in which we all find ourselves, women will be forgotten if they forget to think of themselves!

Join with me, my sisters, so that we are not left behind, as everything around us is moving forward. We want to demand and earn our *share* in saving the world that will at long last come to all of humanity, of which we are one half. [...]

I *invoke* my life, my work as a writer since 1843 – anyone who is familiar with it knows that I am not a so-called 'liberated' woman, someone who has discredited the words 'women's liberation' by making woman into a caricature of man."

Quoted from: Margrit Twellmann, Die Deutsche Frauenbewegung im Spiegel repräsentativer Frauenzeitschriften, Hain: Meisenheim am Glan 1972 (zugl. Diss. Philos. Fak. Univ. Marburg) p. 34f. (transl. by Deanna Nebert).

Vocabulary

midst: middle
upheavals: uprisings
share: part
to invoke: to call on, to refer to

M 5 Louise Otto (1819 – 1895)

When Louise Otto started a newspaper, an 1850 law made it illegal for women to publish newspapers ("Lex Otto"). Drawing

Tasks

1. **Class Differences Among Women**
   a) Make a list of the different classes of women (text).
   b) Show how these differences made the women have different goals (text).
2. **Women's Right to Vote**
   a) Explain why many people did not think women's right to vote was important in Imperial Germany (text).
   b) Find out more about Louise Otto, Helene Lange, Hedwig Dohm, or Clara Zetkin and report back to your class about her.
3. **Cartoon of "the Women's Movement"**
   Divide your class into five groups. Then let each group deal with one of the five pictures in the cartoon (M3).
   a) Tell (or write) a short story explaining what your picture shows.
   b) Describe the artist's solution to the problem.
   c) Find your group's solution to the problem.
   d) Assess how effective it was to make the goals of the women's movement seem ridiculous.
   e) Compare the cartoon to our present situation and find out if it is still up to date.
4. **Louise Otto's Principles**
   a) Sum up Otto's text briefly (M4).
   b) Identify her goals in 1849.

Suffragettes – looking towards Britain

M 6
Suffragettes' Movement
Demonstration in London, 1910

M 7
Suffragettes' Movement
Cartoon, about 1910

Tasks

1. Suffragettes in Britain

a) Describe the pictures. Point out how the suffragettes' movement is shown.

b) Look up the suffragettes' movement and find out when women in Britain got the right to vote.

Vocabulary

to saturate: to fill to the maximum capacity

nightmare: bad dream

to mediate: to help others solve a problem

reinsurance: buying insurance for an already made insurance policy

status quo: things as they are at the moment

foresight: ability to see sth. clearly before it happens

puppeteer: person who makes a puppet or marionette move

Principles of Bismarck's Alliance System

German unity seemed dangerous at first because it made Europe unstable. France was humiliated by defeat, high reparations and the loss of Alsace-Lorraine. A war of revenge seemed to be the next logical step for France. British diplomacy tried to keep the continent stable so that European wars would not interfere with Britain's colonial affairs. Russia seemed neutral and almost friendly towards Germany. Austria was no longer interested in German affairs and was expected to look for a diplomatic understanding. According to Bismarck, who was German Chancellor and Foreign Secretary, German foreign policy had three principles:

- The German Empire was "*saturated*": Germany after 1871 claimed no territory in Europe or in colonies abroad.
- The German Empire had to keep neighbouring powers from forming alliances against her. Bismarck called such a situation his *nightmare*. France had to be isolated.
- The German Empire had to keep the powers in the centre of Europe calm by directing tensions to the outer edges – the periphery – or to the colonies.

The Alliances (1873–1890)

In 1873 Germany, Austria-Hungary, and Russia agreed in the Three Emperors' League that republicanism and socialism were common enemies and promised to cooperate in future.

In 1877–78 a war between Russia and the Ottoman Empire nearly grew into a larger conflict with Britain and Austria-Hungary. Bismarck *mediated* the dispute as an "**honest broker**" at the Congress of Berlin in 1878. Although a peaceful Balkan solution was found, the Russians were disappointed that Bismarck did not support their goals at the congress. Slav nationalists also criticized Bismarck's role.

In 1879 the Dual Alliance, a defensive alliance between Germany and Austria, was signed for five years. In fact it lasted until 1918. It stated that if Russia attacked either Austria or Germany, the remaining partner would provide military assistance. If France attacked Germany, Austria would remain neutral.

In 1881 Russia returned to an alliance with Germany and Austria (whom she had abandoned after 1878) in the Three Emperors' Alliance. It stated that if Germany, Russia, or Austria were at war with another power, the partners would remain neutral. In addition, the powers agreed to

- keep the Black Sea closed to foreign warships,
- only allow territorial changes in the Balkans if the partners agreed beforehand,
- divide the Balkans into **spheres of influence** with Russia in the east, Austria in the west,
- let Russia make Bulgaria larger and Austria annex Bosnia-Herzegovina.

The alliance was renewed after three years in 1884, but a new dispute over Bulgaria made it inactive by 1885.

In the 1882 Triple Alliance, Germany, Austria, and Italy agreed that if a partner were attacked by two or more powers, the other partners would give assistance. In a war between Austria and Russia, Italy would remain neutral. If France attacked Germany, Italy would give assistance. If Italy were attacked by France, Austria and Germany would assist her.

M 1 **"Au Revoir"**
Cartoon in "Punch", 27 September 1873

In the 1887 secret *Reinsurance* Treaty, Germany and Russia agreed to remain neutral if either were at war with a third power. Neutrality was not promised if Germany attacked France or Russia attacked Austria. The treaty also recognized Russian interests in Bulgaria. The agreement was made for three years, but was not renewed in 1890.

Bismarck also encouraged the Second Mediterranean Agreement in 1887, but Germany did not take part. In it Britain, Austria, and Italy guaranteed the *status quo* in the Mediterranean and Near East. This treaty was really directed against Russia, if she tried to create a crisis in Bulgaria or the rest of the Balkans.

Historical Terms

honest broker:
ehrlicher Makler

sphere of influence:
Interessensphäre

Evaluation of the Alliance System

Through complex treaties and diplomatic agreements, Bismarck consolidated the position of the German Empire in Europe without war for twenty years. But the alliances were sometimes confusing and contradicted each other. After he left office in 1890 future chancellors did not manage German foreign policy as well as Bismarck had. His successors did not have Bismarck's *foresight*. That meant that they did not see when the alliances worked against Germany by forcing her to keep her promises instead of acting on her own interests.

M 2 **"Bismarck, the Pointsman"**
(refers to Bismarck's role at the Congress of Berlin)
Caricature in "Punch", 1878. The trains show the Union Jack of Great Britain and the Double-Eagle of Russia

M 3 **Bismarck, the *Puppeteer*, Pulls the Strings**
(refers to Bismarck dealing with the Three Emperors' Alliance)
Caricature in "Punch", 1884

Assessments of Bismarck's Foreign Policy

M 4 Two Historians

a) Historian Gordon A. Craig (1978):

"Bismarck chose his aides with care and with an eye to their intelligence, their technical skills, and their judgement; he protected their rights against attacks from outsiders. [...] But it was always his policy, and they were always only instruments; and he placed so much emphasis on this that, in the long run, he *stunted* initiative and judgement in his Foreign Service. [...] There is no more *striking* proof of [this...] than the result of the debate over the renewal of the Reinsurance Treaty in 1890, after his fall from office. One might have supposed that [the men of...] his diplomatic corps would have tried to defend the tie with Russia, *upon* which he had always *put* such *store*. They neither did so nor seemed even to appreciate what was at stake. Familiar only with the problems of their own posts, they were incompetent to make judgements about greater issues of policy."

Gordon A. Craig, Oxford History of Modern Europe VII: Germany 1866–1945, Clarendon Press: Oxford 1978, p. 137ff.

b) Historian Koppel Pinson (1966):

"Bismarck's [foreign] policy was limited [...] and *intelligible*, and therefore essentially peaceful in character. After the victory of 1870 Bismarck realized that the new German Reich needed a long era of peace. He therefore was satisfied to contain German energy within the European continent. Even the Balkans were not considered by him to be a direct field of German interest. [...] Bismarck had concrete and *tangible* 'interests'. A policy based only on 'prestige' or 'power' was *denounced* by him in a speech in the Reichstag of February 6, 1888, as completely unrealistic."

Koppel S. Pinson, Modern Germany: Its History and Civilization, Macmillan: New York 1966, p. 295.

Vocabulary

to stunt: to keep sth. from growing
striking: clear
to put store upon: to value sth. highly
intelligible: clear to understand
tangible: clear and definite, real
to denounce: to criticize

Tasks

1. **The Principles of Bismarck's Alliance System**
   a) List the principles of the alliance system (text).
   b) Explain Bismarck's "nightmare" of coalitions.
2. **The Alliances**
   a) Make a table of the different alliances (text).
   b) List what each alliance agreed on.
   c) Point out where some of the alliances might conflict with others.
   d) Analyse the strengths and weaknesses of the alliance system.
3. **"Bismarck, the Pointsman"**
   a) Describe the cartoon briefly (M2).
   b) Discuss the symbols and persons shown.
   c) Interpret the artist's intention.
4. **"Bismarck, the Puppeteer, Pulls the Strings"**
   a) Describe the caricature briefly (M3).
   b) Discuss the symbols and persons shown.
   c) Interpret the artist's intention.
   d) Compare and contrast the two interpretations of Bismarck's diplomacy.
   e) Draw your own conclusion about Bismarck's alliance system.
5. **Assessments of Bismarck's Foreign Policy**
   a) Sum up Gordon A. Craig's opinion (M4a).
   b) Sum up Koppel Pinson's opinion (M4b).
   c) Compare and contrast the two historians' views on Bismarck's achievements in foreign policy.

Analysing Historical Monuments

Monuments are historical evidence we can see every day, but we need to place them into a larger context. Each monument has its own history and shows how people felt about historical events at the time the monument was erected. Perhaps more important for us, the way a monument is respected and cared for shows how people feel about these events today. Try analysing a monument on a field day excursion.

Bismarck Monument in Hamburg

The world's largest Bismarck monument, designed by sculptor Hugo Lederer, stands 34 meters high in Hamburg St. Pauli. It is on a base built by architect Emil Schaudt. The 625-ton granite colossus shows Bismarck as a Roland figure leaning on a sword and looking westward toward the mouth of the Elbe and England, rather than eastward toward Berlin. Hamburg's city fathers wanted a large monument to impress William II. But the emperor disliked Bismarck and Hamburg (Bismarck criticized him after 1890 from nearby Friedrichsruh); also, he disapproved of Social Democratic successes in Hamburg elections.

But William's favourite seaport, Bremen, had erected a monument to his unloved father, Frederick III. Hamburg businessmen hoped that their monument to Bismarck would increase the money from the German Empire spent to improve the seaport and harbour facilities in their city. Private citizens raised 500,000 German marks to pay for the monument. When the dedication ceremony was held in 1906, the emperor did not attend.

M 1 Bismarck Monument in Hamburg St. Pauli

The cost of repairing the monument in 2007 is estimated to be about two million Euros, which makes the city of Hamburg ask whether the monument is worth it. As one reporter wrote, "Hardly a postcard shows it, no city brochures praise it – it stands there, dirty, in a blind corner ... like something set aside."

Historical Workshop

Analysing Historical Monuments

1. Description

a. Assess the importance of the monument's location.
b. Find out what material it is made of and what it represents.
c. Name the figures or objects which are used on the monument and what they symbolize.
d. Note how the figures or objects are portrayed, their size, where they are placed in the monument, their body language, their clothing, objects placed near them, etc.
e. Write down any inscriptions you find on the monument – texts, quotations, names, etc.
f. Describe the impression the monument makes on you.

2. Finding Information

a. Find out as much about the building of the monument as you can: sculptor, architect, date built, sponsors, reasons for building it, name or title of the monument, its artistic style.
b. Find out who supported building the monument and who paid for it.
c. Look for evidence on how people felt about the monument at the time it was built: Find documents dealing with its dedication, its history, public debates about it.
d. Note whether the monument is used in ceremonies or formal occasions, who maintains it, and any nicknames it has.
e. Assess the importance of the location today.
f. Examine why people visit the monument today – ask visitors why they have come and how they feel about the monument.

3. Interpreting the Monument

a. Analyse the impression the monument makes on a visitor today.
b. Assess the importance of the monument's symbols to visitors today.
c. Estimate which people will be enthusiastic about the monument today and which groups will not.
d. Formulate what the monument stands for and your response to it in your own words.

1870 | 1875 | 1880 | 1885 | 1890

1871: German Empire is proclaimed

Bismarck's Alliance System

1888: Year of Three Emperors: William I Frederick III William II

1890: Bismarck leaves office

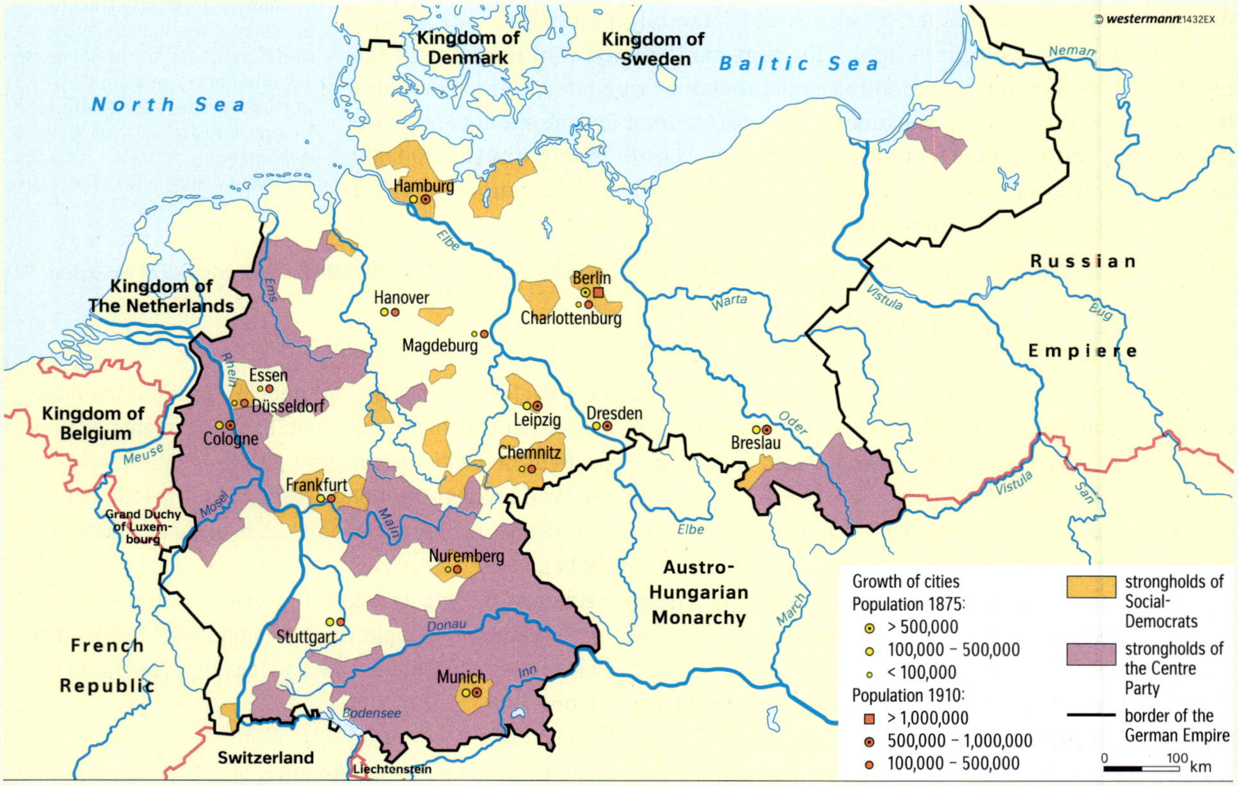

Imperial Germany – the historical map

1900 | 1905 | 1910 | 1915 | 1920

1878–1890:
Socialist Law
in effect

Naval race between
Germany and Britain

1914–1918:
First World War

Summary

After the revolutions of 1848 failed, the German states tried to renew the old German Confederation from 1815. But democratic movements continued to press for change within the different parliaments in the separate states. In Prussia, a conflict between the king and parliament led to a constitutional crisis. Liberals in the Prussian parliament refused to pass a budget unless the king could agree with the parliament on his plans for military reform. The king and his advisors worried that the weak Prussian army could be attacked and beaten by another power, such as Austria, which was the strongest rival to Prussia within the Confederation. The king appointed Otto von Bismarck as Prussian Minister-President in the hope that a strong conservative would be able to keep the parliament under control.

Through Bismarck's leadership and the strength of the Prussian army, three wars (against Denmark, Austria, and France) were won and with them German unity came in 1871. German nationalists had hoped for this goal for years. When Bismarck achieved it, the Prussian constitutional crisis ended in favour of the king. The Confederation ended. Austria turned to interests outside of Germany. But France, badly beaten and shamed in the war, remained a fearsome enemy. Bismarck's answer to keep the new Germany safe from attack (from France or from others) was to manage a complex system of alliances. By the end of his time in office, he seemed to be the only leader who could understand all of the features of the separate agreements.

The new German Constitution of 1871 had authoritarian and democratic features. Its system of voting (universal male suffrage) was a model for democratic voting at the time. Bismarck saw his political opponents in negative terms. He called them "enemies of the empire". Especially Roman Catholics and then Social Democrats were objects of domestic oppression. The German Empire did not integrate its ethnic minorities well. Danes, Poles, and people in Alsace and Lorraine often felt like second-class citizens. Jews, though no longer discriminated against specifically by laws, remained social outsiders in spite of their efforts to improve their status. The military in Imperial Germany had an exaggerated social role – society on the whole was influenced by military thinking. Women found it difficult to make their demands heard in a society which considered them only in terms as wives and mothers.

By 1890 when Bismarck left office, it was unclear which directions the new country would move toward. Some signs seemed positive, others seemed negative. The events which followed led to unexpected results.

DATES

1864: War with Denmark

1866: War with Austria

1870/71: War with France

1871: German Constitution

1871–1878: Kulturkampf

1878–1890: Socialist Law

HISTORICAL TERMS

reparations
Realpolitik
ambassador
guerrilla
suffrage
Kulturkampf
Socialist Law
anti-Semitism
reserve officer
sphere of influence

PERSONS

Otto von Bismarck

William II

Louise Otto

Helene Lange

Clara Zetkin

August Bebel

HISTORY WORKSHOP

Analysing Historical
Monuments

M 1 **"The World's Plunderers",** US cartoon by Thomas Nast, 1885

M 2 **"France Will Bring Culture, Prosperity and Peace."**

Front page of the French paper "Le Petit Journal", 1911

M 3 **Advertising Sign of the Company Bergmann & Co,** around 1899

07 THE NEW IMPERIALISM AND THE SCRAMBLE FOR AFRICA

1880 – 1914

On 1 October 2015 members of the Herero and Nama tribes sent a petition to the German government demanding reparations for the mass killings during the German colonial period at the beginning of the 20th century. The Age of Imperialism, although a hundred years ago, has changed the world and as we can see from the petition still affects politics up to the present day. There have always been periods of colonialism or expansion in human history and quite often they resulted in cruelty and bloodshed rather than cultural exchange and enrichment. Although also the United States of America and the Empire of Japan engaged themselves in colonial expansion in Asia during the late 19th and early 20th centuries, the following chapter focuses on how the "new imperialism" of the European powers changed Africa and the lives of its peoples.

This chapter deals with many questions such as:

- Why did the European powers engage in colonialism?
- What happened in Africa?
- Why is German rule in Southwest Africa still an issue?
- Why did tensions among European powers arise?
- What were the consequences of imperialism on Africa and on the colonizing countries in Europe?
- How can you do credible research on the Internet (history workshop)?

Historical Terms

Scramble for Africa:
Wettlauf um Afrika

Social Darwinism:
Sozialdarwinismus

The "New Imperialism"

The "new imperialism" was a hectic competition among European nations, Japan and the USA for territorial gains in Africa and Asia. The "**Scramble for Africa**" changed the map of the continent profoundly.

Before 1880 only 10% of Africa was controlled by European powers. Colonies spread along the coast of West Africa from the former slave trade, settlements in southern Africa by the Dutch, English and Portuguese, and Algeria in the north, conquered by the French. By 1900 only Ethiopia and Liberia remained free of European control. That left 90 per cent of all African territory under European rule. What did expansion mean to the European powers and to the African peoples?

M 1 **"The English Paw is Grabbing the World"**
French cartoon, 1899

Why Expansion?

The causes of the new imperialism are still hotly debated and extremely complex. Most major European powers saw this expansion as a battle for wealth, growth, power and survival. Although some Europeans bitterly criticized imperialism as a *betrayal* of Western *ideals* of freedom and equality, most people and politicians believed that to remain a great power, or to become one, the possession of an empire was necessary.

Business men, bankers and investors encouraged imperial expansion and expected their governments to support their interests and activities; Cecil Rhodes and George Goldie asked the British government for help. Carl Peters, a German explorer and merchant, called on Bismarck to protect the gains of his German East Africa Company. Their aim was to exploit the continent´s natural resources and profit economically from the colonies.

Many ordinary people were interested in the colonies as somewhere to settle. Life was becoming quite hard for working people in many European countries, partly because of a fast increase in the population and the negative effects of the Industrial Revolution. So the idea of emigrating to other parts of the world became quite popular. Since most of the emigrants went to North America, European governments hoped that colonies might attract some of the settlers instead. Thus they could be kept as citizens in the colonies and social problems in Europe could be eased.

Explorers and missionaries were also interested in the lands overseas. In the 19th century Africa was a mysterious place – "the Dark Continent". Because of diseases and the difficulties of crossing deserts and jungles, Europeans knew little about the interior. Missionaries followed the explorers in order to convert the African people to Christianity. They believed that the natives were "*heathen*" and had to be saved. The civilization of "backward" peoples was also justified with the idea that the white race was superior. This idea was based on the theories of evolution developed by British scientist Charles Darwin (1809–1882), who had focused on the evolution of plants and animals. His ideas of a process of natural selection were applied to human societies, claiming that only the fittest race would survive the permanent conflict among them. This theory was called **Social Darwinism**.

Vocabulary

betrayal of sth.: act of ignoring principles or beliefs in order to achieve something or gain an advantage for yourself

ideals: something that is believed to be perfect

heathen: (here) people who have no religion or who believe in a religion that is not Christian

M 2 **Cecil John Rhodes**
Photograph, around 1890

Biography

Cecil John Rhodes (1853–1902)

He was a British businessman, mine owner and politician in South Africa. He served as Prime Minister of the Cape Colony from 1890 to 1896. Favouring British imperialism, Rhodes and his British South Africa Company founded the southern African territory of Rhodesia, which the company named after him in 1895.

M 3 "Finest Race"

Cecil Rhodes (1853–1902), British businessman and the colonizer of the state of Rhodesia, today's Zambia and Zimbabwe (1902):

"I say that we are the finest race in the world and that the more of the world we *inhabit* the better it is for the human race. Just imagine what change there would be if those parts that are at present inhabited by the most *inferior* human beings were brought under Anglo-Saxon influence. Think of the extra employment a new country added to our dominions would give [...].
The *acquisition* of the greater part of the world under our rule would simply mean an end to all wars. [...] Africa is lying ready for us, it is our duty to take it."

Quoted from: W.T.Stead (ed.), The Last Will and Testament of Cecil John Rhodes, "Review of Reviews" Office: London 1902, p. 58. (adapted by Thomas Söhrnsen).

M 4 "A Solution of Our Social Problem"

Joseph Chamberlain (1836–1914), businessman and British Secretary of State for the Colonies from 1895 to 1903 (1897):

"Our colonies cannot be developed without our assistance. I will consider any case in which investment of British money may help to develop colonies. In such development I see a solution of our social problems: there is no way of securing more employment than by creating new markets and developing old ones."

Joseph Chamberlain, Foreign and Colonial Speeches, George Routledge: London 1897. (adapted by Thomas Söhrnsen).

M 5 "All Human Life is a Struggle for Existence"

Herbert Spencer (1820–1903), English philosopher and prominent liberal political theorist, chiefly remembered as the "Father of Social Darwinism" (1896):

"There is a struggle of race against race and of nation against nation. All human life is a struggle for existence in which only the fittest survive."

Herbert Spencer, The Principles of Biology, Vol. 1&2, Williams and Norgate: London 1896. (adapted by Thomas Söhrnsen).

M 6 "Hammer or *Anvil*?"

Prince Bernhard von Bülow (1849–1905), German Chancellor 1900, speech before the Reichstag on 11 December 1899:

"In our nineteenth century, England has increased its colonial empire – the largest the world has seen since the days of the Romans – further and further; the French have put down roots in North Africa and East Africa and created for themselves a new empire in the Far East; Russia has begun its mighty course of victory in Asia [...].
The English prime minister said a long time ago that the strong states were getting stronger and stronger and the weak ones weaker and weaker. [...] We don't want to step on the toes of any foreign power, but at the same time we don't want our own feet *tramped* on by any foreign power (Bravo!) and we don't intend to be *shoved* aside by any foreign power, neither in political nor in economic terms. (Lively applause.) [...] The means, gentlemen, for a people of almost 60 million – *dwelling* in the middle of Europe and, at the same time, stretching its economic antennae out to all sides – to battle its way through the struggle for existence without strong armaments on land and at sea, have not yet been found. (Very true! from the right.) In the coming century the German people will be a hammer or an anvil."

Quoted from: Michael Behnen, Quellen zur deutschen Außenpolitik im Zeitalter des Imperialismus 1890–1911, WBG: Darmstadt 1977, p. 231ff. (adapted and transl. by Thomas Söhrnsen).

Vocabulary

to inhabit: to live in a particular place
inferior: lower in rank, opp.: superior
acquisition: here: the act of getting land and power
anvil: heavy iron block on which metal is hammered into certain shapes
to tramp: to walk with heavy steps for a long time
to shove: to push with force
dwelling: living

Tasks

1. **Reasons for Expansion**
   Work in groups and draw a diagram that shows the different motives of the European powers to take part in this scramble for territorial gains. Be prepared to introduce the different sources (M1–M6) and to explain your diagram.
2. **Biographies**
   Prepare a short presentation on Cecil Rhodes or Bernhard von Bülow.
3. **Good Reasons?**
   Discuss in class the reasons why the Europeans wanted to take over Africa.

Vocabulary

division: dividing into separate parts

purchase: the act of buying something

dependency: area or country controlled by another one

annexation: the act of taking control, occupation

administrator: a person whose job is to manage and organize the public or business affairs

labour recruiters: (here) white men forcing Africans into work

to subdue: to bring sb. under control by using force

to stride: walk with long steps

Europeans in Africa

Annexation of Territory and Exploitation in Africa

In 1885 the Berlin Conference agreed upon Africa's *division* among the European powers. White people came to rule millions of black people and the speed of expansion was enormous. By the means of *purchase* and war the colonial powers turned all of Africa into *dependencies* and began to exploit the land and its people. The *annexation* of African territories meant the establishment of new states. New borders were drawn that lasted beyond the colonial period.

Colonial rule was executed by policemen and soldiers, *administrators*, tax collectors, traders and *labour recruiters*. Railroads connected the coast with the interior and opened up new markets. The economic exploitation of Africa mainly took place in mines, where the colonists searched for gold, diamonds or copper, and on plantations, which produced coffee, cocoa or rubber.

The hard work was done by Africans, who were forced to labour and were poorly paid. Quite often the natives' land was taken away from them and they had to pay high taxes. The punishments for disobedience were harsh and many Africans were killed or driven off their land. But in some places, attempts to *subdue* the native population were not successful and led to long and bloody wars. The overwhelming majority of African leaders strongly opposed colonial rule and decided to fight for their sovereignty and independence. One tragic example was the rebellion of the Herero and Nama in German Southwest Africa.

	Great Britain	Germany	France
1881	670,953		320,972
1895	5,965,519	2,385,100	2,381,476
1912	6,209,602	2,657,300	6,480,200

Wolfgang J. Mommsen, Imperialismus, Hamburg 1977, p. 37. 147GX

M 1 Acquisition of Colonial Territory in Africa (in km²)

M 2 "The Rhodes Colossus – *Striding* from Cape Town to Cairo"

British cartoon, 1892.

The Rhodes Colossus depicts British colonialist Cecil Rhodes as a giant standing over the African continent.

Europeans in Africa – working with maps

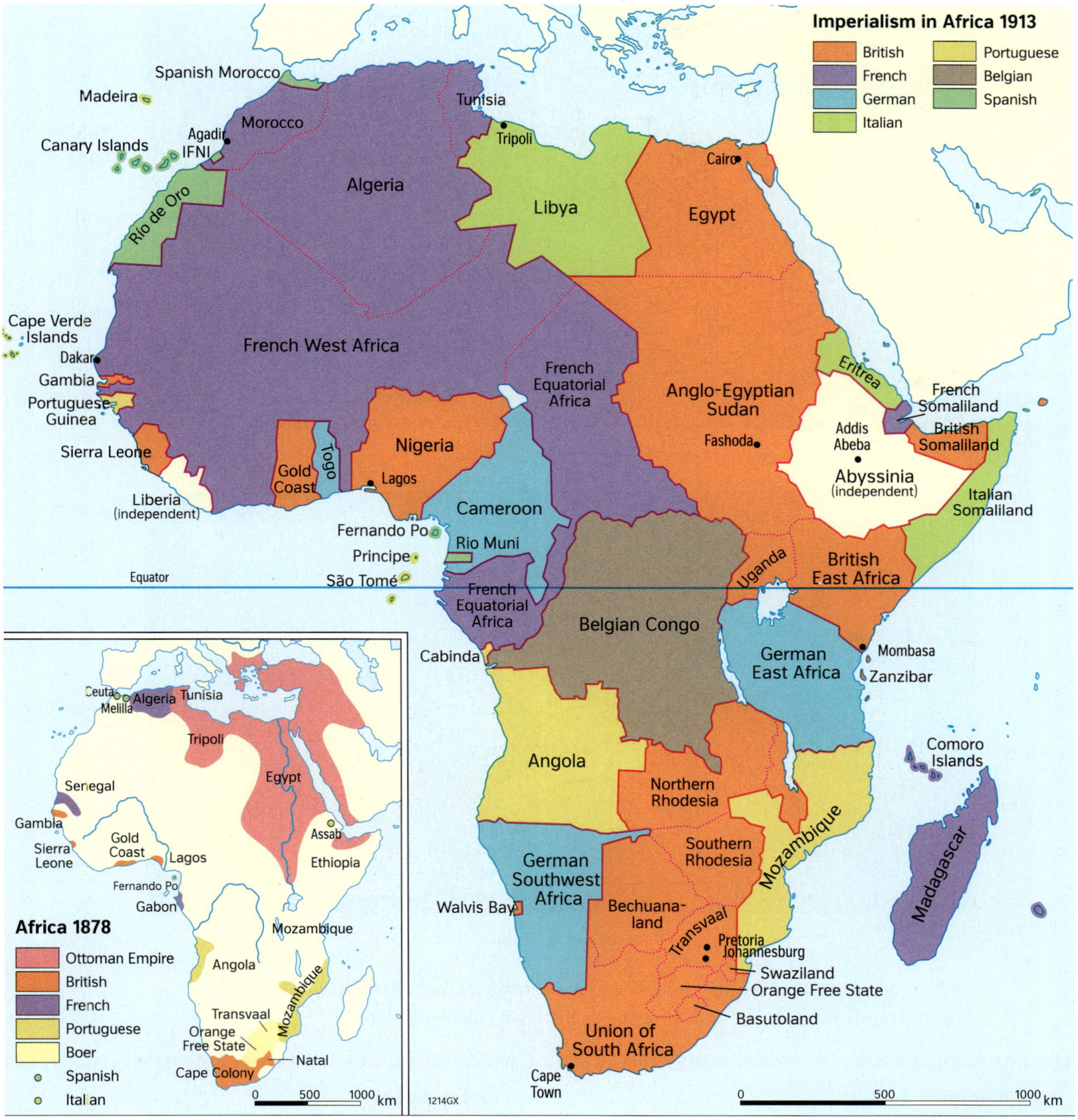

M 3 **Imperialism in Africa (1878 and 1913)**

Tasks

1. Colonial Race

a) Make a diagram showing the growth of colonial territory in Africa (M1).

b) Interpret the development in the diagram.

2. Europeans in Africa – working with maps

a) Describe the two maps.

b) Compare the two maps and name the changes between 1878 and 1913.

Europeans in Africa – working with cartoons

So kolonisiert der Deutsche.

So kolonisiert der Engländer.

M 4 Cartoon by Thomas Theodor Heine in the German Journal "Simplizissimus"
"How the German colonizes" and "How the Englishman colonizes", 1905

Vocabulary

useful words
a palm tree
to parade
to stand in neat rows
to muzzle sb. (jdn. einen Maulkorb anlegen)

Vocabulary

useful words
business man
colonial civil servant
clergyman
pressing board (Pressbalken)
capstan (Drehkreuz)
to give one's blessing (seinen Segen geben)
to torture sb. (quälen, foltern)
to pour sth. down sb.'s throat (jdm. etwas einflößen)
to squeeze sth. out of sb. (etwas aus jdm. herauspressen)

African Perspective

M 5 Statements from African Chiefs

a) In the face of the French invasion of his territory in 1883 and the demand for permission to build a railway across his territory Lat Dior, the Damel of Cayor in modern Senegal, wrote to the French Government:

"As long as I live, be well assured, I shall oppose with all my might the construction of this railway [...]. That is why, every time I receive a letter from you concerning the railway, I will always answer no, no, and I will never make you any other reply. Even when I go to my rest, my horse Malaw would give you the same answer."

b) In 1890, King Machemba of the Yao in Tanganyika (United Republic of Tanzania) told the German commander Hermann von Wissman:

"I have listened to your words but can find no reason why I should obey you – I would rather die first [...]. If it should be friendship that you desire, then I am ready for it, today and always; but to be your *subject*, that I cannot be [...]. If it should be war you desire, then I am ready, but never to be your subject [...]. I do not fall at your feet, for you are God's creature just as I am. I am Sultan here in my land. You are Sultan there in yours. Yet, listen, I do not say to you that you should obey me, for I know that you are a free man. [...] As for me, I will not come to you and, if you are strong enough, then come and fetch me."

c) Hendrik Wittbooi, a king in Southwest Africa, told the Germans in 1894:

"The Lord has established various kingdoms in the world, therefore I know and believe that it is no *sin* or crime that I should wish to remain the independent chief of my land and people."

M 6 Fight between the Herero and German troops 1904

d) In 1895, Wobogo, the king of the Mossi, told the French Captain Destenave:

"I know the whites wish to kill me in order to take my country, and yet you claim they will help me organize my country. But I find my country good just as it is. I have no need of them. I know what is necessary for me and what I want. I have my own *merchants*. Consider yourself fortunate that I do not order your head to be cut off. Go away now and, above all, never come back."

a) – d) Quoted from: UNESCO Courier 5/1984, Paris, p. 33ff.

Vocabulary

subject: (here) a person who is under the rule of a sovereign

sin: the act of breaking a religious or moral law

merchant: businessman, a buyer and seller of goods for profit

Tasks

1. Contemporary Criticism – working with cartoons
- a) Describe the two cartoons (M4).
- b) Compare their messages.
- c) Show who is criticized and why.

2. What can you find out about the African perspective?
- a) Name the arguments of the African chiefs against their oppression by the Europeans (M5).
- b) Assess the chiefs' arguments after reading their statements
- c) Describe the picture (M6).
- d) Discuss the helplessness of the Africans in the face of the colonial threat.

German Rule in Southwest Africa – Consequences for Today?

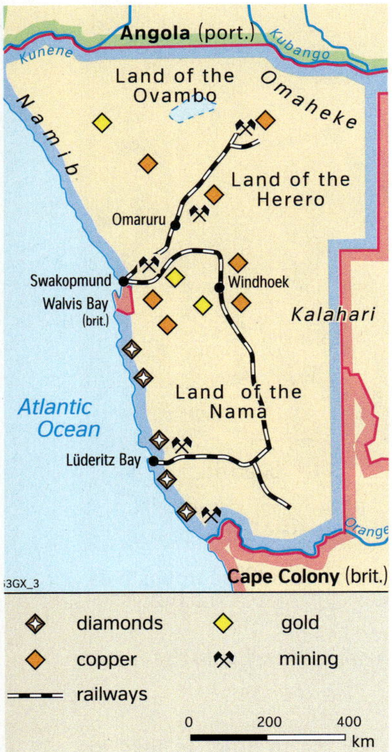

M 1 **German Southwest Africa**

A German Colony

In 1883 the German merchant Adolf Lüderitz bought land from a native chief and asked the German government to protect his interests in Africa. Although the German Chancellor Bismarck was very sceptical about colonies he agreed. In 1884 Southwest Africa became a German colony. It was larger than the German Empire of that time and became the only German colony where Germans settled in great numbers. They hoped for a better life and jobs in the mining (diamonds and copper) and the farming business. By 1902 about 2,600 of the 200,000 inhabitants were Germans and in 1914 their number had increased to 12,000. The native Africans living in the colony were the Herero, the Ovambo and the Nama, also called Hottentots. During the First World War it was administered by South Africa and in 1990 it became the independent state of Namibia.

Herero Uprising

On 11 January 1904, Herero tribal leader Samuel Maharero called for his people to rise up against their German colonial rulers. Angered by the growing number of German settlers, the dividing of their land by new railroads and the killing of their herds of cattle, the Herero killed 100 German civilians and 13 soldiers in just a few days.

Completely unprepared for the unrest, Governor General Theodor Leutwein was unable to keep the uprising from spreading quickly all over the colony. After an unsuccessful six-month bush war the government in Berlin ordered 14,000 German soldiers, equipped with modern weapons, to the region to put down the rebellion. Heading the force was the hard-line Lieutenant General Lothar von Trotha. After the decisive battle near the Waterberg on 12 August 1904, the surviving Herero fled into the dry Omaheke desert.

M 2 **German Soldiers in Southwest Africa**
1904

M 3 **A Group of Herero Starving to Death in the Omaheke Desert**
Photograph, about 1904

Vocabulary

to exterminate: to kill

malnutrition: poor condition of health caused by lack of food

to sue: to make a legal claim

apology: word or statement saying sb. is sorry for sth. that has been done wrong

atrocity: a cruel and violant act, especially in a war

reconciliation: an end to a disagreement and the start of a good relationship again

recipient: a person who receives something

Historical Terms

genocide:
Genozid, Völkermord

Confronted with the very real possibility of dying in the desert, many hoped to surrender to the Germans and headed back to their lands. But on October 2, von Trotha ordered all Herero, armed or unarmed and including women and children, to be shot if they attempted to return. Although the German Emperor William II and Chancellor von Bülow supposedly disagreed with this decision, they apparently did little to stop von Trotha, who was now willing *to exterminate* the Herero. The Africans who survived were put in chains and taken to camps where they suffered under forced labour, from disease and *malnutrition*. Between 75 to 80 per cent of the Herero population died and this tragic event was to become the first **genocide** of the 20th century.

The Herero in Namibia Today

The Herero never completely recovered from the conflict. Around 100,000 – about 7% of the total population - live in Namibia today. Many are poor or work on the farms of white landowners. In 2001, tribal leaders tried *to sue* Germany for compensation in US courts, but the claim for $4 billion (€3.12 billion) was not successful. In 2004 Germany offered a formal *apology* for the *atrocities* but rejected direct payments to victims' descendants. Since Namibia's independence in 1990, Germany has supported the Namibian government in its policy of national *reconciliation*. By 2013 German developmental cooperation with Namibia - governmental and non-governmental programmes taken together - amounted to around €800 million, making Namibia the largest *recipient* of German developmental cooperation in Africa.

M 4 **Hendrik Witbooi**
Chief of the Nama, 1904

Herero Uprising – why war broke out

M 5 **General von Trotha**
Chief of the German troops

M 6 Herero Uprising

a) General von Trotha in an appeal to the Herero, 1904:

"I, the great general of the German soldiers, send this letter to the Herero people. The Herero are no longer German subjects. They have murdered and stolen, have cut off the ears and noses and other parts of injured German soldiers and now they refuse to fight out of *cowardice* [...]. The Herero nation must [...] leave the country. If they do not leave, I will force them out with cannons. Every Herero, armed or unarmed [...] will be shot dead within the German borders. I will no longer accept women and children, but will force them back to their people or shoot them."

Quoted from: Conrad Rust, Krieg und Frieden im Hererolande, Kittler: Leipzig 1904, p. 25. (transl. by Thomas Söhrnsen).

b) Statement of Hendrik Witbooi (Nama chief) on the German administration:

"The German himself [...] makes no *requests* according to truth and justice and asks no permission of a chief. He introduces laws into the land [... which] are entirely impossible, [...] unbelievable, unbearable, *unmerciful* and unfeeling [...]. He personally punishes our people at Windhoek and has already beaten people to death for *debt* [...] it is not just and right to beat people to death for that. [...] He *flogs* people in a shameful and cruel manner. We stupid and unintelligent people, for so he thinks us to be, we have never yet punished a human being in such a cruel and improper way for he stretches people on their backs and flogs them on the stomach and even between the legs, be they male or female, so Your Honour can understand that no one can survive such a punishment."

Vocabulary

cowardice: lack of courage
request: the action of asking for something formally and politely
unmerciful: showing no kindness
debt: money that sb. owes
to flog: to beat with a whip

c) The following letter was written by Samuel Maharero on 6 March 1904 in reply to a letter of the German Governor Leutwein asking him why he had started the war:

"The beginning of the war is not just in this year begun by me, but by the whites, for you know how many Herero have been killed by white people, especially [by] traders with rifles and [by guards] in prison. And always when I brought the matter to Windhoek, the blood of my people was always valued at no more than a few head of [cattle] [...]. The traders increased the trouble in the way that they [...]gave my people credit. After they had done this they robbed them, going so far as to take away by force, to repay themselves, two or three head of cattle for a debt of one pound sterling. These are the things which have caused the war in this land."

b) and c) quoted from: http://namibweb.com/germans.htm [Oct. 2017].

M 7 **Samuel Maharero**
Chief of the Herero

Tasks

1. **Why War Broke Out**
   a) List the reasons the German general and the African chiefs (M6) offer for the outbreak of the war.
   b) Assess the question of guilt.
2. **Biography**
   Find out more about Chief Maharero (M7) on the Internet and present your results in class.
3. **German Responsibility**
   Work in groups and discuss the role the Germans played in Southwest Africa (M1–M7).

Colonial War Against the Herero und Nama – dealing with war and genocide

M 8 Monument from 1912

The statue was put up in 1912 in memory of the colonial wars. It was removed in 2013.

M 9 Monument from 2014

This is the back wall of the Genocide Monument in Windhoek. The monument replaces the statue from 1912 and was erected in 2014.

M 10 "Ten Namibia Dollars"

Chief Witbooi and the Nama revolted against German rule in Namibia in 1904. Today he is one of the national heroes of Namibia, the former German Southwest Africa.

Tasks

1. **The Monument from 1912**
   a) Describe the monument (M8).
   b) Look for similar monuments you know or find on the Internet.
   c) Explain why the monument was removed in 2013.
2. **The Monument from 2014**
   a) Describe the back wall of the Genocide Monument.
   b) Find a picture of the monument in Windhoek on the Internet to see what the whole monument looks like.
   c) Explain the political message of the new monument.
   d) Compare and contrast both monuments (M8, M9).

Vocabulary

to be obsessed: to think about sth. constantly

to heighten: to increase/intensify

glorification: extreme praise

Historical Terms

Reinsurance Treaty: Rückversicherungsvertrag

Entente Cordiale: (französisch für herzliches Einverständnis) auch im Deutschen: Entente Cordiale

Rising International Tensions

Rivalry Among the European Powers

The scramble for colonies in Africa or Asia intensified the rivalry among the European powers. The dispute between France and Great Britain over the Sudan almost led to war at Fashoda in 1898 and Anglo-Russian relations often reached the point of war over disagreements in Asia. Russia and Japan actually engaged in a war in 1904/05. All the imperial powers became *obsessed* with gaining further territory and showing no sign of weakness. An atmosphere of *heightened* patriotism and *glorification* of armed forces spread and undermined any forms of criticism and rational thought.

"New Course" in Germany – new reasons for trouble

This was most noticeable in Germany. Chancellor Bismarck, who had subordinated colonial policy to the goal of stability in Europe, was dismissed in 1890. The **Reinsurance Treaty** with Russia was not renewed. Emperor William II started a "new course" announcing that Germany would adopt a "world policy". Attempting to find "a place in the sun", William's policy aimed at building a strong German navy and making Germany a major imperial power by expanding overseas. The new policy, however, showed little success. The only colonies added between 1897 and 1899 were some islands in the Pacific. But at the same time Germany's "world policy" created a great deal of tension and damaged Germany's standing in the world.

The French and Russian governments agreed on the Franco-Russian Alliance in 1894. When Imperial Germany engaged in a naval race against Britain, the British finally settled their differences with France over colonial policy. This agreement was called the **Entente Cordiale** and was signed in 1904.

Anglo-French cooperation in the Moroccan Crises (1905–1911) stopped Germany's attempt to gain greater influence in North Africa. When Russia and Britain finally closed a contract on their spheres of interest in Asia, the German government felt "encircled". The balance of power in Europe had turned against Germany, which had only one loyal ally: Austria-Hungary.

M 1 **"How are we going to shake hands?"**
German cartoon from "Simplizissimus", 1912

M 2 **Painting of William II**
"The Emperor during a Naval Manoeuvre", by Willy Stöwer, 1912

"New Course" in Germany – analysing maps

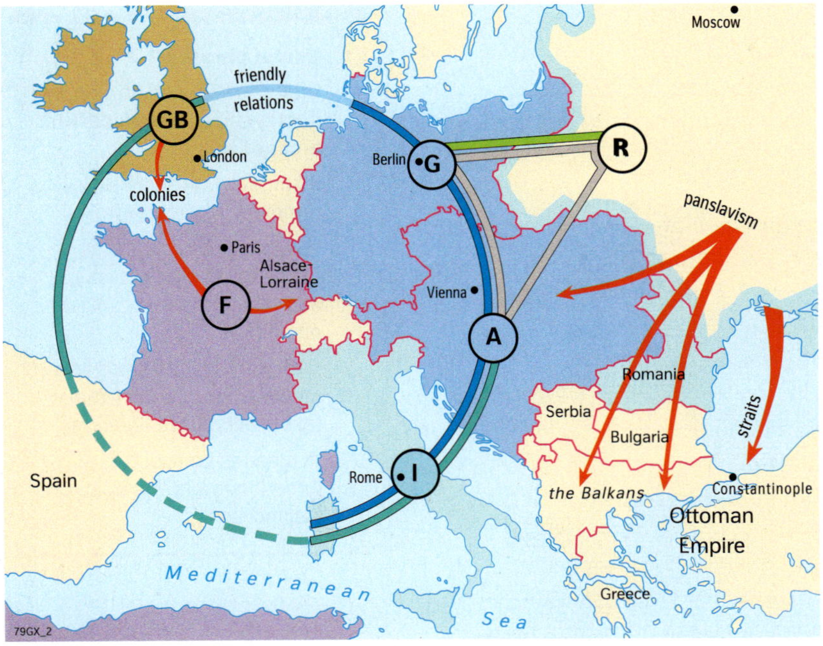

M 3

The European Alliance System in 1887

- Three Emperors' League (1873)
- Dual Alliance (1879)
- Triple Alliance (1882)
- Romania joined the Triple Alliance (1883)
- Reinsurance Treaty (1887)
- Mediterranean Agreement (1887)
- tensions and conflicts

0 500 km

79GXa_2

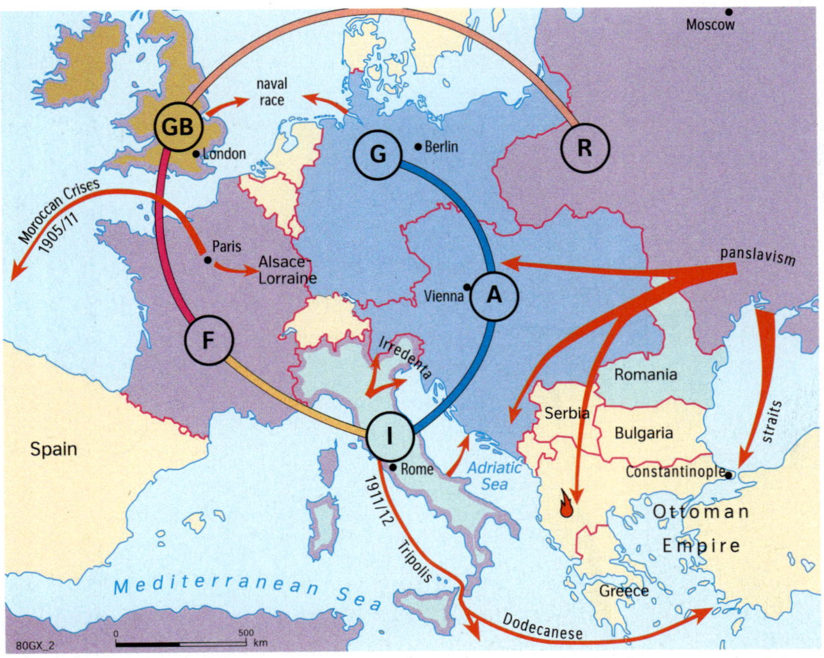

M 4

The European Alliance System in 1914

- Dual Alliance
- Triple Alliance
- Franco-Russian Alliance (1894)
- Treaty of Neutrality (1902)
- Entente Cordiale (1904)
- British-Russian Alliance (1907)
- Balkan Wars 1912/13
- tensions and conflicts

80GX_2

Tasks

1. Tensions Among European Powers

a) Look up the Fashoda Crisis on the Internet.

b) Prepare a short report on the crisis and its background.

c) Describe the cartoon and work out its message. Relate it to events mentioned in the text (M1).

d) Describe the picture and show the artist's intention (M2).

2. The Changing European Alliance System

a) Compare the two maps.

b) Write a short text about the changes in international relations in Europe between 1887 and 1914.

"New Course" in Germany – analysing cartoons

M 5 **"Dropping the Pilot"**

English cartoon by John Tenniel in "Punch", 1890

Vocabulary

Useful phrases

pilot: (here) a person who guides ships through difficult areas of water

dismissal: (here) the act of removing sb. from office

gangway: a bridge placed between the side of a ship and land so people can get on and off

railing: barrier on ships as a means of protection against falling overboard (Reeling)

to steer: to control the direction in which a boat, car, etc. moves

"New Course" in Germany – Emperor William II

Biography

Emperor William II (1859–1941)

William was born in 1859 as the son of German crown prince Frederick (later Emperor Frederick III) and Victoria, the oldest daughter of Britain's Queen Victoria. He was emperor of Germany from 1888 until the end of World War I. During his rule, Germany's relations with Britain, France and Russia became difficult. During the war, Wilhelm allowed his military advisers to dictate German policy. Wilhelm had to abdicate in November 1918 and fled to the Netherlands, where he died in 1941.

M 7 William II

Portrait in the uniform of a Guards Officer.
Painting by Vilma Parlaghy, 1895

M 6 Emperor William II

Review by the English paper "The Economist" on John Röhl's biography "Kaiser Wilhelm II: A Concise Life" (2014):

"How much of the Kaiser's deeply unattractive personality was the result of psychological damage done during childhood can only be guessed at. But it would have been surprising if things had turned out well. In their efforts to repair the left arm crippled at birth, the doctors inflicted one well-intentioned torture after another. [...] Terrifying machines were used to stretch his head and arm without result. His mother, Queen Victoria's daughter, Vicky, tried and failed to hide her *revulsion* at his deformity. [...]

The Kaiser grew up to be emotionally needy, bombastic, choleric, hyperactive and hypersensitive. His personality combined with the militaristic, authoritarian culture of the Prussian court to create a monarch who was extraordinarily *ill-suited* to lead the most powerful country in Europe at the end of the 19th century. His belief in his powers as a great strategist and the absence of anyone prepared to challenge him were major factors in helping to create the conditions and the alliances that led directly to the catastrophe of 1914."

https://www.economist.com/news/books-and-arts/21627552-how-kaiser-led-hitler-toxic-monarch [Oct. 2017].

Vocabulary

revulsion: a strong feeling of disgust or horror
ill-suited: unfit

Tasks

1. Analysing Cartoons

a) Describe the cartoon (M5):
   - who is depicted,
   - what are they doing,
   - how do they appear,
   - what do their faces say?

b) Explain the message of the cartoon.

c) The English title "Dropping the Pilot" was translated as "Der Lotse geht von Bord". What do you think of this translation? Explain your answer and give another translation.

d) Find suitable thought bubbles for the two figures.

2. Biography

a) Do some research to find out how William's upbringing prepared him for the role of the emperor (M6).

b) Find out more about William II on the Internet.

c) Assess his influence on German policy during his rule.

Vocabulary

legacy: sth. from the past that affects life today

impact: powerful effect

decade: period of ten years

provision: the act of supplying sb. with sth. that they need or want

The Legacy of Imperialism

What *legacy* did colonialism leave to Africa? There is no doubt that the economic, social and political *impact* of imperialism was very strong, but there is still bitter controversy over the different effects. To some historians its impact was positive or at least not harmful for Africa. To others colonialism in Africa had only negative consequences. Latest research shows that a more balanced assessment is necessary.

Politics, Infrastructure and Trade

The impact of imperialism varied: Some poor nations have enjoyed greater economic benefits from contact with the colonizing countries than others. India, Brazil, and other developing nations have even begun to compete economically with their former colonial powers. In Africa the first positive political impact was the establishment of a longer lasting peace and stability than before. The nineteenth century was a century of tribal wars which caused a great deal of instability and insecurity. The first two or three *decades* of the colonial era (from 1880 to 1910) intensified this instability, violence and disorder and caused destruction and loss of population. But after the colonial occupation and the establishment of civil services, most parts of Africa, especially after the end of the First World War, enjoyed a great degree of continuous peace and security.

The second positive effect was that the colonial system introduced a new judicial system and a new bureaucracy or civil service into most parts of Africa. The spread of Christianity was closely linked to western education. Certainly, by the end of the colonial regime, there were relatively few areas without at least elementary schools. The spread of western education had far-reaching social effects such as an increase in the westernized educated African elite. This elite now runs governments and makes up the backbone of the civil service in African states. The impact on economics was equally important. The first and most obvious positive effect was the *provision* of a basic infrastructure of roads, railways, telegraph, telephone services and, in some cases, even airports. Completed by the 1930s, this infrastructure moved not only goods, the new cash crops (crops grown for selling), and troops, but people, too. Also the impact of colonialism on the **primary sector** of the economy was realized during the colonial period. The African mining industry boomed while the cultivation of cash crops such as cocoa, coffee, tobacco, peanuts, sisal and rubber spread.

The Economic Importance of the German Colonies	
Raw materials imported from the colonies as a proportion of total raw materials imported	1.6%
Colonies' share of German Empire's exports	0.5%
Colonies' share of German Empire's capital exported	2.0%
German settlers in the African colonies until 1913 as a proportion of all the emigrants from the German Reich 1871-1914	0.03%

R. v. Albertini, Europäische Kolonialherrschaft 1880-1940, Zürich 1976 141GX

M 1

Historical Terms

primary sector:
primärer Wirtschaftssektor = Landwirtschaft, Forstwirtschaft, Fischerei und der Bergbau

M 2 **"Light of Civilization"**
Schoolboys at the German School in Togo, about 1900

Exploitation and Suppression

Primarily, colonialism was a period of suppression and the murder of thousands of African natives. Although there were positive effects, the negative effects were even greater. The economic exploitation of Africa´s natural resources was and still is quite often controlled by western companies. European powers pushed for the economic exploitation of colonized nations to benefit the mother country. There was little interest in the welfare of the colonized peoples, instead imperial states sought to maximize their profits and gains, regardless of what that meant for the colonized countries and peoples. The colonies were only sources of cheap raw products to be later used in European industries. The unwillingness of imperial powers to reinvest the profits in the industrial development of the colonies has had far-reaching consequences until today. Colonies were forcefully kept in a *fragile* agricultural economy and *cash crops* replaced the food crops, which often resulted in famine.

Often the borders of the African states were *arbitrary* and many of the states were artificial creations made up of various peoples with different cultures, traditions, origins and languages. The negative consequences can still be seen today. Civil wars within and among African states have become part of daily life. Worse still was the impact of colonialism in the cultural field. Throughout the colonial period, African art, music, dancing and even history were not only ignored, but actively discouraged or rejected. Imperialism has destroyed traditions and ways of thinking and has replaced them with the habits and mentality of the western world. As one speaker at the Second Congress of Negro Writers and Artists in Rome declared in 1959: "Among the sins of colonialism, one of the most *pernicious*, because it was for a long time accepted by the West, was the concept of people without culture."

Disaster or Benefit?

It is an exaggeration to consider colonialism as a disaster for Africa that caused only underdevelopment and backwardness. On the other hand, colonial *apologists overstate* the facts when they see colonialism as an unqualified *blessing* for Africa. The question of whether a colony benefited from colonialism has to be examined on a case-by-case basis. However, colonial rulers did not see the development of Africans as a priority. The impact of colonialism could be positive as well as negative. But most of the positive effects were rather accidental by-products of activities or measures taken *to promote* the interests of the colonizers. They do not outweigh the negative impacts of imperialism.

Consequences on Europe and Germany

Some British colonies like India or South Africa proved to be economically rather profitable, but German colonial engagement did not live up to expectations. It did not help to solve the Social Question in Germany and did not boost the economy. Financially the colonies became a losing game. The German government had to invest more money than it could take in. Of course, products from Africa enriched the range of goods in shops which sold goods from overseas ("Kolonialwarenläden"). Even today museums and botanical gardens have their roots in Germany´s colonial past. But the political consequences were disastrous. At the time German imperialism led to isolation in foreign policy and contributed to the outbreak of the First World War.

Vocabulary

fragile: weak

cash crop: crop grown mainly for sale

arbitrary: not based on reason, system or plan, seeming to be unfair

pernicious: very harmful

apologist: sb. who defends or justifies sth.

to overstate: to exaggerate

blessing: something that is good or helpful

to promote: to help sth. to happen

The Legacy of Imperialism – disaster or benefit?

M 3 Cartoon Critizing Colonialism

Germania nurses a black baby. German Cartoon by Thomas Theodor Heine, 1904

Vocabulary

to cavil: to argue about unimportant details

staggering: very amazing, extremly surprising

contention: opinion

M 4 Two Different Views

a) The English historian P.C. Lloyd:

"It is easy *to cavil* today at the slow rate of economic development during the half-century of colonial rule [...]. Nevertheless, the difference between the condition of African society at the end of the nineteenth century and at the end of the Second World War is *staggering*. The colonial powers provided the infrastructure on which progress in the 'independence' period has depended: a fairly efficient administrative machine, reaching down to villages in the most remote areas, a network of roads and railways, and basic services in health and education."

b) The black Guyanese historian Walter Rodney:

"The argument suggests that, on the one hand, there was exploitation and oppression, but, on the other hand, that colonial governments did much for the benefit of Africans and that they developed Africa. It is our *contention* that this is completely false. Colonialism had only one hand, it was a one-armed bandit."

a) and b) UNESCO Courier 5/1984, p. 33 ff.

Tasks

1. Benefits for Germany's Economy

a) Working in pairs, transform the data (M1) into text.
b) Evaluate the importance of the colonies for the German economy.
c) Describe the cartoon and relate it to your assessment (M3).

2. Discussing the Impact of Imperialism

a) Which positive and negative effects of imperialism do the author's text and the two historians describe? Make a list (M4).
b) Add further aspects that should be considered.
c) Discuss the legacy of imperialism in class and the lessons that should be learned for today's world.
d) Compare your results with the images on the introductory pages and evaluate their messages.

The Renaming of Streets

The era of imperialism is over and Germany no longer has any colonies. But there are still signs and reminders of colonial times. There are monuments or streets named after German colonists in many cities; and they led and still lead to controversial discussions. In Schleswig-Holstein's capital Kiel, such a controversy over the "Carl-Peters-Straße" arose in the summer of 2006. "The name is full of bloody history" was the headline of an article in the local paper and different political groups wanted to rename the street. With the help of the Internet we can inform ourselves about Carl Peters.

M 1 **"The name is full of bloody history"**
Headline "Kieler Nachrichten", 27 July 2006

Historical Workshop

Research on the Internet

The World Wide Web

The World Wide Web offers users access not only to information from universities, libraries, government and the press but also to information from firms or private persons wishing to share their ideas and views. Keep in mind:

- Anyone can put something on the Internet – an unintelligent person or an expert.
- He can say anything he likes – be it true or false.
- He can leave it there as long as he likes – even if it is out of date.

Therefore, it is necessary to check how credible a source is. It is important not to trust everything you read on the Internet. Be careful about which information you use.

Trust

So how do you decide whom or what to trust? Ask yourself the "three Ws": who, where, when? Who has written the information (author's name, organisation, About Us section, URL)? Where is the information coming from? When was the information produced? Has it been updated?

Develop a Search Strategy

1. What exactly is the topic you're searching for? Example: Carl Peters and his actions in Africa.

2. What are the three or four keywords for your topic? Example: German colonist, imperialism in Africa, 19th century, Carl-Peters-Straße in Kiel

3. How can you combine these keywords to start a search? Despite differences among search engines, most of them have tools in common. (A) Putting a phrase in QUOTATION MARKS tells the search engine to list only sites that contain those words in that exact order.
(B) Using "operators" like AND or OR: For example: "Carl Peters" AND "German colonialism in Africa" returns web pages containing both words.
(C) Using the operator OR returns pages containing only one key term. For example: "Carl Peters" OR "German colonism".
Start your search with a search engine.

Minding the "Netiquette"

- Whenever you download information or texts, graphics, etc. you should be fair to those who created them.
- Do not simply copy and present information without citing: You have to document where the material comes from. Not doing so is an academic offence called plagiarism.

How to Cite Correctly

Web pages are cited in the following way: Author's last name, author's first name, title or site of page, name of institution or organization, date of visit to site, URL of page. Example: Boddy-Evans, Alistair, Biography: Carl Peters, About.Com, New York Times Company, 2 March 2007, http://africanhistory.about.com/cs/biography/p/bio_peters. htm?terms=carl+peters

Results

a. Explain the background of the controversy in Kiel.
b. Give an account of Carl Peters's biography.
c. State your opinion and decide whether the street in Kiel should be renamed.

1870 1875 1880 1885 1890

1884: First German colonies: Southwest Africa, Togo, Cameroons, Islands in the Pacific

1878: Berlin Conference

1890 Bismarck´s dismissal

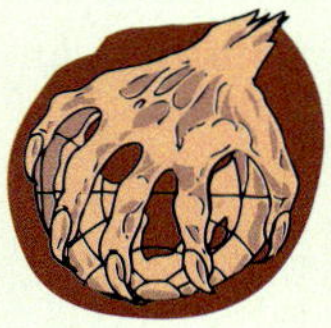

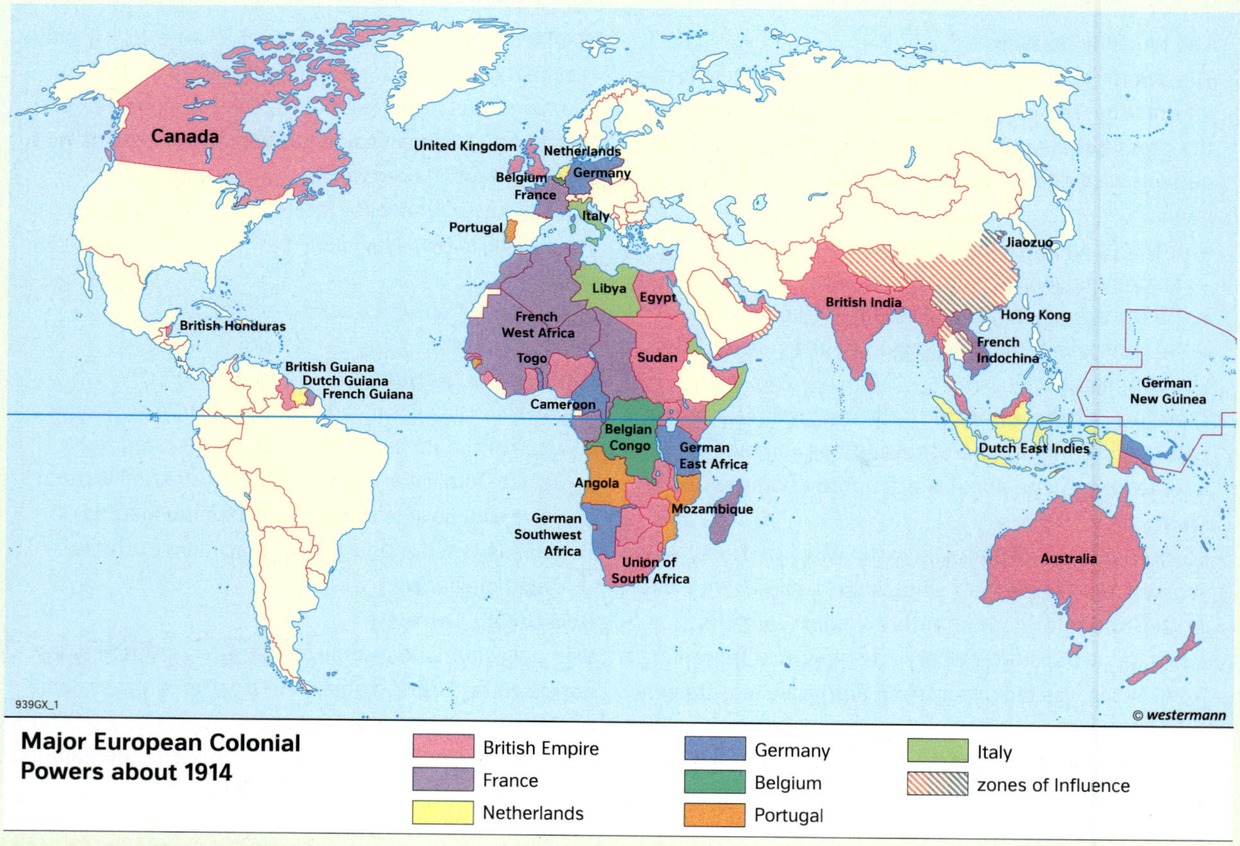

The New Imperialism and the Scramble for Africa – the historical map

1900 1905 1910 1915 1920

Naval race between Germany and Britain

1904: Herero Uprising; Entente Cordiale

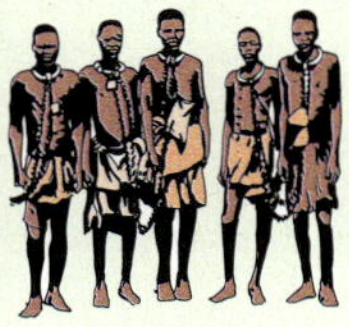

1911: Second Moroccan Crisis

1914 – 1918 First World War

Summary

The New Imperialism was a period of colonial expansion by the European powers, the United States of America and the Empire of Japan during the late 19th and early 20th centuries. The policy of those powerful countries was to extend their power beyond their own borders. Imperialism aimed at the creation of an empire. When imperialist countries took control of other countries they usually used military force. They had economic, nationalist, social and religious motives and used Social Darwinism and racist theories to justify their policy.

Large empires increased national pride. Colonies offered cheap raw materials, new markets for finished goods and capital investments. Human resources were also gained since colonized peoples were often forced into slavery or into low-wage work. They could also be called into military service on behalf of the empire. In some cases African peoples became victims of mass killings.

Thus, a policy of imperialism could enrich the imperialist country, but – as the German colonies showed – did not always do so. For most colonized peoples imperialism turned out to be a period of oppression and exploitation. After World War II most of the former colonies became independent, but the new order could not offer peace and prosperity. Today the consequences of imperialism affect our world. Often enough terrorism and civil wars in developing countries have their origins in the colonial policies from many decades or even a century ago.

1884: First German colonies

1890: Bismarck's dismissal

1904: Entente Cordiale

1914 – 1918: First World War

HISTORICAL TERMS

Scamble for Africa

Social Darwinism

Reinsurance Treaty

Entente Cordiale

primary sector

genocide

PERSONS

Cecil John Rhodes

Hendrik Witbooi

William II

HISTORY WORKSHOP

Research on the Internet

M 1 **"Horrors of War"**

Painting by John Singer Sargent, 1918/19

M 2 **"Destroy this Mad Brute"**

US poster, 1917

M 3 **"News of a Soldier's Death"**

Drawing by Käthe Kollwitz

M 4 **"Dogfight over France"**

Watercolour, 1917

M 5 **Propaganda Postcard**

1914

M 6 **War Cemetry in Douaumont near Verdun**

In the building the remains of 100,000 unknown soldiers are stored

08 THE FIRST WORLD WAR

The War to End All Wars or „the Great Seminal Catastrophe of this Century"?

2014 marked the 100th anniversary of the outbreak of the **First World War.** In many countries around the world people remembered what started out as a local European war but soon became a global war that lasted from 1914 to 1918. This war was very different from conflicts in the past and was called the **Great War** or the War to End all Wars. It was not only particularly bloody, but it also introduced a new era of warfare, involving tanks, aircraft and even chemical weapons. More than 15 million people died and many more were wounded.

Great political and social changes turned the post-war world into a different one. Germany, Austria and Russia had entered the war as authoritarian monarchies, four years later in 1918 they had collapsed. Poles, citizens of the Baltic countries, Czechs and Slovaks emerged as sovereign nations from the murderous conflict between the Entente and the Central Powers. Finally, hunger riots, strikes and revolutions shook Europe. The long-term consequences of the war were to affect Germany and the whole continent for a generation.

This chapter deals with many questions such as:

- Why did the war break out?
- How did the peoples in Europe react?
- What made the war so different and destructive?
- In which ways did it affect the people at home?
- How did it change world politics and the situation in Germany?
- How should we remember the First World War?

Historical Terms

First World War or Great War:
Erster Weltkrieg oder Großer Krieg

Historical Terms

The Schlieffen Plan:
Der Schlieffenplan

July Crisis:
Julikrise

M 1 **"The Boiling Cauldron"**
English Cartoon, published in "Punch", 1908

M 2 **The Assassination in Sarajevo**
Police arrest Ferdinand Behr for interfering in the arrest of the Sarajevo assassin Gavrilo Princip. Behr proved that he was not involved.
Photograph, 28 June 1914

The Road to War

The First World War – "Hell's Last Horror"

In August 1914, when war broke out in Europe, the British Foreign Minister Sir Edward Grey said: "The lamps are going out all over Europe; we shall not see them lit again in our lifetime." He was one of the few who realized that this war would be totally different from former ones and would turn out to be, in the words of the British poet, Siegfried Sassoon, "Hell's Last Horror". The Great War or World War I became a global military conflict which left millions dead and shaped the modern world. But who was to blame?

The Origins of the War – who is to blame?

The causes of the war were complicated and historians still suggest different interpretations about who was responsible for its outbreak. As shown in the last chapters, colonialism had negative effects on the relationships between European nations. Tensions rose, a massive arms race began and an inflexible system of opposing alliances created an atmosphere of fear and insecurity. There was a general sense that war was likely to break out.

Germany feared an attack on two fronts: from France in the west and from Russia in the east. To win such a war would be difficult, because it meant splitting forces in two. Therefore, General von Schlieffen drew up a war plan in 1905 which proposed to knock out France first and then turn against Russia. In order to avoid French *fortresses*, German troops had to invade France via Belgium, whose neutrality was guaranteed by Britain. **The Schlieffen Plan** was a calculated *gamble* and included risks. The general thought that it would take Russia at least six weeks to mobilize its forces and prepare for war which would give Germany enough time to beat the French. The second risk was that Britain would join the war in order to protect Belgium. The acceptance of the plan meant that as soon as the Russian troops started to mobilize, Germany had to attack France. This dilemma left little room for diplomacy to solve conflicts.

The Balkans – the *powder keg* of Europe

The spark that finally *ignited* the war was the assassination of the Austrian heir to the throne, Archduke Franz Ferdinand, and his wife in Sarajevo. The Bosnian assassin was supported by a group of Serbian nationalists. Although a number of conflicts like the Moroccan Crises had been solved peacefully, the Balkans in south-eastern Europe were a dangerous trouble spot. The states had been part of the *crumbling* Turkish Ottoman Empire. Therefore powers like Austria and Russia tried to expand into this area. Russia encouraged a movement to form a Pan-Slavic union of all Slavs under the protection of Russia. This would include Bulgarians, Serbs and the majority of the population in Montenegro and Bosnia. Since many Slavs lived in Austria-Hungary its government saw Slav nationalism as a serious threat to the empire and a potential cause of war. The assassination of the Austrian Archduke set into motion a series of fast-moving events – the **July Crisis** – which eventually led to war.

Austria consulted Germany. William II promised support for every Austrian action, a "*carte blanche*" was given. In the light of this promise Austria used the murder as an excuse to attack Serbia. An *ultimatum* was sent to Serbia which contained terms that were impossible to accept. The most important demand was

Chronology

Chronology of Events during the July Crisis 1914

28 June	Archduke Franz Ferdinand of Austria is assassinated in Sarajevo.
6 July	Germany gives Austria 'carte blanche'.
20–23 July	French President Poincaré visits St. Petersburg and declares that France will be on Russia's side whatever happens.
23 July	Austria sends an ultimatum to Belgrade (Serbia): (1) that Serbia was to ban all societies organizing anti-Austrian propaganda (2) that Serbia was to dismiss all officials to whom Austria objected (3) that Austrian police and officials were to enter Serbia to make sure that these two demands were carried out.
25 July	Russia promises to help Serbia. Serbia accepts (1) and (2) of the Austrian ultimatum, but refuses to accept (3) for reasons of her sovereignty. Austria mobilizes part of her troops.
28 July	Austria declares war on Serbia.
29 July	Russia mobilizes part of her troops (against Austria-Hungary). In an ultimatum to Belgium, Germany demands the right for her troops to march through Belgian territory in case of war against France.
30 July	Russia mobilizes all her forces (directly against Germany).
31 July	In two ultimata Germany demands that a) Russia demobilize and b) France declare her neutrality in case of war between Germany and Russia.
1 August	a) Russia does not answer the German ultimatum and b) France mobilizes her forces and rejects the ultimatum. Germany mobilizes her forces. Germany declares war on Russia.
2 August	Great Britain mobilizes her fleet.
3 August	Germany declares war on France and invades Belgium.
4 August	Great Britain declares war on Germany because she has violated Belgian neutrality.

Vocabulary

fortress: a strong building or place to protect against attacks

gamble: a risky action

powder keg: small barrel of gunpowder

to ignite: to start to burn

to crumble: to break off

"carte blanche": complete freedom to act as one thinks best

ultimatum: a final threat to use force if sb. does not do what is wanted

to reject: unwilling to accept sth.

that Austrian officials should be allowed into Serbia to arrest the murderers. After Russia had offered support for Serbia, Serbia *rejected* the Austrian demand because it violated Serbian sovereignty. On 28 July Austria declared war on Serbia and one day later Russia mobilized its army. This development brought Germany into the conflict. When Russia refused to stop the mobilization, Germany declared war on Russia on 1 August. Germany invaded Belgium and France two days later. On 4 August the British government declared war on Germany. The automatic sequence of mobilization by the great powers destroyed any hope of a political settlement. The First World War had begun.

M 3 "War"

Mobilized troops in Paris, 1914

M 4 "Trip to Paris"

German soldiers on their way to the front, 1914

Who Was Responsible for the Outbreak of War?

M 5 **"I did not want war!"**
German postcard, 1914

M 6 **"!!Danger!! – Dynamite, The All-European Store House of War Equipment and Explosives"**
American cartoon, 1914. The figures in the back represent European States.

M 7 An Assessment

Australian historian Christopher Clark published his best-selling book on the outbreak of World War I, "The Sleepwalkers: How Europe Went to War in 1914" in 2013. In an interview with Radio Free Europe/Radio Liberty in June 2014 he said (www.rferl.org):

RFE/RL: During July 1914, following Franz Ferdinand's assassination, tensions steadily mounted, leading to the outbreak of World War I by the end of the month. In your view, who was most responsible for getting Europe to the point of no return?

Clark: In the end, we're looking at a Europe inhabited by great powers, each of which was, in a very egotistical and *autistic* way – without respect, really, to the interests of the others – pursuing its own interests and each of which was willing, for the sake of the pursuit of its own interests, to take the risk of a major conflict.

RFE/RL: But could we speak in terms of who was most responsible? Was it Germany?

Clark: A friend of mine asked me this the other day. He said, "Let's draw up percentages of responsibility" and he wanted it divided up between Germany and France and Russia and so on. I think if we are looking at the July crisis itself [...]. I think the (German) "Blank Check" would be at the top of the list.

The next one is the Russian mobilization. I think the Austrian declaration of war has to come fairly high up as well. In the end I would be *apportioning* the responsibility fairly evenly.

But the thing is, it's not just about the July crisis. The July crisis occurs after the assassination, but by the time the assassination occurs the Balkans is already very seriously stirred up and the international situation is already very unstable and the peace is very fragile.

The reasons for the fragility of peace, those reasons are very complex [...]. Why are the French paying the Russians? Why did the French in autumn 1913 agree to pay the Russians the largest loans in the history of finance? These are the largest international loans ever, and whose purpose is to grow a vast Russian Army of 2.8 million men with *quadruple* strategic railway lines leading to the German front. That's not a very good way of keeping the peace.

RFE/RL: [...] Do you see parallels to the world today?

Clark: This is what's so disturbing about 1914 for today, that we are in a world which is very like the world of 1914, more and more so. [...] We've seen in the last few weeks, the Ukrainian crisis has revealed the complete incapacity of the EU to form a shared view on these sorts of questions. My own view – and in this I see a parallel with 1914 – is that the causes of this crisis don't simply lie in [Russian President] Vladimir Putin's power plays, but that this is a complexly caused crisis. And I don't want to assign blame, but I think the actions of the EU also helped to destabilize the situation in Ukraine.

RFE/RL: What lessons can we draw from World War I today?

Clark: We mustn't be confident that we will see the next war coming 18 months in advance and have plenty of time to try and avoid it. It's not necessarily going to be like that. You know, we saw how rapidly the relationship between Russia, the EU, and the United States has been transformed by the Ukrainian crisis. It's a few months. The situation in the west Pacific, – in the China Sea – we've seen a *deterioration* now in relations with Vietnam because of the ramming of several Vietnamese frigates by Chinese ships. That situation could deteriorate very drastically, very, very fast.

So I suppose one of the lessons of the book is that bad stuff can happen very fast and we need to be extremely *vigilant* and we need to focus not so much on recognizing that a war is coming in advance, but even before those signs appear, on building structures that can avoid naked, armed conflict.

M 8 The Peace Treaty of Versailles (1919) Contained a "war guilt clause": Article 231

"The Allied and Associated Governments *affirm* and Germany accepts the responsibility of Germany and her allies for causing all the loss and damage to which the Allied and Associated Governments and their nationals have been subjected as a consequence of the war *imposed* upon them by the aggression of Germany and her allies."

http://net.lib.byu.edu/~rdh7/wwi/versa/versa7.html [Oct. 2017].

Vocabulary

autistic: unable to communicate with or react to other people

to apportion: to divide something among people

quadruple: (here) four times as many

deterioration: the fact or process of becoming worse

vigilant: very careful to notice any signs of danger or trouble

to affirm: to state publicly that sth. is true

to impose upon: to force sth. on someone

Tasks

1. Before the War

a) Describe the situation in the cartoon (M1) and identify the nations which the figures on the cauldron represent.
b) Explain the message of the cartoon.
c) Look at the chronology (p. 189) and assess which measures encouraged war, which were intended to prevent war.
d) Describe the photos (M3, M4) and explain why many people were enthusiastic about the war.

2. The Question of Guilt

a) Assess William's statement (M5).
b) Describe the cartoon and explain how the cause of war is illustrated (M6).
c) Discuss this assessment (M7) and the question who was to blame for the outbreak of the war.
d) Comment on Lloyd George's quote: "The governments of Europe stumbled and staggered into war" (Lloyd George was English Prime Minister).
e) Compare the statement in M8 with those in M5 and M7.

The Modern War

"The Spirit of 1914" – enthusiastic about war?

The war had long been expected and when it finally came patriotic enthusiasm took hold and created the "Spirit of 1914". Many people in Europe seemed to be delighted at the prospect of war. Especially in major cities a general rejoicing became visible. Demonstrations in support of the war took place in the streets and, driven by the propaganda of the time and a sense of patriotism, honour and duty, millions of young men volunteered for military service and marched off to the front singing patriotic songs. The glamour of the uniform, the chance for adventure and the idea that the war would be over by Christmas of 1914 also attracted many men. Others, usually workers, were more critical, but their protests and marches against the war had only a limited effect.

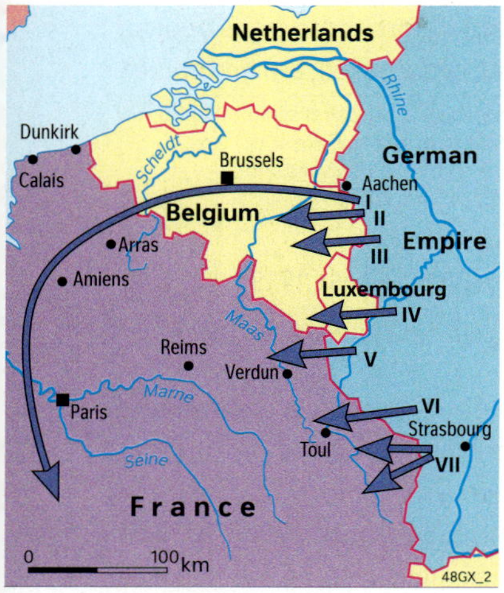

M 1 **The Schlieffen Plan**

The War in the West

The war began on 3 August 1914, when German troops invaded Belgium. On the one side were the Central Powers: Germany and Austria, later joined by Turkey and Bulgaria. On the other were the Allies or Entente Powers: France, Russia and Britain, later joined by Japan, Italy, China and the United States (1917).

At first it looked as though the Schlieffen Plan would work. The German armies swept into Belgium but their progress was slower than expected. They met strong Belgian resistance at Liège and then the British Expeditionary Force held them up at Mons. Even worse, the Russians mobilized more quickly than expected and on 19 August the Russian army attacked. The Germans had to send two divisions to try to stop them on the eastern front. Despite all this, by 4 September German troops had almost reached Paris. When they were just sixty kilometres from the French capital, the French and British counter-attacked along the River Marne. The Battle of the Marne was the most important battle of the war. It lasted a week and involved two million men. Finally, the Germans were forced back to the River Aisne, where they dug *trenches* and built defences. When the Allies found they could not advance any further, they also dug themselves in facing the German positions. By the end of 1914 these trenches stretched from Belgium to Switzerland. There was little change in these positions until 1918. Both sides were locked in a *stalemate*. The German defeat at the River Marne ruined the Schlieffen Plan and General von Moltke, the German Chief of Staff, told the Emperor "Germany has lost the war". William II did not take the consequences and von Moltke resigned.

M 2 **French Soldiers in the Trenches**
Lorraine, June 1915

Trench Warfare – a new type of warfare

The war became a static *war of attrition*. Each side tried to break through, to gain land and advantage. In 1915 and 1916 the major battles took place at Ypres, Verdun and at the River Somme. There was no breakthrough in the lines but the fighting cost the lives of millions of soldiers. Life in the trenches was hard. Soldiers had to cope with the extremes of the weather. Heavy rain could leave the trenches knee deep in water and in the hot summer there was no chance for refreshment. Soldiers ate basic food, stood guard and slept in mud. Hunger, rats, lice and the penetrating smell of dead bodies characterized daily life. Again and again exhausted soldiers were sent "over the top". This meant climbing out of the trenches, crossing the stretch between the lines, the so-called No Man's Land, and attacking the enemy lines. The defenders protected themselves with *barbed wire* and machine guns.

Heavy artillery fire, gas or aeroplane attacks proved to be traumatic and horrifying. Modern warfare was much different from former wars and much more murderous. There was no decisive battle and no quick end to the fighting. Instead, there were unlimited *casualties* and endless killing of millions of soldiers.

The invention of the *tank* eventually gave protection for the attacking troops and offered a chance to break the standstill. But it took another two years, when finally Allied tanks broke through the defences at Amiens on 8 August 1918. The German army suffered its "black day" and was forced to retreat to the defensive positions along the "Siegfried Line" in northern France.

The War in the East and the War at Sea

In the east, the German army was initially on the defensive, but after the successful battles of Tannenberg and the Masurian Lakes, General von Hindenburg could stop the Russian advance. In 1915, German and Austrian troops moved into Russia and brought the Russian Empire near collapse. Although its soldiers fought bravely, the huge Russian army could not stop the invaders. Badly equipped and led by incompetent generals, the Russians suffered enormous losses and the fighting spirit was low. *Mutinies* in the army and riots and strikes at home prepared the ground for the Communist Revolution in October 1917. The new government, headed by Vladimir Lenin, made peace with Germany and had to accept the harsh terms of the Treaty of Brest-Litovsk in March 1918. Russia agreed to pay reparations for war damage, lost its western provinces and accepted an independent Ukraine. Germany could now transfer armies to the western front where they were immediately needed. But it was too late to change the course of events.

Wilhelm II had built up the German navy before the war, but the British fleet was still much stronger. When the war started the British navy blockaded all German ports to cut off supplies of raw materials and food to Germany. From 1915 on German submarines tried to stop supplies reaching Britain by sinking merchant ships in the Atlantic. When they sank the passenger liner "Lusitania" in May 1915 many Americans were also killed. After US protests Germany promised to restrict U-boat warfare. On 31 May and 1 June 1916 the British and German deep-sea fleets finally met off the coast of Denmark. This Battle of Jutland (Skagerrakschlacht) was the only major naval battle of the First World War. Both sides claimed the battle as a victory. The Royal Navy suffered heavier losses than the German navy, but remained in control of the North Sea. The German fleet failed to end the British blockade and rested at anchor until the war ended.

In 1917 the Germans returned to unrestricted U-boat warfare sinking British merchant ships in high numbers without warning. The Allies introduced the new convoy system, in which merchant ships sailed in large groups escorted by destroyers. This improved the situation because it made it more difficult for U-boats to attack. When American ships were torpedoed again, US President Wilson declared war on Germany in April 1917.

Vocabulary

trench: a long, deep hole dug in the ground

stalemate: situation in which neither side can win or make any progress

war of attrition: wearing the other side down by killing so many men that they could not be replaced

barbed wire: strong wire with short sharp points on it, used especially for fences

casualties: killed, wounded or missing soldiers

tank: a military vehicle covered with strong metal and armed with guns

mutiny: a refusal by a group of soldiers or sailors to accept orders

M 3 "Hero's Death on the High Sea"

Painting by Hans Bohrdt, about 1915

Tasks

1. **The Modern War**
   a) Analyse the map (M1) and explain the course of the war.
   b) Point out which areas were particularly affected by the war (text, M1).
   c) Describe the pictures (M2, M3) and comment on what they express.

The War in the West

M 4 **Panorama of a Trench System**

M 5 "All Quiet on the Western Front"

Extract from Erich Maria Remarque's Novel "All Quiet on the Western Front" 1929. Remarque was a German soldier in the First World War:

"We occupy a crater and get surrounded. Two fellows with a flame-thrower move towards us. One carries the tin of petrol on his back, the other has a hose from which the fire spouts. If they get near enough to use it, we are done for, since we cannot retreat across the open ground.
We open fire on them, but they work nearer; things look bad. Bentinck is lying in the hole with us. When he sees that we cannot escape, he takes a rifle, crawls out of the crater and, lying down propped on his elbows, he takes aim. He fires – the same moment a bullet smacks into him. Still he lies there and aims again; at last he fires, lets the gun drop and slips back into the hole. One of the flamethrowers is hit, he falls, the hose slips, squirting fire on all sides and he burns.
Bentinck has a chest wound. After a while a shell fragment hits him and smashes away his chin. The same fragment carries on to tear open Leer's hip. He bleeds quickly, like an empty tube; after a couple of minutes he collapses."

Erich Maria Remarque, Im Westen nichts Neues, Propyläen: Berlin 1928. (transl. by Thomas Söhrnsen).

M 6 **Trenches at Ypres, 1917**

M 7 **Battleground at Ypres, 1917**

Tasks

1. Modern Warfare

a) Explain why it was difficult for each side to attack and capture the enemy's position (M4).

b) Describe the photos (M6, M7) and read the text (M5) carefully. Then write a report about the life of a common soldier on the front line.

c) Compare the soldiers' lives with their enthusiasm before the war (M5 – M7 and text p. 192).

d) Describe the postcard and discuss the artist's intention (M3).

M 1 Women Producing Grenades
Photo, 1917

The War at Home

World War I – the first total war?

Once the war began, the countries taking part mobilized their entire populations and economic resources to achieve victory on the battlefield. The term "home front" was used for the first time during World War I. It perfectly expressed this new concept of a war in which the civilian population behind the lines was directly involved in the war *effort*. Governments forced men to enlist in the army and took control of important industries. Women found themselves doing jobs that they would never have dreamed of doing before the war: They drove ambulances, took jobs in arms factories and on buses and trains. During the war women gained more confidence in their abilities and began to challenge traditional ideas about female behaviour and roles in society. After 1918 they gradually gained the right to vote in Britain and a year later in Germany.

Shortages in Germany

As soon as the war started the British navy blockaded all German ports. This cut off supplies of raw materials and food to Germany. Expecting a short war, the German economy was not prepared for a long war on two fronts. *Stocks of supplies* were low and soon they had to be rationed. In 1917 the daily food ration sank to one-third of the peace time ration. The meat supply collapsed completely and was finally limited to nineteen grams a day. When the bread ration had to be reduced, hunger strikes broke out. The winter of 1916/17 was called the "*turnip* winter", because turnip syrup was used as a substitute for coffee and jam; turnips were added to meat and bread *dough*. Children were asked to collect all sorts of things to be recycled. The shortages in food and raw materials played an important part in Germany's decision to end the war in 1918.

M 2 "Selling Potatoes on the Alexanderplatz"
Photo, 1917

Vocabulary

effort: activity to achieve sth.

stocks of supplies: reserves of food

turnip: a round root vegetable

dough: a kind of bread or pastry made of flour, water, etc.

M 3 Economic Situation in Germany

British secret agents in Germany reported to the Foreign Office in September 1918:

"In addition to other hardships, the German public is threatened this winter by an almost complete lack of lights of every description: electric light, gas, lamp oil and candles. The lack of soap and washing powder makes personal cleanliness impossible and helps the spread of disease. Medicines are difficult *to obtain* [...]. In the industrial district of Westphalia many of the women have hardly any clothing and are going about in a thin blouse and skirt, barelegged with wooden shoes."

The Foreign Office, The Economic Situation in Germany and Austria-Hungary, 1914–1918, Confidential Report no. 11025, September 1918.

M 4 A Strike in Berlin 1918

Towards the end of the war protests in Germany increased. The paper "Vorwärts" of the Social Democratic Party reported on a workers' strike meeting in Berlin on 29 January 1918:

"The meeting formulated the following demands:

- The speedy bringing about of peace [...].
- Better food supplies [...].
- The complete restoration of the right of assembly as well as the right of free discussion [...].
- An end to military control of industries.
- The immediate *release* of all persons convicted or arrested for political action.
- The right to vote in the Prussian parliament for all men and women over 20 years old."

Quoted from: Josh Brooman, Germany 1918–45: Democracy and Dictatorship, Longman: Harlow 1996, p. 9.

M 5 Women Urged to Quit Home for Factory

A British report from 1915:

"March 18. The Government has issued an urgent appeal to the women of Britain to serve their country by signing on for war work. The aim is to get as many women as possible doing vital jobs so that men can be freed for fighting. Women are desperately needed in trade, industry, agriculture and above all in armaments, where thousands could be employed immediately making shells.

The Government is now setting up a Register of Women for War Service. Any woman, trained or untrained, can sign on at her local Labour Exchange. The move has been warmly welcomed by leaders of the women's movement including Emmeline Pankhurst who said: 'Women are only *anxious* to be recruited.'

During her recent visit to France she had seen many jobs previously done by men now being done by women, including bank telling and cabdriving. Another official of the Women's Social and Political Union, Mrs Dacre Fox, said: 'We believe women can be employed in almost any capacity of intellectual or physical work.'

Mrs Fawcett, president of the National Union of Women's Suffrage Societies, said it would raise the standard for women in both work and wages. 'This war has really had a good effect in bringing men and women together and making them *rely upon mutual* friendship and cooperation.'"

Quoted from: Chronicle of the 20th Century, Dorling Kindersley Ltd.: London 1995, p. 200.

M 6 "Home Front": A Coalwoman

Photo, during First World War

Vocabulary

to obtain: to get
release: the act of setting free
anxious: wanting sth. very much
to rely upon: to depend on sb./sth.
mutual: shared by two or more people

Tasks

1. **Fighting at Home**
   a) How did the war affect the life of people at home? Analyse the sources to find answers (M1–M6).
   b) Make a mindmap with the term "home front" as a starting point.

Vocabulary

descent: a person's family origins

to cut back: to reduce

Towards Allied Victory – 1917, an Epochal Year

US Entry into the War?

1917 was a year of change with the tide turning against Germany. Communist Russia left the war, but the USA decided to join it against Germany. The US had never before been an ally in European wars, and had remained neutral in 1914. Many Americans were of German *descent* and approved of the policy of "isolation". When the war began, President Woodrow Wilson said, "We have to be neutral. Otherwise our mixed population would wage war on each other." But at the same time, many Americans, including Wilson, wanted the Allies to win the war. They preferred democratic governments to the old-fashioned rule of the monarchies in Germany and Austria. American business interests realized that big profits could be made by trading with the Allies, and when they were asked to supply raw materials, food and weapons they agreed. Payment was arranged in the form of generous loans which had to be repaid after a victorious war.

Unrestricted Submarine Warfare

So the USA became the arsenal of Great Britain and France and thousands of ships sailed across the Atlantic. This did not seem neutral to the Germans and they used submarines to sink all merchant ships bringing supplies to Britain. The sinking of the passenger ship "Lusitania" in 1915 – over 1000 people including 128 Americans died – caused some anti-German feeling in the States.

The German emperor ordered the submarine warfare to be *cut back*, but two years later the Germans returned to unrestricted U-boat warfare. Believing that Britain could be brought to her knees in six months, they declared that any ship sailing to Britain would be attacked. The German U-boats were very successful, but the sinking of neutral ships bringing supplies to Britain greatly angered the USA. On 2 April 1917 President Wilson asked the Congress to declare war on Germany. "The world must be made safe for democracy," he announced, and four days later the USA entered the war.

The American decision to take part in European matters was one reason that made 1917 an important year. The other one can be found in Russia.

M 1 **"US Troops at War"**
US troops in France, 1917

Propaganda Posters

M 2 "Irishmen Avenge the Lusitania"
British poster, 1915

M 3 "Destroy this Mad Brute"
US poster, 1917

M 4 "I Want You For U.S.Army"
US poster, 1917

Entering the War

M 5 Different opinions

a) President Woodrow Wilson's War Message (April 1917):

"Our object [...] is *to vindicate* the principles of peace and justice in the life of the world as against selfish and autocratic power [...]. We are glad [...] to fight [...] for the ultimate peace of the world and for the liberation of its peoples, the German peoples included: for the right of nations great and small and the privilege of men everywhere to choose their way of life and of obedience. The world must be made safe for democracy [...]."

Abridged from:http://historymatters.gmu.edu/d/4943/ [Oct. 2017].

b) Speech by Senator George W. Norris opposing US entry into the war:

"[...] I am opposed to taking any step that will force our country into the useless and senseless war now being *waged* in Europe [...]. No *close* student of recent history will deny that both Great Britain and Germany have, on numerous *occasions* since the beginning of the war [...] *violated* in the most serious manner the rights of neutral vessels and neutral nations under existing international law [...]. The reason given by the President in asking Congress to declare war against Germany is that the German government has declared certain war zones, within which, by the use of submarines, she sinks, without notice, American ships and destroys American lives. [...] The first war zone was declared by Great Britain [...]. This zone so declared by Great Britain covered the whole of the North Sea. [...] Both of these orders declaring military zones were illegal and contrary to international law.

There are a great many American citizens who feel that we owe it as a duty to humanity to take part in this war. Many instances of cruelty and inhumanity can be found on both sides. Men are often *biased* in their judgment on account of their sympathy and their interests [...].

We have loaned many hundreds of millions of dollars to the Allies [...]. The enormous profits of munition manufacturers and *stockbrokers* [...] must be still further increased by our entrance into the war [...].

To whom does war bring *prosperity*? Not to the soldier who [...] goes into the trench, there to shed his blood and to die if necessary; not to the broken-hearted widow who waits for the return of her husband; not to the mother who weeps at the death of her brave boy [...].

War brings no prosperity to the great mass of common and patriotic citizens. It increases the cost of living of those who *toil* and those who already must strain every effort to keep soul and body together. War brings prosperity to the stock *gambler* on Wall Street – to those who are already in possession of more wealth than can be realized or enjoyed".

Abridged from: https://www.mtholyoke.edu/acad/intrel/doc19.htm [Oct. 2017].

Vocabulary

to vindicate: to prove that sth. is true
to wage: to begin and continue a war, a battle, etc.
close: (here) knowing well
occasion: a situation that allows sth. to happen
to violate: to do sth. that is not allowed by law
to be biased: having or showing prejudice, unfair attitude
stockbroker: sb. whose job is to buy and sell shares of stock (money) for other people
prosperity: the state of being wealthy, rich
to toil: to work very hard, physically
gambler: sb. who likes to play and risk his money

Tasks

1. **Entering the War**
   a) Describe the propaganda posters (M2–M4).
   b) Explain the effect they should have on the people in Britain and the United States.
   c) Read the speeches (M5) and list the arguments in your own words.

Making Peace

M 6 **Thomas Woodrow Wilson**

28th President of the United States from 1913–1927

M 6 The Fourteen Points

President Woodrow Wilson, 8 January 1918:

"We entered this war because violations of right had *occurred* [...] and made the life of our own people impossible unless they were corrected and the world made secure once and for all against their *recurrence*. What we demand in this war, therefore, is [...] that the world be made fit and safe to live in [...] The program of the world's peace, therefore, is our program; and that program, the only possible program, as we see it, is this:

1. No more secret treaties
2. Free *access* to the sea at all times
3. No restrictions on trade between countries
4. Disarmament by all countries
5. Colonies to have a say in their own future
6. Russia to be free of German troops and to choose her own system of government
7. Belgium to be evacuated and *restored* as an independent country
8. Alsace-Lorraine to go back to France [...]

10. The peoples of the Austro-Hungarian Empire to be free
11. *Self-determination* for the peoples in the Balkans [...]

14. A League of Nations should be set up to settle *disputes*."

Adapted from: https://archive.org/stream/americanismwoodr00unitiala/americanismwoodr00unitiala_djvu.txt [Oct. 2017].

Vocabulary

to occur: to happen

recurrence: when sth. that has happened before happens again

access: the right to enter a place, use sth., see someone, etc

to restore: to make sth. return to its former state or condition

self-determination: the right of the people in a country to choose their own government

dispute: a serious argument or disagreement

Tasks

1. Making Peace

a) Wilson's Fourteen Points can be summarized under the following principles:
   1. safeguards (against war for the future)
   2. no discrimination against any nation
   3. no occupation of foreign territory
   4. self-determination of the peoples

   Together with a partner, find the points showing these principles.

b) Discuss Wilson's peace programme. Can it help to prevent future wars?

The Russian Revolution

M 1 **Tsar Nicholas II (1868–1918)**
Photograph, about 1900

The February Revolution 1917

In 1917, two revolutions swept through Russia, ending centuries of imperial rule and leading to political and social changes that would later lead to the formation of the Soviet Union.

The February Revolution began on 8 March 1917 (or 23 February in the Julian calendar). Most Russians had lost faith in Tsar Nicholas II. He refused reforms, his government was undemocratic and corrupt and the Russian economy remained backward. In addition, there was extreme poverty among peasants and miserable working and living conditions for the workers in towns. However, the immediate causes of the February Revolution were Russia's military defeats with millions of *casualties*, which led to an immense *war-weariness*. Growing civil unrest, coupled with chronic food shortages, turned into open revolt in St. Petersburg. Supported by huge crowds of striking industrial workers, the protesters called on the czar to abdicate. When soldiers were commanded to shoot at the rioters, they refused and joined in the strike. Workers and soldiers elected their own councils, called "**soviets**", in the big cities. Tsar Nicholas saw that he had lost the support of the army and that he had no choice. He abdicated and a new "provisional government" was formed by Alexander Kerensky.

Historical Terms

soviets: Sowjets, Räte
Bolsheviks: Bolschewiki, Anhänger Lenins

The October Revolution: "Peace – Land – Bread"

The new government and the Petrograd Soviet promised some democratic and social reforms but did not take Russia out of the war. The situation changed when radical revolutionaries, the **Bolsheviks**, returned from *exile* and demanded a Communist revolution. Led by Vladimir Lenin, who the German government allowed to travel from Switzerland through Germany to Russia, the Bolsheviks put forward their own demands. Lenin said that the war was a war of capitalists and should be stopped. The real enemies were not the Germans, but the landowners and capitalists in Russia. His slogan "Peace – Land – Bread" was very attractive to workers, soldiers and peasants. Lenin promised that he would end the war, give people enough food to eat and share out the land among the peasants. When food prices continued to rise and a new military offensive failed, soldiers deserted the army. Strikes and protests broke out again. Lenin was ready to act. Red Guards

M 2 **Alexander Kerensky**
Photograph, about 1917

M 3 **Lenin at his Arrival in St. Petersburg**
Photograph, April 1917

M 4 **Victims of the Russian Civil War**
Photograph, about 1922

"stormed" the Winter Palace on 7 November and arrested members of the "Provisional Government". Kerensky went into exile, and Lenin took full control of the government in what is called the Bolshevik Revolution. Russia was now the first communist country in the world.

Lenin's government made peace with Germany at Brest-Litovsk in March 1918, *nationalized* industry and *distributed* land, but beginning in 1918 had to fight a *devastating* civil war against anti-Bolshevik White Army forces. In 1920, the anti-Bolsheviks were defeated, and in 1922 the **Union of Soviet Socialist Republics (USSR)** was established.

An "Epochal Year"

The American decision to become involved in European matters and the communist *seizure of power* in Russia had far-reaching consequences for the history of the 20th century and thus 1917 is called an "epochal year".

Vocabulary

casualties: people who are killed or injured in war

war-weariness: being tired of war

exile: a situation in which you are forced to leave your country or home and go to live in a foreign country

to nationalize: to put an industry or a company under the control of the government, which becomes its owner

to distribute: to give things to people; to share sth. between a number of people

devastating: causing a lot of damage and destruction

seizure of power: act of suddenly taking control of a country, esp. by force

Historical Terms

Union of Soviet Socialist Republics (USSR): Union der Sozialistischen Sowjetrepubliken (UdSSR)

M 5 **"Lenin on Stage"**
Painting by A. M. Gerassimow, 1930

"The Bolshevik" – analysing propaganda

M 6 **"The Bolshevik"**
Painting by Boris Michailowitsch Kustodijew, 1920

Vocabulary

Useful phrases

a gigantic figure / a colossus

to seem unyielding, energetic, full of strength and will

to stride through a city (here: Moscow)

to look like Lenin

facial expression: decisive and aggressive

to carry a red banner

people follow him through the streets / gather at his feet / push on together to a common goal

in the left foreground stands a tower of the Kremlin

Vocabulary

in the right corner stands the Pashkov House (later home of the V.I. Lenin State Library of the Soviet Union, renamed the Russian State Library in 1992)

to show Bolshevism as a mass movement

masses of people and the Bolshevik move together toward the Kremlin

the Bolsheviks made the Kremlin their seat of power in 1918

Moscow returns to importance after 100 years

to show the path of the Bolsheviks to power

clear message is almost like a cartoon

Lenin's April Theses 1917

M 7 What Were the Bolsheviks Fighting for?

Lenin's April Theses 1917 (excerpt):

One
[...] the war on Russia's part remains an [...] imperialist war.

Two
[...] the present situation in Russia [...] represents a transition from the first stage of the revolution – [...] to its second stage which is to place power in the hands of the *proletariat* and the poorest [...] of the peasantry [...].

Five
Not a parliamentary republic – a return to it from the Soviet of Workers' Deputies would be a step backward – but a republic of Soviets of Workers', Agricultural Labourers' and Peasants' Deputies throughout the land, from top to bottom.

Six
Confiscation of private lands. Nationalization of all lands in the country, and management of such lands by local Soviets of Agricultural Labourers' and Peasants' Deputies.

Seven
Immediate *merger* of all the banks in the country into one general national bank, over which the Soviet of Workers' Deputies should have control [...].

Eight
Not the "introduction" of Socialism as an immediate task, but the immediate placing of the Soviet of Workers' Deputies in control of social production and distribution of goods [...].

Ten
Rebuilding *the International*. Taking the initiative in the creation of a revolutionary International [...]."

Abridged from: http://www.firstworldwar.com/source/apriltheses.htm [Oct. 2017].

Vocabulary

proletariat: working class people
confiscation: the act of officially taking sth. away from somebody
merger: the process of combining two or more companies
the International: an international socialist organization

Tasks

1. **Biographies**
   Find out more about Tsar Nicholas II or Vladimir Lenin and write a short profile.
2. **Explain Why the Revolution Started**
   a) Why was the tsar overthrown in 1917? Draw a diagram that shows the causes for the February revolution.
   b) It is 1917. You live in St Petersburg as a factory worker, soldier or nobleman. What do you think about the strikes, the war or the tsar? Write entries for your diary saying what you saw, did and thought on Sunday, 9 March and on 8 November.
3. **What Did the Communists Want?**
   a) Read Lenin's April Theses (M7) and fill in this table:
   – Lenin's position on the war
   – The system he demands and the one he rejects
   – The measures he suggests to transform Russia into a communist state
   b) Discuss possible reactions to Lenin's programme by the western democracies.
4. **"The Bolshevik" – Analysing Propaganda**
   a) Describe the painting (M6).
   b) Explain its message.

The End of the War

Allied Superiority

The support of the USA was a huge *boost* to Allied morale when it was badly needed. The economic and military strength of America encouraged the Allies in their hope of victory in 1918. The US navy was very important for breaking the German submarine blockade, and in the summer of 1918, the fresh and well-equipped American troops played a decisive role on land. After the German spring offensive was halted the Allies began counter-attacks in August 1918. They forced the Germans to withdraw their demoralized troops to a specially constructed area of defences known as the Hindenburg Line. By October 1918, an American army of over 1,750,000 soldiers was in France. The German commander General Ludendorff finally called on his government to ask the Allies for an *armistice* before the fighting reached Germany itself.

Vocabulary

boost: sth. that helps or encourages sb.

armistice: a formal agreement during a war to stop fighting and discuss making peace

influenza: an infectious disease

mutiny: a refusal by a group of soldiers or sailors to accept orders

primordial: existing at the beginning of time or the beginning of the Earth

disillusionment: having no ideals and becoming disappointed or bitter because of this

Revolution in Germany – the end of monarchy

In Berlin, political leaders saw that the situation was hopeless. Bulgaria and Turkey had asked for peace and the Austro-Hungarian Empire was falling apart. An epidemic of *influenza* had added to the problems of the starving German people. Over 1700 Berliners died in one day. A naval *mutiny* in Kiel and revolutionary uprisings in Munich began. On 9 November, a republic was proclaimed, marking the end of the monarchy. The situation was so grave that Emperor William fled to exile in the Netherlands. On 11 November, the armistice was agreed to and signed in a railway carriage at Compiègne. After four long years the First World War was over. It has been called the "*primordial* catastrophe of the twentieth century" and was the largest global conflict yet seen, leading to the deaths of millions and the devastation of parts of Western Europe. Three great empires – the Austro-Hungarian, the Russian, and the Ottoman – had collapsed.

New boundaries were drawn and America became a world power. Europe's dominance in the world was destroyed, and the war's political, economic, and social consequences were felt throughout the century. The "war to end all wars" caused widespread *disillusionment* and produced burdens that finally added to the even worse disaster of World War II.

M 1 End of the Great War

Crowds of people celebrating Germany's signing of the armistice on 11 November 1918 ending WWI. Photograph, London, 1918

143GX Countries	Total Mobilized	Killed & Died	Wounded	Prisoners & Missing	Total Casualties	Casualties % of Mobilized
Allied Powers (Without: Japan, Romania, Belgium, Greece, Portugal)						
Russia	12,000,000	1,700,000	4,950,000	2,500,000	9,150,000	76.3
France	8,410,000	1,357,800	4,266,000	537,000	6,160,800	76.3
British Empire	8,904,467	908,371	2,090,212	191,652	3,190,235	35.8
Italy	5,615,000	650,000	947,000	600,000	2,197,00	39.1
United States	4,355,000	126,000	234,300	4,500	364,800	8.2
Serbia	707,343	126,000	133,148	152,958	331,106	46,8
Montenegro	50,000	3,000	10,000	7,000	20,000	40.0
Total	42,188,810	5,152,115	12,831,004	4,121,090	22,104,209	52.3
Central Powers						
Germany	11,000,000	1,773,700	4,216,058	1,152,800	7,142,558	64.9
Austria-Hungary	7,800,000	1,200,000	3,620,000	2,200,000	7,020,000	90.0
Turkey	2,850,000	325,000	400,000	250,000	975,000	34.2
Bulgaria	1,200,000	87,500	152,390	27,029	266,919	22.2
Total	22,850,000	3,386,200	8,388,448	3,629,829	15,404,477	67.4
Grand Total	**65,038,810**	**8,538,315**	**21,219,452**	**7,750,919**	**37,508,686**	**57.6**

M 2 **Casualties in the First World War**

M 3 The "Stab in the Back" Legend

a) Diary notes of Colonel von Thaer, who attended a meeting of the German Supreme Command on 1 October 1918:

"As we were gathered together, (General) Ludendorff stood up in our presence, his face was *pale* and filled with deep worry, but his head was still held high [...].
He said *roughly* the following: It was his duty to tell us that our military condition was terribly serious. Any day now, our Western Front could be *breached*. He had had to report this to His Majesty the Kaiser recently [...] that the Supreme Army Command and the German Army were at an end; the war could no longer be won, but rather an unavoidable and conclusive defeat awaited. [...] Therefore, the Supreme Army Command demanded of His Majesty the Kaiser and of the Chancellor that a proposal for the bringing about of peace be made to President Wilson of America without *delay*, for bringing about an armistice on the basis of his Fourteen Points".

Abridged from: https://wwi.lib.byu.edu/index.php/From_the_Diary_Notes_of_Oberst_Thaer [Oct. 2017].

Vocabulary

German Supreme Command: group of highest army officers

b) The former German Commander-in-Chief Paul von Hindenburg on 18 November 1919:

"In *spite of the* superiority of the enemy in men and materials, we could have brought the struggle to a favourable conclusion if *determined* and *unanimous* co-operation had existed between the army and those at home. The German army was stabbed in the back. It is plain enough on whom the blame lies".

Adapted from: Herbert Michaelis/Ernst Schraepler (eds.), Ursachen und Folgen Bd. 2: Der militärische Zusammenbruch und das Ende des Kaiserreichs, Dokumenten-Verl. Wendler, Berlin 1959, p. 7f. (transl. by Thomas Söhrnsen).

Vocabulary

pale: having a very white skin

roughly (adv.): saying sth. without giving exact details or information

to breach: to get through, to break

delay: a period of time sb. has to wait

in spite of: without being affected or prevented by sth.

determined: having a strong desire to do sth., so that you will not let anyone stop you

unanimous: a unanimous decision, vote, agreement etc is one in which all the people involved agree

Tasks

1. **German Defeat**
   a) Explain why the general asks for an armistice based on Wilson's Fourteen Points (M2a).
   b) Comment on Hindenburg's point of view (M2b). List possible reasons why Germany lost the war.
2. **The War in Perspective**
   a) Study the table on casualties in the First World War (M2).
   b) It was called "The Great War" and certainly there has never been anything like it in history. Take notes on aspects that made this war so extraordinary.
   c) Looking back: Look at the introductory pages of this chapter again and explain the context and message of each source.

How to Remember World War I

M 4 First World War: How Countries across Europe Will Mark Centenary

The English paper "The Guardian" on 16 January 2014:

From exhibitions and concerts to a movie and football match, a host of events will take place *to commemorate* [the] anniversary.

Germany is lagging behind its European partners in devising plans to commemorate the *centenary* of the First World War. A press conference in Berlin yesterday has revealed a single concrete event – a small-scale "exhibition" telling the story from 1914 right through to the eastern expansion of the EU in just 26 posters [...].

Angela Merkel's spokesperson, Steffen Seibert, *hinted at* the reason for her government's reluctance to take a lead in shaping events last week, when he said that Germany did not have a "staatliche Geschichtspolitik", a state-approved policy on historical matters. Commemorative events are usually organised at federal level, rather than *decreed* by Berlin. The only public event scheduled for a German official won't even happen in Germany: the president Joachim Gauck will join François Hollande in Alsace on 3 August for an event to start the commemorations.

Germany's bureaucratic *stasis* contrasts with a *welter* of events, official and unofficial, digital, public and private, in the other former belligerent countries.

France has two big commemorations to mark the centenary: the first, involving more than 1,500 exhibitions, concerts, ceremonies, debates and public events to be run by an official body created for the purpose, the Mission du Centenaire ("centenary mission"). For the second it will invite thousands of descendants of war from 31 countries, from Albania to Yemen, to organize marches commemorating the destiny and suffering of their men.

[...] Britain's official commemorations will include the centenary of the first day of conflict on 4 August, the start of the Battle of the Somme on 1 July 2016 and further events to mark the battles of Jutland, Gallipoli, Passchendaele and Armistice Day in 2018.

Funds are being distributed to hundreds of groups and communities for large and small schemes, including a grant that will allow the twinned towns of Newark in England and Emmendingen in Germany to recreate the Christmas 1914 football match in which opposing forces from the trenches on the western front came together in an unofficial armistice [...].

However, the plans are not without critics, most vocally in the form of anti-war activists who have come together in a No Glory campaign backed by high-profile supporters such as the actors Jude Law and Alan Rickman and the poet laureate, Carol Ann Duffy [...].

https://www.theguardian.com/world/2014/jan/16/first-world-war-europe-centenary [Oct. 2017].

Vocabulary

to commemorate: to remind people of an important person or event from the past

centenary: the 100th anniversary of an event

to hint at: to suggest sth. in an indirect way

to decree: here to order

stasis: a condition in which there is no movement or change

welter: a large and confusing amount of sth.

scarlet: a bright red

moat: a deep wide hole surrounding a castle for protection

poignant: giving you feelings of sadness

M 5 Circled by a Sea of *Scarlet*

This picture shows the Tower of London *moat* filled with nearly 900,000 poppies to commemorate the First World War. Up to four million people have already visited the *poignant* tribute at the Tower which will be finished on 11 November 2014.

M 6 "Terrible and Bitter Lessons"

Federal President Joachim Gauck at a ceremony in Liège/ Belgium commemorating the centenary of the First World War, 4 August 2014:

[...] We are here today to commemorate the terrible "Great War", which became the first of the two world wars. This war began in western Europe with Germany's completely unjustifiable invasion of neutral Belgium. The invasion only followed military logic, and it thus became apparent on the very first day of the conflict how quickly treaties became worthless and how quickly the standards of civilisation were rendered *null and void* [...].

Nationalism had blinded almost everyone's hearts and minds. Neither the standards of culture and civilisation, nor religious faith, nor reason were strong enough to sway people's consciences in another direction. On the contrary, people actually believed that they were morally and religiously in the right. In the clash of cultures, feelings of superiority and extreme national egoism triumphed over empathy.

The utter failure of diplomacy; the ill fated Schlieffen Plan; [...] the erroneous belief in a short military campaign to resolve international disputes; and finally, propaganda that knew no bounds and demonised the enemy in a way hitherto unknown – all of this led Europe into a *fratricidal* war, which ultimately spread far across the world.

With the invasion of Belgium by German troops at the latest, and as in Greek mythology, Pandora's box had been opened, bringing misfortune, misery, *crippling* injuries and death to millions of people.

Along with representatives from all over the world, we commemorate those killed in action, the wounded, and those left physically and emotionally *mutilated* by the war. We will always remember and honour them. We are grateful to have been able to live together in peace for so long here in Europe. [...] Europe is now governed by the strength of the law rather than by the law of the strong. The fact that small and large member states of the European Union now strive to find joint solutions and agree on joint policies in a peaceful manner in Brussels is an achievement of civilisation that cannot be overstated.

We know all this from our own terrible history. But we are also aware of it when we look at the current state of the world. We see war, terrorist brutality and civil war in so many places. Millions of people are afflicted by violence and terror; millions have fled their homes. Political, ethnic and religious beliefs are still being exploited to justify violence and murder. Extremism and fanaticism continue to spread fear and terror. And once again, international law is being violated in a region, while in other parts of the world *martial* law or excessive violence is used in conflicts. We are therefore not only united here today in commemoration as representatives of so many countries, but also as witnesses to the greatest political, cultural and moral success of the old Europe, to the fact that peace and reconciliation are possible. A continent marked by perpetual *animosity* and the repeated outbreak of war has become a continent of peace. However, what we have witnessed should also remind us that we share responsibility for the world. We cannot remain indifferent when human rights are violated or when violence is threatened or used. We must actively champion freedom, the rule of law, awareness, tolerance, justice and humanity.

Ladies and gentlemen, the two great wars taught us terrible and bitter lessons. Let us show not merely through words of remembrance and commemoration, but also through our actions in the present and future, that we truly learned our lesson.

www.bundespraesident.de/SharedDocs/Reden/EN/JoachimGauck/Reden/2014/140804-Belgium-Commemoration.html [Oct. 2017].

Vocabulary

null and void: having no legal force; not valid

fratricidal: killing members of your own family or social group

crippling: damaging sb.'s body so that he/she is no longer able to walk or move normally

to mutilate: to hurt or damage badly

martial: connected with fighting or war

animosity: a strong feeling of opposition, anger or hatred

Tasks

1. How to Remember World War I

a) List the activities each country plans to commemorate the centenary of World War I (M4, M5).

b) Discuss why official remembrance of the First World War is different in Germany.

c) Which lessons, according to President Gauck, does the First World War teach us today (M6)?

1910 1911 1912 1913 1914

Imperialism

Anglo-German naval rivalry

28 June Assassination of Archduke Franz Ferdinand in Sarajevo

July Crisis and declarations of war

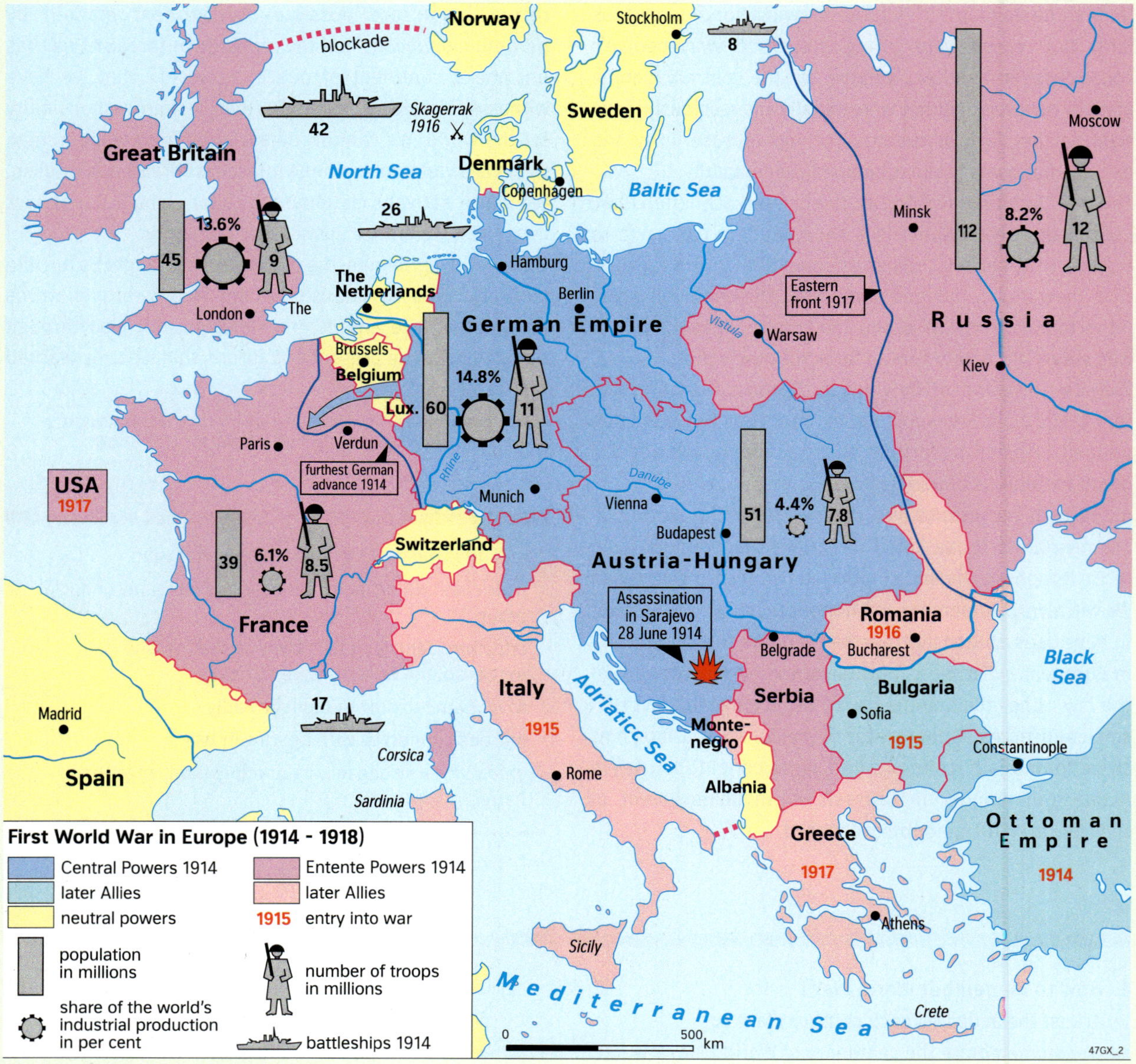

The First World War – the historical map

1916 | 1917 | 1918 | 1919 | 1920

nking of the usitania" German submarine

Battles of Verdun and the Somme;
war of attrition

Unrestricted submarine warfare,
US enters the war,
Russian Revolution

German spring offensive failed
Sailor's mutiny in Kiel
Proclamation of a republic in Berlin
Emperor William II abdicated
Armistice signed, end of war

Summary

The First World War was the first global and one of the deadliest conflicts in history. It paved the way for major political changes, including revolutions in many of the nations involved. Although there were a number of causes for the war, the assassination of Austrian Archduke Franz Ferdinand in June 1914 was the trigger. In the following July Crisis the European powers failed to find a diplomatic solution to the conflict. They seemed to accept the war as inevitable.

The fight between the Allies and the Central Powers turned out to be the first modern war making use of the most advanced technology like machine guns, tanks, poison gas, submarines and aircraft. The effect was devastating. Over 9 million soldiers died. More were injured – many of them were left permanently disabled.

The violence and blockades of the war also led to the deaths of millions of civilians and the large-scale destruction of property and land. Politically the war had far-reaching consequences.

The international system was totally transformed. Germany became a republic, a communist Soviet Union emerged, America became a world power and Britain started a slow decline. At the peace conferences of 1919, the German, Turkish, and Austro-Hungarian empires were broken up. New boundaries were drawn in Europe and the Middle East, boundaries – as in Iraq and Kuwait – which were still intact at the end of the century.

DATES

1914 – 1918: World War I

1917: US entry into the war

1917: October Revolution

HISTORICAL TERMS

Great War or World War I

The Schlieffen Plan

July Crisis

soviets

Bolshevik

USSR

PERSONS

Woodrow Wilson

Vladimir Lenin

HISTORY WORKSHOP

abolition of serfdom: Reforms of the 18th and 19th centuries which freed the peasants from serfdom and hereditary subservience. The reforms also ended the manorial system.

absolutism: (lat. absolutus: loose, unlimited) Form of government in which a monarch rules as sovereign with unlimited authority. The monarch is responsible only to God, derives his authority from God ("king by the grace of God") and demands complete obedience from his subjects. Absolutism was the prevailing system of government in Europe from the 16th to the 18th centuries, and is the term given to the same era ("the Age of Absolutism"). The French king Louis XIV is considered the leading example of this type of government. He centralized monarchical power by bringing the politically independent nobility under his control and rescinding the right of the estates to approve taxation. He extended his power through a standing army, a professional bureaucracy and the economic system of mercantilism.

bourgeoisie (English: middle class): A diverse concept which includes the Third Estate during the Age of Absolutism as well as middle social groups in the Age of Industrialization. The concept is further defined when speaking of "grand" or "petite bourgeois" or "educated and propertied" classes. In Marxism it is the bourgeoisie which exploits the proletariat. Today we speak of social groups, as a class society no longer exists.

capitalism: Economic system in which capital is invested in business to earn profit. Supply and demand determine the price of wares, the state does not take any role in the system. To Marxists capitalism is a system of profit-oriented property which exploits the workers and leads to their impoverishment. Productive capital is the central force which includes all means of production such as machines and factories. They belong to private persons – entrepreneurs or capitalists – who oppose the workers or proletariat. According to Marx only class warfare can end this exploitation.

Central Powers (also Dual Alliance): In World War I the allies German Empire and Austria-Hungary, later joined by the Ottoman Empire and Bulgaria.

code civil: A civil set of laws written for Napoleon (1804), based on the principles of the French Revolution (personal freedom, legal equality, separation of church and state). The code (also "Code Napoleon") had great influence on later European laws.

Committee of Public Safety, The: A governing organ of the French Convention and an instrument of terror during the Jacobin dictatorship. The committee consisted of twelve executive commissars. Its leading member was Robespierre.

Confederation of the Rhine: In 1806 sixteen imperial princes declared their withdrawal from the Holy Roman Empire and founded the Confederation of the Rhine under the protection of Napoleon. The Habsburg Franz II gave up the imperial crown of the Holy Roman Empire and became Emperor of Austria instead. After Napoleon's Russian campaign was lost, the Confederation of the Rhine quickly dissolved.

Congress of Vienna: Conference of European rulers and statesmen (1814–15) to determine the political reordering of Europe after the fall of Napoleon. Chairman was the Austrian foreign minister Prince Metternich, who directed the main negotiations. The participants of the Congress of Vienna based their decisions on the principles of legitimacy and restoration.

constitution: The political order of a state which defines the form of government, the use of power and the function of political organs. A democratic constitution is written by a constituent, or national, assembly and is ratified by the voters directly or by their elected representatives in parliament. It is based on the principles of the separation of powers and the right of the people to take part in political decisions.

constitutional monarchy: Form of government in which the monarch is bound by a constitution, which guarantees the participation of a parliament in making the laws.

entrepreneur: Someone who runs a business and is its legal representative is called an entrepreneur. This is also the case with master craftsmen, distributors and business owners in the pre-industrial age. During the Industrial Revolution entrepreneurs, as the leaders of industrial branches, became more important, because they influenced the economy and determined the fates of large parts of the population. Originally, the entrepreneur was the investor of capital ("capitalist") and thus bore the greatest risk in his business. Later capital investment and management of the company were often divided. Joint-stock companies (for example, public limited companies or corporations), in which capital is owned by stockholders, are formed, and the company is managed by employed executives.

estates: Social groups which differ from each other in origin, profession, education and rights. In the Middle Ages there were three different estates: the clergy, the nobility, and the burghers and farmers. After the French Revolution and the reforms of the 19th century the system of estates disappeared. In the 19th century workers came to be called "the fourth estate". (In GB and USA "the fourth estate" refers to the press.) A corporative state is one in which the representatives of certain estates take part in governing.

Estates-General: Assembly of the representatives of the three estates (clergy, nobility, burghers and farmers) in France with the right to approve taxation.

freedom of trade: In pre-industrial times price and production in trades were controlled by trade guilds. During the 19th century guild controls were abolished, and freedom of trade was introduced. Anyone could open a business selling any product.

German Confederation: Loose confederation of thirty-five principalities and four free cities (as well as territory ruled by three foreign states) founded at the Congress of Vienna in 1815. Its only governing organ was the Diet in Frankfurt am Main, where delegates met under the chairmanship of Austria. It was destroyed by Austro-Prussian rivalry in 1866.

German Customs Union: Association of eighteen German states founded under Prussian leadership in 1834. Eventually all German states (except Austria) joined. Its goal was to create a German economic bloc without customs barriers or duties among the member states.

human rights: Opinion rooted in the Enlightenment, in which every person has inalienable rights which the state must preserve and protect. These include equality, personal inviolability, the right to own property, freedom of opinion, freedom of religion, the right to resist oppression. These rights were first formulated in the American Declaration of Independence (1776), taken up in the French constitution of 1791 and in many constitutions since then.

imperialism: The efforts of a state to extend its authority to other countries and peoples. Power is extended through conquest or economic control due to economic superiority. During the Age of Imperialism (1880–1914) the Great Powers established colonial empires and divided the world into spheres of influence.

Industrial Revolution: Decisive economic and social change, starting with industrialization in England around 1760. By 1840 it spread to Germany and later all over the world. It required the use of machinery, which led to new industrial production processes (mass production, division of labour, factories). In its early phase it is connected with social impoverishment, at the same time class differences developed because of the social problems of workers (the Social Question).

Kulturkampf: Conflict led by Bismarck between the Prussian state and the Catholic church, 1871–78.

labour movement: The Industrial Revolution created social problems which made the workers feel a sense of community. They developed class consciousness and organized workers' political parties and trade unions to represent their interests at the end of the 19th century.

liberalism: Political movement with roots in the Enlightenment which came to prominence in the 19th century. It states the right of the individual to develop freely without state control. It demands religious freedom, freedom of opinion, guaranteed human rights and participation in political decisions. Economic liberalism demands a free market without state controls or customs barriers.

Marxism: Theory of scientific socialism founded in the 19th century by Karl Marx and Friedrich Engels. Its main tenet is "historical materialism", which calls for a socialistic society following social and economic development (class warfare, communism). Marx also criticizes capitalist means of production and their effect on society (capitalism) in "A Critique of Political Economy" (Capital, vol. 1).

National Assembly: Elected parliament of a country, especially one which writes a constitution, for example, the French National Assembly of 1789-92 or the Frankfurt National Assembly of 1848–49.

nationalism: Usually negative concept for exaggerated national feelings and attaching too much importance to one's own nation.

North German Confederation: Confederation of Prussia and all states north of the Main, created by Bismarck in 1867. The executive power lay in the Federal Council of the allied governments, whose president was the king of Prussia. Bismarck was the chancellor. Legislative power lay with the Federal Council and the Diet, which was elected directly according to universal male suffrage. This constitution was the basis of the Imperial Constitution of 1871.

parliament: A freely elected popular assembly in a democratic state. It is the supreme organ for the laws and checks the power of the executive (separation of powers).

pauperism: (lat. pauper = poor) Term formulated around 1840 for the continuing poverty of large groups of people. Because of this mass poverty people were unable to earn even a meagre living and had to depend on charity.

political parties: Organized associations of citizens with similar political ideas to influence the state. Modern political parties developed at the beginning of the 19th century as loose associations of prominent personalities. The socialist parties were formed by the labour movement as a new type of mass party, which also was found among Catholic or religious parties (such as the Centre Party). Parties received important political functions as parliamentarianism established itself securely in the 20th century.

popular sovereignty: Unlike the sovereignty of a monarch, popular sovereignty rests in the hands of the people. Therefore, the election of a government by the people is the expression of popular sovereignty. Next to the separation of powers, popular sovereignty is the hallmark of the modern democratic state. The theoretician of popular sovereignty in modern times was J.J. Rousseau, who explained it in his work, "The Social Contract".

proletariat: In ancient Rome the lowest strata of the population, without property. In the 19th century it is defined by Marxism as the class of dependent wage labourers in capitalism. According to Marx the proletarian has only his work to sell and therefore depends on the bourgeoisie which owns the means of production and exploits him. Only class warfare and the "proletarian revolution" can end this oppression.

reaction: Term for the political attempts to turn back all progressive developments begun during the French Revolution. In Germany this is especially the time from 1819–30 and 1850–58. An anti-progressive attitude which defends outdated conditions is called "reactionary".

restoration: Attempts to bring back earlier conditions. The concept refers to the era between 1815 and 1848 when statesmen tried to return to the political principles which prevailed before the French Revolution.

revolution: A violent overthrow of the political order, which leads to thorough political and social changes. It is supported by large sections of the population – unlike a coup d'état or a Putsch, in which only a new group of political leaders takes power. Typical examples are the French Revolution in 1789 and the Russian Revolution in 1917.

secularization: Making church goods worldly property. In France a far-reaching secularization occurred during the French Revolution. In Germany this occurred after 1803 and later.

separation of powers: Division of governmental power into law-giving (legislative), law-fulfilling (executive) and law-judging (judicative) branches. The principle stems from the Enlightenment and is to prevent the abuse of governmental power. Constitutional organs independent from one another, such as parliament, the government and courts, result from this principle.

social laws: In general all the laws passed to secure the social well-being of citizens. In Imperial Germany the social laws refer to the legal measures passed by Bismarck to ease problems caused by age, illness and disability.

Social Question, The: Term for the unresolved social problems of labourers following the Industrial Revolution in the 19th century. Among them were: poverty because of low wages and high unemployment, extremely long working hours, unreasonable working conditions, unfit living conditions, heavy labour for women and children. The lack of security in case of illness, disability, labour accidents or old age made the conditions even worse. Attempts to solve the Social Question came from individual factory owners, the Church, and after 1883 from the government, with its social laws. The workers themselves founded trade unions, political parties and various self-help organizations to protect their interests and further their goals.

socialism: A political movement begun in the 19th century to change society in order to achieve social equality and justice. In Marxism this is the transitional phase between capitalism and communism. After the end of the 19th century moderate and radical socialist groups tried to realize different goals from reform of the capitalist system to overthrow of the existing social order (class warfare).

Socialist Law: A law introduced by Bismarck to combat Social Democracy. It forbade all Social Democratic, socialistic or communistic organizations, assemblies and publications and threatened to ban "agitators" from a district. The goal was the destruction of Social Democratic organizations and trade unions; however, the Social Democratic Party remained in the Diet. The law proved a political failure, as Social Democracy continued to grow even after the law was revoked in 1890.

steam engine: Steam was used at the end of the 17th century to pump water out of coal mines. James Watt invented a machine for use in industry in 1769. Water and manpower were replaced by steam, making industrialization possible.

strike: A plan for a large number of labourers to refuse to work in order to get higher wages or better working conditions from their employer(s). In the 19th century industrial strikes led to the founding of trade unions; the strike became one of the most important means to emphasize union demands. In Germany prior to 1918 strikes were illegal and punished by law. Today the right to strike is recognized in many countries and has become an important part of democratic thinking.

student society (German: Burschenschaft): Student fraternity movement founded first in Jena in 1815 which quickly extended to all German universities. The movement demanded university reform as well as national unity in Germany and proclaimed its liberal goals at the Wartburg Festival in 1817. The Carlsbad Decrees in 1820 made the student societies illegal, but the movement continued in secret. After the founding of the German Empire in 1871 conservative groups had a dominant role in the movement.

terror (lat. = frighten): Violent form of political conflict to cut off all resistance by frightening people. It can be introduced by the state (state terrorism) or by extreme organizations to overthrow the political or social order. Typical examples are the Terror of the Jacobins during the French Revolution from 1793-94 or terror under the regimes of fascism, National Socialism and communism.

three-class-electoral system: Electoral system for the Prussian House of Deputies valid from 1849 to 1918. Voters in each electoral district were divided into three classes, each of which paid one-third of the taxes in the district. Each class chose electors who then voted for deputies (indirect election). The principle of the system was that those voters who paid the highest taxes should have the most prominent voice in parliamentary decision-making.

trade unions: Organizations of workers to protect their economic interests. In England workers organized at the end of the 18th century; in Germany various local unions were established after 1848. After 1890 (when the Socialist Law was revoked) the unions became large mass organizations.

War of Secession: American civil war caused by the controversy between the northern and southern states on the question of slavery. Armed conflict began in 1861 with the withdrawal (secession) of the southern states from the Union and ended in 1865 with the victory of the northern states.

women's rights movement: Organized struggle of women for political and social equality. The movement began during the French Revolution and grew during the Industrial Revolution. Its main demands aimed at attaining full political citizenship for women, as well as entrance to all professions, trades and educational institutions. In 1865 a national German women's association was founded, in 1897 an international group followed.

(to) abandon: to desert, to leave alone

(to) abdicate: to give up the throne

(to) abolish: to end a law officially

access: the right to enter a place, use sth., see someone etc.

account: version

acquisition: the act of getting land and power

administrator: a person whose job is to manage and organize the public or business affairs

(to) affirm: to state publicly that sth. is true

ain't: verb form of isn't or aren't (considered grammatically incorrect today)

ambassador: an official who represents his country in a foreign one

animosity: a strong feeling of opposition, anger or hatred

(to) annex: to add a territory to another state

annexation: the act of taking control, occupation

anvil: heavy iron block on which metal is hammered into certain shapes

anxious: wanting sth. very much

apologist: sb. who defends or justifies sth.

apology: word or statement saying sb. is sorry for sth. that has been done wrong

(to) apply the whip before offering the carrot: to punish first and then reward sb. ["Zuckerbrot und Peitsche"]

(to) apportion: to divide something among people

arbitrary: not based on reason , system or plan, seeming to be unfair

ardently (adv.): intensely

armistice: a formal agreement during a war to stop fighting and discuss making peace

armour: covering (usually metal) to protect the body from weapons

arsonist: sb. who sets things on fire

assassination: murder, killing

(to) assert: to state firmly

atrocity: a cruel and violant act, especially in a war

attributes: features

autistic: unable to communicate with or react to other people

avarice: greed, extreme desire for wealth

(to) avert: to prevent

axle: long piece of wood or metal connecting wheels

(to) backfire: to have the opposite effect

banquet: large, formal dinner

barbed wire: strong wire with short sharp points on it, used especially for fences

bear: animal, symbol of Russia

bedroom slipper: soft shoe worn in the house

beloved: dear

benediction of God: blessing, approval of God

(to) bequeath (formal): to give sb. property

betrayal of sth.: act of ignoring principles or beliefs in order to achieve something or gain an advantage for yourself

(to) be biased: having or showing prejudice, unfair attitude

blast furnace: a large structure like an oven in which iron ore is melted in order to take out the metal

blessing: something that is good or helpful

blight: plant disease

bloodshed: people losing blood

blueprint: draft, model

(to) blur: to make sth. unclear

board and lodging: a place to stay and get food

boost: sth. that helps or encourages sb.

border barrier: a barricade keeping people and goods from passing a border

border guard: government official who protects the border and keeps people from entering the country without permission

border sign: sign showing where the border of a country begins or ends

Borussia: female symbol for Prussia

branch: a special section or department

brass: money

(to) breach: to get through, to break

(to) breed (bred, bred): to mate, to couple

breeding: the controlled reproduction of animals

brick: a kind of stone made to build walls/ houses

brisk: busy

(to) broadcast: to throw by hand

bugbear: sth. that keeps annoying you

candidacy: being a choice for an office

capture: taking sb. prisoner

cart: a vehicle pulled by a horse for carrying loads

"carte blanche": complete freedom to act as one thinks best

cash crop: crop grown mainly for sale

casualties: people who are killed or injured in war

cause: reason

(to) cavil: to argue about unimportant details

census: an official count of the people with details such as age, sex, occupation, etc.

centenary: the 100th anniversary of an event

character trait: good/bad character traits make a person what they are like

charcoal: coal made from burnt wood

close: knowing well

(to) coalesce: to unite

coffin: box to bury a dead person in

(to) commemorate: to remind people of an important person or event from the past

(to) compensate: to provide sth. good in order to balance a loss

compensation: payment, making up for sth.

(to) compose: to make up

comprehensive: broad, thorough

(to) conceive: to form an idea, plan, etc. in your mind, to imagine

concise: clear and short, focused

conclusion: decision

(to) confiscate: to officially take away sb.'s possessions

confiscation: the act of officially taking sth. away from sb.

conquest: the act of taking control of a country or a city

consideration: thinking carefully about sth.

(to) consolidate: to combine, to unify

constituent assembly: group which writes a constitution

consummator: sb. who finishes a job

contemporaries: people living at that time

contention: opinion

(to) contribute: to give sth., esp. money or goods

(to) convert: to change religion

conviction: a strong opinion or belief

core: most important, central part

(to) covenant: to legally agree to do sth.

covered wagon: a wagon, drawn by horses or oxen, covered with heavy material, like canvas, to keep out wind and rain

cowardice: lack of courage

cradle: baby's bed on rockers, place of origin, beginning

crippling: damaging sb.'s body so that he/she is no longer able to walk or move normally

(to) crumble: to break off

(to) crush: to defeat sb. completely, to get rid of sth., to wipe it out

curious: wanting to know about sth.

customhouse: office where customs duties are collected, or where customs officers can wait

customs officer: government official who checks goods at the border and collects customs duties on them

(to) cut back: to reduce

debt: money that sb. owes

decade: period of ten years

(to) deceive oneself: to refuse to admit to yourself that sth. unpleasant is true

decisiveness: ability to decide

(to) decree: to order

delay: a period of time sb. has to wait

demagogue: a leader who misleads the people

(to) denounce: to criticize, speak against

dependency: area or country controlled by another one

(to) deport: to send away to a foreign country by force

descent: a person's family origins

deterioration: the fact or process of becoming worse

determined: having a strong desire to do sth., so that you will not let anyone stop you

devastating: causing a lot of damage and destruction

devious: dishonest

(to) devour: to eat, to consume very eagerly

(to) digest: to absorb, to take sth. in

diligence: working hard

disability: the state of not being able to use body or mind fully

disillusionment: having no ideals and becoming disappointed or bitter because of this

dismissal: the act of removing sb. from office

dispatch: message, official letter

dispute: a serious argument or disagreement

dissolution, decomposition: falling apart, rotting

(to) dissolve: to dismiss a parliamentary body

(to) distribute: to give things to people, to share sth. between a number of people

disturbance: trouble, disorder

division: dividing into separate parts

donation: money given by people in order to help

dough: a kind of bread or pastry made of flour, water, etc.

dues: charges, money that you owe sb.

dwelling: living

efficient: well-organized, effective

effort: activity to achieve sth.

eligible: suitable, fit for military service

emanation: origin, beginning, outpour

(to) emigrate: to leave one's country

emulation: competition

(to) encircle: to surround, form a circle

encouragement: giving support or hope to sb.

encyclical: an official announcement by the pope in form of a letter

engineering works/factory: a factory that produces machines, etc.

(to) enshrine: to make sth. seem important

entirely: totally, completely

envoy: diplomat who represents his country

(to) envy: to be jealous of sb., to hate sb. or sth.

(to) escort: to go with sb. to keep him from escaping

ethnic: having a common cultural background (customs, language, history, etc.)

(to) exaggerate: to overdo, overdraw, overstate, overemphasize

executive: leading

(to) exceed: to be greater than ...

exile: a situation in which you are forced to leave your country or home and go to live in a foreign country

(to) exploit: to use sth. in order to gain as much from it as possible

exploitation: overuse of a person or a thing

(to) exterminate: to kill

external apparatus: outside machinery

fair (n.): people's festival,travelling entertainment, exhibition

faithful: loyal

fallow: not used for growing crops

famine: little or no food for a long time

(to) famish: to die of hunger, starve

ferocious: very aggressive and violent

fertilizer: substance added to soil to make plants grow better

fine: a sum of money that must be paid as punishment

firing squad: a group of soldiers who shoot a prisoner

flat: room to live in

(to) flog: to beat with a whip

foresight: ability to see sth. clearly before it happens

formidable: sth. impressive or powerful, because it is very difficult/complicated

fortress: a strong building or place to protect against attacks

fortune: success, luck, wealth

fragile: weak

fratricidal: involving killing members of your own family or social group

free colonist: a colonist who was not an indentured servant and therefore had the right to vote

furnace: a kind of oven

gamble: a risky action

gambler: sb. who likes to play and risk his money

gangway: a bridge placed between the side of a ship and land so people can get on and off

geneticist: a scientist who studies genetics

German Supreme Command: group of highest army officers

Germania: female symbol for Germany

(to) "Germanize": to make sb. more German

(to) give vent to: to express a feeling, esp. anger, strongly

glorification: extreme praise

governess: woman employed in a private home to train and teach children

(to) grasp: to understand sth. completely

gravedigger: sb. who digs a grave for the dead

guardian: protecting

gulp: a quick swallow of a large amount of a drink

gutter: edge of street carrying water and waste

habeas corpus: legal principle that a court must decide whether sb. can be imprisoned

hard coal: coal found in the ground

hath: has

haughtiness: pride

(to) have a preference: to like sth., to prefer

(to) head: to get ahead of sb.

headache: pain in the head

heathen: people who have no religion or who believe in a religion that is not Christian

hegemony: being the most important country dominating the others

(to) heighten: to increase/intensify

heraldry: the study of the coats of arms and of old families

(to) hint at: to suggest sth. in an indirect way

house of cards: structure made of playing cards

(to) be humiliated: losing pride, seeming foolish

(to) hunt: seek out animals to kill or capture, search for sth.

ideals: something that is believed to be perfect

(to) ignite: to start to burn

ill-suited: unfit

immaturity: the state of not being fully developed

(to) immigrate: to come into a country

impact: powerful effect

impeachment: the act of formally accusing a public official of a serious crime

impetus: push

(to) impose upon: to force sth. on someone

improvement: sth. made better

in defiance of: against

in face of: regarding

in flagrante delicto: in the very act of doing wrong

in spite of: without considering, without being affected or prevented by sth.

incorruptibility: never doing sth. illegal or immoral, cannot be made dishonest

indentured servant: person who agrees to work for sb. for a number of years to pay back money borrowed

indiscriminately: without any purpose, randomly

(to) indulge: to enjoy, to give in to

inefficient: not effective

infallibility: not being able to make a mistake in beliefs *infant mortality:* deaths of small children and babies

inferior: lower in rank, the opposite of superior

(to) inflict: to cause sth. unpleasant to happen

influenza: an infectious disease

(to) inhabit: to live in a particular place

inhabitants: people living in a place

inherited: passed from parent to child

(to) initiate: to begin the process of passing laws

innumerable: uncountable

insolent: disrespectful

intelligible: clear to understand

interest: money you have to pay when you have borrowed money

interrelated: closely connected and affecting each other

intervention: getting involved in order to help

intimidation: frightening, threatening

invention: production of sth. new that has not existed before

(to) investigate: to find out about sth.

(to) invoke: to call on, to refer to

issue: a topic that is talked about

jealousy: wanting sth. belonging to another person

Jim Crow: an unpleasant name for Negro

joint stock company: a company that is owned by all the people who have shares in it

journeymen: a person who learnt a handicraft and travels to find work or works for a master

jury: a group of people, usually 12, who judge a court case

laborious (adj.): taking a lot of time and effort

labour recruiters: white men forcing Africans into work

lash: whip or hit with a whip

laundress: woman who does the washing and ironing in a household

legacy: sth. from the past that affects life today

legitimate sentiment of retaliation: rightful feeling of paying sb. back for doing sth. wrong

(to) levy: to ask for, to use official authority to collect payments

life tenure: holding a job for as long as sb. lives

Lippe-Schauenburg: principality of Lippe-Schauenburg (today called Schaumburg-Lippe) in Westfalia; it was one of the smallest German states at this time, which is why it is often used in cartoons making fun of the many small German states

loom: a machine to weave cloth

malnutrition: poor condition of health caused by lack of food

martial: connected with fighting or war

martial law: law of war

masters: leaders (ironical)

(to) mediate: to help others solve a problem

(to) mediatize: to join a smaller state to a larger one

mercenary: a soldier who will fight for anybody for money

merchant: businessman, a buyer and seller of goods for profit

merchant clothier: a person who sells clothes or cloth

merely: only, just

merger: the process of combining two or more companies

meticulousness: paying attention to details

midst: middle

militia: citizen's army

moat: a deep wide hole surrounding a castle for protection

(to) mobilize: to assemble troops at the start of a military action

(to) modify: to change sth. slightly

monotonous: one-sided, boring

mortality: the number of deaths in a period of time

muck: dirt or mud

(to) mutilate: to hurt or damage badly

mutiny: a refusal by a group of soldiers or sailors to accept orders

mutual: shared by two or more people

NAACP: National Association for the Advancement of Colored People

(to) nationalize: to put an industry or a company under the control of the government, which becomes its owner

navigable: easy for a ship to travel on

necessity: the fact that sth. must happen

nightmare: bad dream

no man's land: area between two borders which belongs to neither country

null and void: having no legal force, not valid

nursemaid: woman hired to care for children in a household

(to) be obsessed: to think about sth. constantly

obsolete: no longer used because sth. new has been invented

obstacle: sth. that hinders you

(to) obtain: to get

occasion: a situation that allows sth. to happen

(to) occur: to happen

old maids: women who did not marry

oligarchy of sovereigns: a small group of rulers

on a spa: at a health resort with a mineral spring

on account of: because of

option: sth. you can choose to have or do

out of kilter: not right in some way

(to) outlaw: to make sth. illegal

(to) overstate: to exaggerate

(to) overthrow: to get rid of a government by force

pace: the speed at which sb. walks, moves, runs, etc.

Palatinate: German "Pfalz"

pale: having a very white skin

pamphlet: a leaflet containing a political message to influence people

peasant: a farm worker of low status

(to) perish: to die

pernicious: very harmful

perpetual: never-ending

(to) persecute: to treat sb. in a cruel or unfair way

petition: an official document asking for sth. to be done

(to) picket: to take part in a protest

pigtail: hair braided together, symbolizing authority

pinnacle: the most successful part

plant: factory

(to) plead: to ask urgently

poignant: giving you feelings of sadness

policies: principles for political decisions

(to) pout: to show unhappiness, often by sticking out the lower lip

powder keg: small barrel of gunpowder

prairial: 9th month in the calendar of the French Revolution

predecessor: a person or thing that came/was there before

prefect: a public official

pregnancy: the state of a woman with a child inside her body

preliminary: coming before

premium: amount of money paid regulary for insurance

preservation: keeping sth. the way it is

(to) prevail: to dominate

primordial: existing at the beginning of time or the beginning of the Earth

principality: a country ruled by a prince

procedure: the way sth. is done

(to) proceed: to carry on

prohibition: forbidding sth. by law, e.g. alcoholic drinks

proletariat: working class people

(to) promote: to help sth. to happen

prosperity: the state of being wealthy, rich

provision: the act of supplying sb. with sth. that they need or want *punctuality:* always being on time

puppeteer: person who makes a puppet or marionette move

purchase: the act of buying something

(to) pursue: to follow and persecute sb.

(to) put store upon: to value sth. highly

quadruple: four times as many

(to) quadruple: to multiply by four

(to) quarter: to give soldiers a temporary home

racket: noise, illegal doing

(to) rage: to continue in a violent way

railing: barrier on ships as a means of protection against falling overboard

reactionary: strongly opposed to any political or social changes, the opposite of progressive

(to) reap: to cut and collect a crop from a field

recipient: a person who receives something

reconciliation: end to a quarrel and start of a good relationship again

record: written document

recurrence: when sth. that has happened before happens again

redress: payment for sth. wrong that has happened to people

reinsurance: buying insurance for an already made insurance policy

(to) reject: unwilling to accept sth.

release: the act of setting free

relocation: moving to a new place

reluctant: unwilling, not wanting to do sth.

(to) rely upon: to depend on sb./sth.

(to) renounce: to state formally that you no longer have a particular belief or position

(to) repeal: to state officially that a law has ended

(to) repulse: to push back

request: the action of asking for something formally and politely

resembling: similar to

resistance: opposition

resolution: parliamentary decision

resolved: determined, firmly decided

(to) restitute: to establish again or to restore

(to) restore: to make sth. return to its former state or condition

(to) revoke: to cancel

revulsion: a strong feeling of disgust or horror

rider: person who sits on top of a horse and leads it

ridiculous: laughable, silly

roughly (adv.): saying sth. without giving exact details or information

(to) rub one's eyes: to wipe away tears when crying

rump parliament: a smaller parliament left over from a larger parliament

(to) safeguard: to protect sb. from loss

(to) sanitize: to make sth. clear

(to) saturate: to fill to the maximum capacity

savage: a primitive, brutal, or cruel person

scapegoat: a person who is blamed unjustly

scarlet: bright red

scourge: a thing that causes trouble or suffering

seamless: with no spaces between one part and the next

(to) sear: to burn the surface

(to) secularize: to take sth. away from religious control and put it under civil authority

seizure of power: act of suddenly taking control of a country, esp. by force

self-determination: the right of the people in a country to choose their own government

sentinel: guard

serf: a person who is tied to the land he works on

share: part

sharecropper: a worker who works on sb. else's land and has to give them a big part of the harvest

shares: units of equal value sold by a company to raise money

shelling: shooting with big guns

shortcoming: a fault in a plan or system

(to) shove: to push with force

shuttle: a wooden stick that pulls the thread back and forth in a loom

sin: the act of breaking a religious or moral law

skilful: good at doing sth.

slogan: a short phrase easy to remember and often used by a political party

social companion: person employed to live or travel with sb.

soil: the earth on the fields

sojourn: (literary) a period of time when you stay in a place that is not your home

sovereign: having independent power

spark: a piece flying out of a fire

spiked helmet: helmet worn by Prussian soldiers

spring: source or origin of sth.

spur: motivation

(to) spy: to find out secret information

stagecoach: a large carriage pulled by horses for carrying people

staggering: very amazing, extremly surprising

stalemate: situation in which neither side can win or make any progress

(to) stall: to stop sth. from happening until a later date

standing army: army on permanent duty

stasis: a condition in which there is no movement or change

status quo: things as they are at the moment

(to) stay in charge: to keep control over a situation

(to) steer: to control the direction in which a boat, car, etc. moves

(to) stir up: to make people feel strong emotions

stockbroker: sb. whose job it is to buy and sell shares of stock (money) for other people

stocks of supplies: reserves of food

(to) stride: walk with long steps

striking: clear, impressive

(to) stunt: to keep sth. from growing

(to) subdue: to bring sb. under control by using force

subject (n.): a person who is under the rule of a sovereign

(to) subject: to put sth. under the control of sb.

subsidies: money the state gives people for investment

(to) succumb: to give in, to surrender

(to) sue: to make a legal claim

(to) suffer hardship: to have really bad times

superstition: the belief that particular events bring good or bad luck

supply: an amount of sth. that is provided or available

(to) suppose: to imagine

surge: sudden increase

(to) surrender: to give up sth. when forced to

suspect: a person who is thought to have committed a crime

(to) take a toll: to pay a high price

tangible: clear and definite, real

tank: a military vehicle covered with strong metal and armed with guns

tar: a dark, thick liquid with a strong smell

team of horses: group of horses who work together to pull a load

temperance: drinking alcohol in moderation

tenant: a farmer who rents land and has to pay for it

the slain: the people who were killed

thread: long thin string for weaving and sewing

threat: danger that is about to come/happen, declaration of intent to harm

(to) thresh: to separate grain from the rest of the plant

throng: crowd

(to) toil: to work very hard physically

toll: price

top with stick: toy which spins when pushed with the stick

tour de force: masterpiece, triumph

(to) tramp: to walk with heavy steps for a long time

trench: a long, deep hole dug in the ground

(to) trigger sth.: to make sth. happen suddenly

trust: a group of companies working together to reduce competition, control prices, etc.

trustee: supervisor

tsar (czar): Russian emperor

turnip: a round root vegetable

ultimately (adv.): finally

ultimatum: a final threat to use force if sb. does not do what is wanted

unalienable: sth. that cannot be taken away from you

unanimous: agreed by all

undisputed: sth. that cannot be questioned

unique: there is only one of it

unmerciful: showing no kindness

untrammelled: not limited or controlled

upheavals: uprisings

urgency: need to deal with sth. quickly

(to) utilize: to use

utterly (adv.): completely

vaccination: medicine that is given to immunize a person or animal against diseases

(to) vanish: to disappear

vigilant: very careful to notice any signs of danger or trouble

(to) vindicate: to prove that sth. is true

(to) violate: to do sth. that is not allowed by law, to injure

virtue: high moral standards

vital: living, essential

wage: payment for work done

(to) wage: to begin and continue a war, a battle, etc.

wagon wheel: wheel attached to a cart or wagon

war of attrition: wearing the other side down by killing so many men that they could not be replaced

war of succession: war over who will be the next king or queen

warrant: certificate, license

war-weariness: being tired of war

welfare: well-being

well-secured: guaranteed

welter: a large and confusing amount of sth.

whip: strip of leather on a handle used to make an animal move

wicked: evil, bad

(to) winnow: to blow air through grain in order to remove its outer covering

wooden soldier: soldier made of wood

zenith: highlight, highest point (of power or success)

akg-images GmbH, Berlin: Titel.(Vordergrund), 4.1, 4.2, 5.2, 6.1, 10.2, 12.1, 15.1, 17.1, 17.3, 18.1, 21.1, 24.1, 26.1, 28.2, 29.1, 29.2, 32.1, 32.2, 38.1, 38.2, 44.1, 56.1, 56.2, 58.1, 60.1, 60.3, 63.1, 64.1, 65.1, 68.1, 69.1, 71.1, 72.1, 76.1, 77.1, 82.1, 88.2, 91.1, 91.2, 101.1, 104.1, 107.1, 108.1, 108.2, 112.1, 114.1, 115.1, 118.1, 120.1, 123.1, 124.1, 125.1, 132.1, 133.1, 138.1, 140.1, 140.2, 143.1, 144.1, 154.1, 154.2, 159.2, 173.2, 174.1, 174.2, 179.1, 188.1, 188.2, 193.1, 199.3, 202.1, 204.1; A. Held 73.2; British Library 3.1; E. Lessing 26.2; historic-maps 119.2; Lessing, Erich 14.1, 70.1; VISIOARS 73.1; © VG Bild-Kunst, Bonn 2020/Gerasimov, Aleksander Michailowitsch 203.2. |Alamy Stock Photo (RMB), Abingdon/Oxfordshire: Art Collection 3 32.3; B. Daemmrich 47.1; D. MacDonald 53.1; Granger, NYC 6.2, 44.2; K. Sriskandan 208.1; M. Burgess 175.3; The Print Collector 25.1, 100.1, 119.1. |alimdi.net, Deisenhofen: Gerhard 175.1. |Archiv der sozialen Demokratie, Bonn: H.J. Darchinger 82.2. |Archiv der sozialen Demokratie der Friedrich-Ebert-Stiftung: SPD/AdsD, Bonn: AdsD/Friedrich-Ebert-Stitung 152.2. |Baumgärtner, Ulrich Dr., Puchheim: 88.1. |Bibliothek für Hugenottengeschichte, Tübingen: frz. Bible de chignon (La Haye, 1753/1754); Sammlung Prisard 16.1. |Bildarchiv Foto Marburg, Marburg: Stemple, Postkarte Berlin, private Sammlung, Inventar-Nr. BOR13 150.1. |bpk-Bildagentur, Berlin: 29.3, 58.2, 60.2, 74.1, 77.2, 82.6, 112.2, 125.2, 129.1, 129.2, 130.1, 131.1, 138.2, 148.1, 148.2, 149.1, 159.1, 176.1, 178.1, 186.3, 202.3; D. Katz 171.1, 186.4; Gebrüder Haeckl 196.1; H. Buresch/Eduard Thöny Nachlass München 151.1; Katz, D./© VG Bild-Kunst, Bonn 2018 182.1; RMN/Grand Palais/Gérard Blot 9.1; SMB/Kunstbibliothek/© VG Bild-Kunst, Bonn 2018 170.1; SMB/Kupferstichkabinett/Anders, Jörg P. 27.1. |Bridgeman Images, Berlin: 8.1, 128.1; Bibliotheque Nationale, Paris 65.2; British Library, London 23.1; Château de Versailles 19.1; Fogg Art Museum, Harvard University Art Museum, Nachlass G.L. Winthrop 61.1; Musee de la Ville de Paris 3.3; Private Collection/Photo © Christie's Images 186.1. |Brieske, Rainer, Berlin: 17.2. |Cartoon's Magazine, Chicago: 190.2. |Das Bundesarchiv, Koblenz: Plak 001-004-066/Barch 109.1. |DB Museum Fotosammlung, Nürnberg: 90.1. |Deutsches Historisches Museum, Berlin: 152.3, 190.1; A. Psille 82.3. |F1online, Frankfurt/M.: Tips Images 34.1. |fotolia.com, New York: Ana 9.2; blickwinkel2511 11.1, 11.2; picturemaker01 127.1. |Germanisches Nationalmuseum, Nürnberg: 126.1. |Getty Images, München: Bettmann 48.1; Photo 12 10.1. |Historisches Archiv Krupp, Essen: 94.1, 95.1, 97.1. |Historisches Archiv MAN, Augsburg: 152.1. |Imago, Berlin: Caro 28.1. |Interfoto, München: Granger, NYC 121.1; Mary Evans 89.1; Mary Evans/Grenville Collins Postcard Collection 157.2; Sammlung Rauch 82.4; Sammlung Rauch + VG Bild-Kunst, Bonn 2020/Olaf Gulbransson 153.1. |Keystone Pressedienst, Hamburg: 198.1; Topfoto 195.1; TopFoto 195.2, 197.1. |Köhler-Kaeß, J., Flintbeck: 183.1. |Mary Evans Picture Library, London: 96.1, 96.2, 96.3, 186.5. |mauritius images GmbH, Mittenwald: Rossenbach 4.3, 146.1. |Niggemann, Nils, Berlin: Titel.(Hintergrund). |Picture-Alliance GmbH, Frankfurt/M.: akg-images 157.1; dpa 206.1; dpa/Heuse 186.6; dpa/Prado-Museum Madrid 76.2; Fotoreport Bayer AG 82.5; Photoshot 22.1; united archives 166.2. |Shutterstock.com, New York: Soto, Jose Ignacio 6.3. |Staatsarchiv Bremen, Bremen: 180.1. |Süddeutsche Zeitung - Photo, München: Sammlung Megele 156.1, 202.2. |Tonn, Dieter, Bovenden-Lenglern: 30.1, 30.2, 31.1, 31.2, 31.3, 54.1, 54.2, 55.1, 55.2, 55.3, 80.1, 80.2, 81.1, 81.2, 81.3, 81.4, 86.1, 110.1, 110.2, 110.3, 111.1, 111.2, 111.3, 111.4, 111.5, 136.1, 136.2, 136.3, 137.1, 162.1, 162.2, 162.3, 163.1, 163.2, 163.3, 184.1, 184.2, 184.3, 185.1, 185.2, 185.3, 194.1, 210.1, 210.2, 210.3, 211.1. |ullstein bild, Berlin: 95.2, 120.2, 138.3, 140.3, 152.4, 172.1, 173.1, 196.2, 201.1; Archiv Gerstenberg 5.1, 132.2, 134.1, 134.2, 166.1, 189.1, 203.1; Granger Collection 22.2, 37.1, 43.1, 164.1; Granger NYC 186.2, 199.1; histopics 199.2; Kujath 161.1; Photo 12 192.1; ROGER VIOLLET/ A. Harlingue 62.1; The Granger Collection 168.1; United Archives 106.1. |vario images, Bonn: Imagebroker/J. Woodhouse Titel.(Hintergrund). |wikimedia.commons: 3.2, 32.4, 32.5, 32.6, 32.7, 40.1; (John Tenniel: Au Revoir!, Punch 6 August 1881) 158.1; Library of Congress, Washington 49.1, 50.1. |Zeller, J., Berlin: 175.2.

Terms for Discussion

War and peace	
to be responsible for the outbreak of the war	
to set off / trigger a war	
to enter / join the war	
to declare war	
to win / lose a battle / war	
to occupy / take control of / invade / annex / conquer a country / territory	
to volunteer for military service / join the army	
to mobilize / demobilize troops / an army	
to fight for sovereignty / independence	
to demand / pay reparations	
to establish peace / to stabilize a country	

Diplomacy	
to send / serve as an ambassador / (an envoy)	
to have / break off diplomatic relations with a country	
to achieve a diplomatic triumph	
to guarantee neutrality	
to negotiate / sign an agreement / a pact / a treaty	
to stir up / settle a dispute over	
to cause / create rising tensions	
to issue / deliver an ultimatum	
to sign / negotiate an armistice / a peace treaty	
to proclaim a republic	

Economy	
to make an invention / to invent sth.	
to be a pioneer	
to start a business	
to invest money / to go bankrupt	
to increase production / to grow crops / to breed animals	
to exploit natural resources / exploitation	
to open new markets	
to be employed / unemployed / a skilled / unskilled worker	
to enjoy economic benefits	
to suffer from food shortages	